ALL ROADS
LEAD TO
ROME

ALL ROADS LEAD TO ROME

WHY WE THINK OF THE ROMAN EMPIRE DAILY

RHIANNON GARTH JONES

Aurum

Quarto

First published in hardback in 2025 by Aurum,
an imprint of Quarto
One Triptych Place,
London, SE1 9SH
United Kingdom
www.Quarto.com/Aurum

EEA Representation, WTS Tax d.o.o., Žanova ulica 3, 4000 Kranj, Slovenia

A catalogue record for this book is
available from the British Library.

ISBN: 978-1-836-00295-6
Ebook ISBN: 978-1-836-00297-0
Audiobook ISBN: 978-1-836-00621-3

10 9 8 7 6 5 4 3 2 1

Cover design by Two Associates
Maps by Lovell Johns Limited
Typeset in Adobe Garamond Pro by SX Composing DTP, Rayleigh, Essex
Printed and bound by CPI Group (UK) Ltd, Croydon, CRO 4YY

Contents

Maps   vi

Cities of the Roman Empire   xvi

1. Introduction   I

Part One Religion   **13**

2. The New Rome   17

3. The Holy Roman Empire   41

4. The Third Rome   65

Part Two Empire   **89**

5. Conquering Rome: the Ottoman Empire   95

6. Pax Romana, Pax Britannica   117

7. Roman Fasces, European Fascism   141

Part Three Culture   **165**

8. Rivalling Rome: the Empires of Early Islam   169

9. The New Republic: USA Edition   195

10. Conclusion: All Roads Lead to Rome   217

Want to Know More?   229

Full Bibliography   239

Timeline   263

Acknowledgements   271

Index   274

Maps

A Roman view of the world

This nineteenth-century reconstruction, by Konrad Miller, of a map by the ancient Roman geographer Pomponius Mela, reflects the world as understood by Romans in the first century CE.

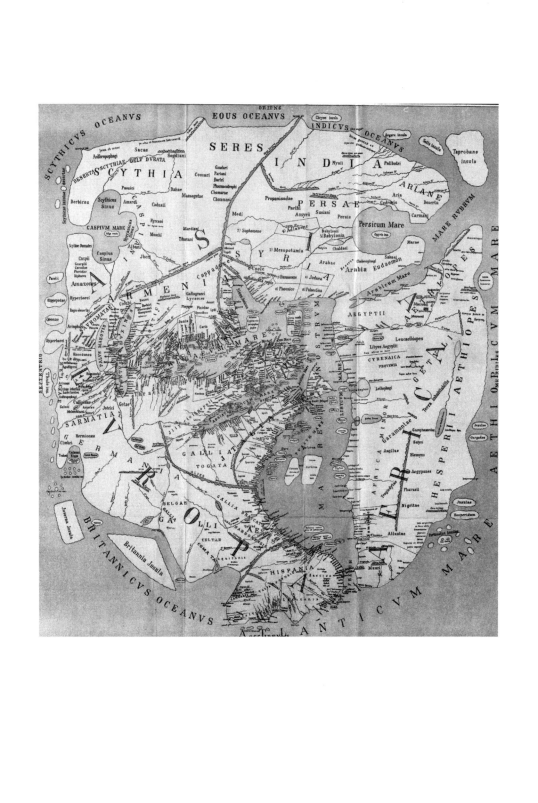

Mare nostrum: 'our sea'

Meaningful control over land and sea ebbed and flowed over time, as with all empires, but Roman rule was well-established in these cities and regions around the time Constantine built New Rome in 330 CE.

The 'medieval' Mediterranean

By the tenth century, rulers around the Mediterranean were using Roman references and traditions, in combination with others, to assert their own authority – frequently in competition with rival rulers.

Umayyad
Caliphate

● Córdoba

Aachen ●

Holy Roman
Empire

Rebel Fatimid
Territory

Rome ●

Romanland

Constantinople ●

● Raqqa

Cairo ●

Damascus ●

● Baghdad

● Nishapur

Abbasid
Calphate

W

S   N

E

0   1,000 km

0   1,000 miles

The 'early modern' Mediterranean

By the seventeenth century, the Habsburg, Ottoman, and Russian empires competed to be the pre-eminent power of the time. Directly and indirectly, claims to Rome were part of this rivalry.

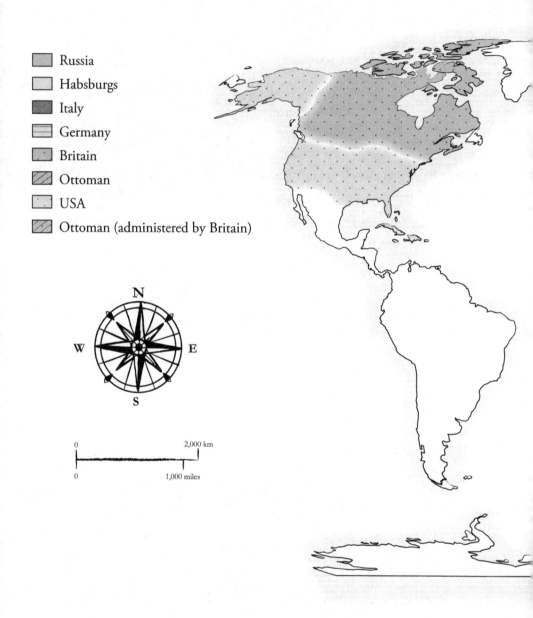

Russia
Habsburgs
Italy
Germany
Britain
Ottoman
USA
Ottoman (administered by Britain)

Rival Roman empires around the world

On the eve of the First World War, much of the globe
was ruled by empires who believed they had inherited
a legacy of Rome – and with it, a right to rule.

Cities of the Roman Empire

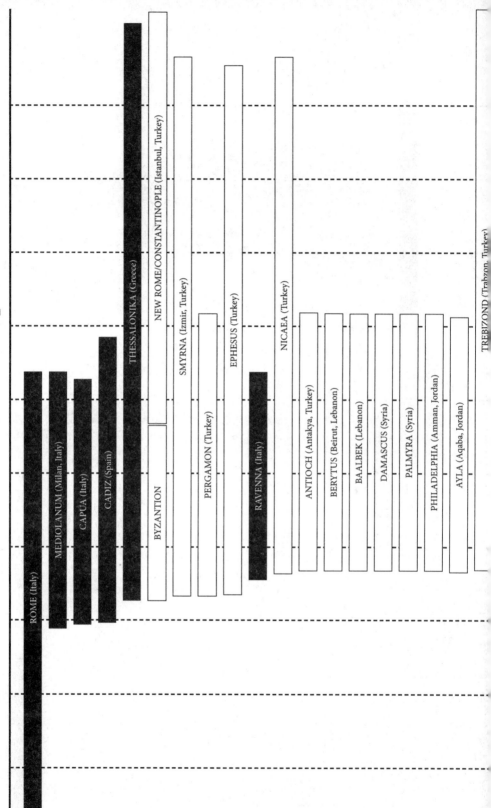

ROME (Italy)

MEDIOLANUM (Milan, Italy)

CAPUA (Italy)

CADIZ (Spain)

THESSALONIKA (Greece)

NEW ROME/CONSTANTINOPLE (Istanbul, Turkey)

BYZANTION

SMYRNA (Izmir, Turkey)

PERGAMON (Turkey)

EPHESUS (Turkey)

RAVENNA (Italy)

NICAEA (Turkey)

ANTIOCH (Antakya, Turkey)

BERYTUS (Beirut, Lebanon)

BAALBEK (Lebanon)

DAMASCUS (Syria)

PALMYRA (Syria)

PHILADELPHIA (Amman, Jordan)

AYLA (Aqaba, Jordan)

TREBIZOND (Trabzon, Turkey)

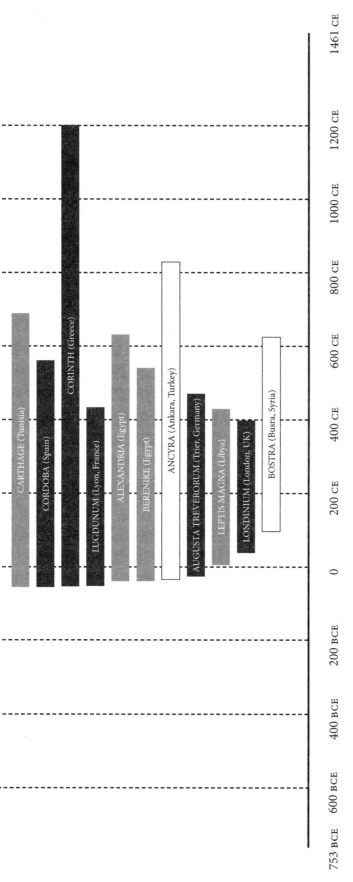

From the legendary founding of Rome in 753 BCE to the conquest of Constantinople in 1453, the Roman empire changed repeatedly, expanding, contracting, and shifting in focus. Consequently, the most significant cities in the empire changed over time. Those listed here were consistently some of the most important urban centres, administratively, culturally, and/or economically.

MODERN 'MIDDLE EAST'

MODERN NORTH AFRICA

MODERN EUROPE

753 BCE   600 BCE   400 BCE   200 BCE   0   200 CE   400 CE   600 CE   800 CE   1000 CE   1200 CE   1461 CE

CARTHAGE (Tunisia)

CORDOBA (Spain)

CORINTH (Greece)

LUGDUNUM (Lyon, France)

ALEXANDRIA (Egypt)

BERENIKE (Egypt)

ANCYRA (Ankara, Turkey)

AUGUSTA TREVERORUM (Trier, Germany)

LEPTIS MAGNA (Libya)

LONDINIUM (London, UK)

BOSTRA (Busra, Syria)

Quid est enim aliud omnis historia, quam Romana laus?
What else is all of human history, except praise of Rome?
Petrarch (1304–1374)

I

Introduction

A gleaming, pale building rises high into the blue sky, its monumental columns creating an imposing entrance. Above it, an enormous dome emerges, defying gravity. White marble statues of gods, goddesses, and leading politicians serenely gaze on, decorating this austere, impressive space. Men in togas gather, discussing the politics of the day. In the forum below, citizens stop at market stalls and around beautiful fountains sculpted from pale stone.

This, in the popular imagination, is ancient Rome. It is an incredibly powerful image, one that connects much of modern Europe and the USA with a Mediterranean empire that thrived nearly 2,000 years ago. Take away the togas and this could describe a scene today in London, Paris, or Washington DC. Important government buildings, public spaces, and the statues that decorate them are often made in the same style. They might not remind everyone who sees them of Rome but, on some level, we all understand that this is a sign of power and identity.

Except ancient Rome didn't look like that. Yes, there were columns and domes, statues and fountains, temples and forums. But they weren't white; they weren't even pale. We would certainly not describe them as austere or serene. The Romans loved colour – the more, the better. And it wasn't just paint – they decorated their statues and buildings with gold leaf, sparkling glass, and brightly coloured gemstones. Imagine those serene, ageless faces painted in with heavy eyeliner and cherry-red lips, their clothes in vibrant, colourful patterns. Rome was bedecked, bedazzled, and generally decorated in a way we would now consider gaudy.

This is not something science has only just revealed to us. The evidence has always been available: it is actually visible to the naked eye, even if chemical analysis, infrared, and ultraviolet techniques can help us reconstruct things more precisely. Roman art shows people painting statues, Roman texts describe the colours of buildings and the role of paint. Nor is it just a popular misconception because we have all watched the film *Gladiator* a few too many times. Many experts will freely admit they can still find it jarring to see ancient Rome in full colour. In the past, some experts have simply refused to believe it.

In 1755, a scholar called Johann Winckelmann arrived in Rome. Over the next thirteen years, he would revolutionize archaeology and art history. He was in the right place at the right time. For centuries, artists living on the Italian peninsula had been encouraging a greater appreciation for all things Roman. Hadn't everything been better and more beautiful when it was ruled from the city of Rome? Shouldn't their art, recreating the art of that glorious period, be the most prestigious?

As PR campaigns go, it had been extremely successful.[1] All over the Italian peninsula – the various Italian-speaking states did not consolidate into one until 1861 – people were digging up ancient Roman antiques for the burgeoning art market. Italian artists were making beautiful paintings and sculptures that 'revived' those of Rome, in contrast to the so-called 'barbarian' styles across the German-speaking lands.[2]

---

1 This period is usually referred to as the Renaissance, the *re-birth* of ancient Roman (and Greek) culture in Europe. As we shall see, things are much more complicated than that.

2 As with the Italian-speaking states, the German-speaking territories in this period do not necessarily overlap with the modern-day nation state of Germany.

Wealthy families were funding architecture, art, and scholarship on incredible scales.

During the previous decades, the Roman cities of Pompeii and Herculaneum, buried under the debris from the volcanic eruption of Mount Vesuvius in 79 CE, had become part of this mania for all things Roman. Winckelmann was on the scene during the early excavations. One of the key early finds was a statue of the goddess Artemis, a statue on which red paint could clearly be seen on the hair, the sandals, and the strap of her quiver. This paint meant the statue could not be Roman, Winckelmann concluded: Roman statues were white, and so the colour must mean this was a statue from an earlier period, perhaps an Etruscan one.

More excavations revealed incredible painted wall frescoes in both cities, whose vibrant colours had scarcely been touched. There was other evidence that the Romans – along with the ancient Greeks – appreciated colour in their art. It was clear that other powerful ancient cultures, like the Assyrians, Egyptians, and Etruscans, embraced lavish amounts of colour – and, indeed, that they had used huge amounts of resources to achieve such colours.

Winckelmann was undeterred. Colour could make something more appealing, he argued, but it was not beautiful in itself. In fact, he famously argued about sculptures that 'the whiter the body is, the more beautiful it is'.

In the more than 250 years since Winckelmann made his claims, archaeology and art history have developed as major areas of study. There have been regular, significant discoveries of colourful paint on buildings and statues, in Rome and throughout the territories that made up the Roman Empire. Scholars are confident that the Artemis Winckelmann saw, with her red hair, shoes, and weaponry, was Roman. The only area of doubt left is just *how* bright the colours that decorated Rome might have been.

And yet, if you visit a museum exhibition where scholars have reconstructed a Roman statue, using state-of-the-art scientific techniques, it is hard not to flinch. Although some European museums in the late nineteenth century did paint copies of statues and altars to recreate the possible colour schemes or displayed them in brightly painted spaces, for a combination of reasons, this quickly fell out of fashion and seems to have made little wider impression. Well-meaning, misguided archaeologists have frequently scrubbed the remaining colour off statues to get to the white marble below, believing themselves to be restoring them. This *idea* of Rome, this interpretation of Rome, is more powerful than what we know to be the reality.

Once you start to look, you can see Rome everywhere in the modern world: in art and architecture, languages and law, politics and philosophy, religion and warfare – even in places incredibly far removed from its Mediterranean territories. Not just in the buildings and statues, not just in the ruins and the foundations of European roads, but in cultural phenomena like *Star Wars*, tech bro Stoics in Silicon Valley, and the counterculture Goths. Rome is so present that one of the biggest internet trends of 2023 asked 'Do you think about the Roman Empire daily?'

But are we seeing Rome in full colour or are we looking at the 'restored' white statues, scrubbed of their paint, their detail, and their meaning?

Eventually, it became an empire and military superpower, whose hegemony stretched across the entire Mediterranean basin and beyond.

At different times and in different ways, the things that made up its identity changed: religions, leading families, political systems, military systems, ideals, art, literature, language. This was true at every level of society and in every province. Roman society was obsessed with tradition, with the *mos maiorum*, the customs of the ancestors – but its idea of tradition changed as its society changed.[3]

These differences and changes mean that a number of very different interpretations of Rome are possible, depending on your focus. The colour spectrum of possibilities is vast. It should therefore not be surprising that a number of different societies have looked at themselves and seen Rome, or a connection to Rome, with a lot of evidence to support that view. In fact, many of those very different societies have claimed Rome at the same time, each using different pieces of evidence.

It is not just Rome itself that we see and think about every day, but these many different interpretations of Rome. How and why these have developed explains much about the modern world and underpins the different ways we understand each other today. Ideas about Rome have been interpreted and re-interpreted, repackaged and repurposed for different reasons in different times and places throughout history – right up to the present day. The only constant is that Rome has remained important.

Rome, of course, is a place. It is the capital city of modern-day Italy, home to millions of people, and beloved by tourists for its architectural marvels and historical charm.

But Rome is also a concept. When Vladimir Putin talks about Moscow as 'The Third Rome', we know he isn't talking about the Italian city. When fundamentalist groups like ISIS declare war on Rome, we know they don't mean the Italian city, either.

When Russia and ISIS fight over Roman remains at Palmyra, they are competing over different interpretations of Rome and its legacy. (Likewise, when they ignore the long Christian and Muslim histories of the city, they are only seeing part of the picture of the place and its people.)

---

3 The same phenomenon can be observed in many societies today, where our view of what we need in the present influences our view of how things were in the past. This is as true of conservatives as it is of progressives, for societies are always complex and multi-faceted and humans are always looking to their past for answers.

The culture war over statues? That has its origins in different interpretations of Rome.

Modern fascism? That, too, has its origins in different interpretations of Rome.

The very *concept* of Rome is about identity, power, and legitimacy and, for more than 1,500 years, governments, rulers, and religions have been using it to legitimize their power – often in direct competition with each other. Understanding this helps make sense of the so-called present-day 'clash of civilizations' between both the West and Russia, and the West and Islam. It helps make sense of the current identity crises of the USA, UK, and EU. It helps make sense of the modern world.

A populist leader believes an election has been stolen from him and encourages his supporters to #CrossTheRubicon, marching on the centre of government to restore the Republic.

In 2021, the attack on Capitol Hill, an attempted coup supporting Donald Trump, failed. In 49 BCE, however, Julius Caesar successfully marched on Rome. His armed forces crossed the river Rubicon, the traditional border of Italy, and he was given the official title of Dictator in the Senate building on Capitoline Hill, the political and religious heart of the Roman Republic.

Donald Trump's supporters and opponents had been comparing him with Julius Caesar long before the result of the 2020 presidential election. After his loss, however, this claimed connection became more meaningful; it became a different way of conferring legitimacy and moral authority.

Many people, at the time and since, considered Julius Caesar to be a political, military, and literary genius who was beloved by ordinary people and was the last hope of the Roman Republic. He was attacked by inferior political rivals who were jealous of his popularity and success, and who put their own personal ambition before the Republic. They attacked him in the Senate, in the law courts, and in the court of public opinion. You can see why this interpretation might appeal to Trump supporters.[4]

In fact, in the United States, a claim to the inheritance of Rome is baked into the nation state's identity. The Founding Fathers consciously modelled the new republic on their interpretation of Republican Rome. The name Capitol Hill is a direct reference to the Capitoline Hill in Rome, the political and religious centre of the city. The neoclassical buildings of Washington DC, all white columns and domed roofs, are modelled on an idea of Roman architecture.

Trump's opponents believe in the importance of Rome as much as his supporters. The fight is over whose interpretation of Rome is the right one – whose *claim* is the right one, not whether that claim is meaningful. Rome, after all, is central to the West's understanding of itself and the United States is the leader of the West. Its right to claim the mantle of Rome is taken for granted.

Except that Vladimir Putin, the leader of Russia, has been claiming Rome for himself to legitimize his war against Ukraine, a war many understand as an attack on Western values. At home and abroad, Putin has been leveraging an ideology with its origins in the fourteenth century, which argues that Moscow represents the Third Rome, the righteous defender of Christian values. According to this ideology, the Orthodox Christianity of Russia claims the moral and religious authority of Rome.

---

4 Of course, other interpretations of Julius Caesar have been put forward – there is general agreement that he was hugely talented but many would argue that it was he who put his personal ambition before the Republic and was the final death blow rather than its last hope.

Putin has been supported in this by an archbishop of the Roman Catholic Church, another institution that claims to have inherited the authority of Rome, in opposition to Orthodox Christianity.[5]

While Americans, Russians, and the Roman Catholic Church might not be able to decide which of them has a better claim to Rome, they would probably all agree that the legacy of the superpower that ruled the Mediterranean underpins Christianity more broadly. As a collective, they would probably agree that Christianity and Christian culture have a better claim to Rome than Islam, for example. Islam and Christianity are, so this logic goes, fundamentally different religions that have generated fundamentally different cultures.

However, if you study a map of the Roman Empire at any point, its cultural, intellectual, and economic centre ran from modern-day Turkey, down the eastern Mediterranean, and back across to Libya. Cities like Leptis Magna in Libya, Timgad in Algeria, Jerash in Jordan, Palmyra in Syria, Baalbek in Lebanon, and Ephesus in Turkey all have stunning Roman ruins.

Most of the Roman emperors[6] between 27 BCE and 476 CE,[7] when we usually say Rome 'fell', were born in Italy. But there were also emperors from modern-day Algeria, Bulgaria, Croatia, France, Germany, Lebanon, Libya, Serbia, Spain, Syria, Tunisia, and Turkey. None, funnily enough, were from the North American continent.

So what gives the United States, a nation state that was formed only around 250 years ago on a completely different continent, a better claim to have inherited Rome more than fifteen centuries after it 'fell' than some of the countries where actual Roman emperors were born? Who decided this interpretation was definitive?

---

5 Archbishop Carlo Maria Viganò was the papacy's official diplomat to the USA from 2011 to 2016. On 5 July 2024, he was officially excommunicated for 'schism', although he retains his title.

6 The number is around eighty, depending on whether you count some as legitimate rulers or consider them usurpers.

7 The events of this year and its significance are discussed in Chapter 2.

The last emperor of what we often call Rome didn't leave a last will and testament, so how do we decide *who* gets to inherit its authority? If we could ask him, what would he tell us was the most important element of his identity: his language, his army, his religion, his ancestors, his geographical location? And would the people he ruled have agreed, or would they have highlighted different elements and customs?

This book considers some of the most important interpretations of Rome throughout history and the ways in which they have frequently competed with each other. In doing so, it reveals the world today more clearly – in a little more colour, if you will.

This means covering a huge amount of time and space. Each chapter is dedicated to an empire that claimed a relationship with Rome and examines some of the key elements of their interpretation. Sometimes those claims are based on a previous entity's claim, sometimes they involve denying a rival's claim. Each chapter is designed to work alone – if you just want to drop in – but the claims, interpretations, and many of the themes overlap in a way that means they work better together.

The chapters are grouped into three broad themes: religion, empire, and culture. Of course, these themes also overlap. But they are structured so it is possible to go into detail about the everyday reality of ancient Rome as well as the interpretations that influence the world today.

By the start of the twentieth century, these differing ideas of the Roman Empire had spread around the world. The British, Ottoman, and Russian empires had a presence on every continent between them. Catholic France, Portugal, and Spain had their own global empires with their own legacy of Rome. The United States had modelled itself on Rome. Islam was one of the biggest religions around the globe. And European fascism was about to tear the world apart.

The First and Second World Wars weren't fought over the legacy of Rome; but they were fought by empires, nations, and people who had spent a lifetime being influenced by Rome. The world that emerged is still influenced by those conflicts and by their ideas about Rome.

Before thinking about the different ways in which Rome has been interpreted by later empires to support their own rule, however, it's worth going back to the start and briefly reviewing the history of Rome – how it was ruled and how that changed over time.

Rome started out as a city-state ruled by kings, a period which, according to Roman legend, began in 753 BCE. In 509 BCE, the leading families rebelled against the tyranny of the last king and founded the Roman Republic. In order to avoid the rule of one man, which they felt would inevitably lead to tyranny, they instituted a system in which two men called consuls were elected to rule together for a year.[8] They would alternate political control in the city, taking a month each, and divide military commands between them according to seniority.

They were supported by men elected to more junior political and military offices and by the Senate, an elite body that advised the consuls and comprised all previous elected officials. Each year, the positions were voted on again and a new set of governing officials took over, helped by the previous office-holders. In 493 BCE, representatives of the people were added to the Senate, also elected every year. Together, they formed the Senate and the People of Rome, the combined expression of Roman authority (in Latin, *senatus populusque romanus* or SPQR for short).

By the time Gaius Julius Caesar marched on Rome in 49 BCE, this system had long shown signs of strain. Military leadership, always hugely important in Rome, now became a way to circumvent the law

---

8 We would not describe this electoral system as democratic; wealthier, more aristocratic citizens literally got to vote first and with a weighted vote. Women were not allowed to vote, nor was the substantial enslaved population, nor the vast majority of those who lived outside the city of Rome. However, lower-class, free, male citizens of the city of Rome were entitled to a vote and they seem to have been very proud of this, even if it was not often that meaningful in terms of the result.

and the one-year restriction on consular rule. By 27 BCE, the system had collapsed entirely. Caesar's heir, Gaius Octavianus,[9] subtly introduced a new system, whereby the Senate was still technically important but the decisive element in government was one man, the *princeps* or First Man: what is now called the emperor.[10]

The Roman Republic became the Roman Empire and historians call this period the Principate, the period where one man ruled alone. The trappings of the Republic remained: the political positions to govern the empire or command military forces were still available but they were now appointed by the *princeps*, not elected. At first discreetly, but soon very clearly, the *princeps* was a hereditary position. Membership of or access to the imperial family was where power lay.

The Senate remained prestigious, however, and the wealthy men who occupied it now found themselves with more time than power. Many of the histories of this period were written by them and they are filled with villainous figures: freedmen, women, and uncouth soldiers whose negative influence on the noble *princeps* led to disasters that would presumably not have happened had they themselves only been consulted.

By the time of emperor Diocletian, in 293 CE, this system had also long shown signs of strain. His solution was in many ways a reversion to the old Republican system but with new names: two men sharing military and political power (the *augusti*[11]), with junior assistants

---

9 Caesar's heir was originally called Gaius Octavius. On adoption he became Gaius Julius Caesar, with 'Octavianus' often added to reference his birth name and differentiate him from his adopted father. Later, he would have the name 'Augustus' conferred upon him by the Senate, which is usually translated as 'majestic' or 'venerable', like an even more impressive version of 'the Great'.

10 The word emperor comes from the Latin *imperator*, which itself comes from the verb *imperare*, meaning 'to order, to command', specifically with reference to military troops. Its use as an important (if not the main) title for the rulers of the Roman Empire came from a Republican military tradition and highlights the importance of military support and success for emperors.

11 After the title 'Augustus', conferred by the Senate on Gaius Julius Caesar Octavianus, the first real sole ruler of the Roman Empire.

(the *caesares*[12]). This time, however, they divided all the territories between them, rather than alternate authority by the month. The imperial families remained hugely powerful while the Senate's actual power declined further (they continued to be wealthy, which, of course, came with its own kind of power). Diocletian's reforms also meant military support for the emperor was now more important than ever.

Since the mid-first century, military competence and the backing of the troops had been essential to leading the Roman Empire. Family connections and wealth helped, but they rarely made up for lack of military ability for very long and they could both be overlooked in favour of military ability. Moreover, success in the military would usually lead to better family connections and increased wealth. It was not a meritocracy or a democracy but a society where military power was decisive.

Roman religion over the 1,000 years covered here was incredibly complex: it was central to everyday life for everyone but also incredibly diverse and varied. Old gods and goddesses would remain, transform, or die out. New gods and goddesses appeared; some took hold and others did not. In different regions, different gods and goddesses were understood in different ways.

The three empires covered in Part One all considered Christianity essential to understanding Rome. More than that, they all understood themselves to be meaningfully Roman – in ways that might seem strange to us – because of their own Christianity.

This is where we start: with religion, and how a city that spent more than a millennium celebrating hundreds of gods became known for only one.

---

12 After Julius Caesar, the adopted father of Gaius Julius Caesar Octavianus. Originally, this was the family name of the dynasty but the dynasty quickly ran out of potential rulers. The prestige of the name remained so the link was maintained by using it as a title.

PART ONE
RELIGION

Incense and the scent of freshly crushed petals float on the air in the sacred grove of the Arval Brothers, one of Rome's most prestigious priestly colleges. Colourful wreaths of flowers, bunches of fresh herbs, and newly picked fruits decorate temples, citizens, and divine statues alike. A priest, dressed in his colourful ritual robes, leads a procession through the ancient streets of Rome, accompanied by racing hares and goats, animals associated with fertility. Petals and herbs are thrown in the air as they walk to the theatre, where a special performance will officially open the festival to Flora, the goddess of spring. Outside the theatre, enormous banqueting tables creak under the weight of the feast that has been provided for citizens to eat before the games begin, all paid for by magistrates hoping to earn favour for the next election. Night falls but the festivities continue for six days.

Floralia, the Roman religious festival that greeted the arrival of spring, particularly captivated the imagination of Renaissance artists and thinkers. There are many famous paintings depicting this now lesser-known Roman goddess and her celebrations, some by painters as famous as Botticelli, Rembrandt, and Titian.

Many Roman religious festivals would have been a less charming sensory experience; no amount of incense and petals can cover the smell of animal sacrifice, for instance. The Lupercalia, perhaps Rome's oldest and most important religious festival, would begin with the sacrifice of a goat and a dog. Before the feasting began, the priests would be anointed with the blood of the slaughtered animals. Then those same priests, supervised by one of the highest religious officials of Rome, stripped the skins of the animals and cut them into thongs. These freshly cut animal-skin strips were then picked up by naked or near-naked young noblemen. Led by the official priests, they ran through the streets of the city and whipped women with the thongs as they passed, hoping to bring fertility, health, and good luck.

This was a major festival of ancient Rome. It was connected with Romulus, the mythological founder of Rome, who, legend said, was suckled by a wolf. Plutarch, writing in the late first century CE, reported that Julius Caesar supervised a Lupercalia festival at the height of his power. Mark Antony, who would go on to fight Augustus for control of the empire and die with Cleopatra at the Battle of Actium in 31 BCE, participated as a young nobleman. Long after most of the elite of the Roman Empire had converted to Christianity, and after the last Roman emperor ruled from the city of Rome, this religious festival was still celebrated in the city, held until at least the sixth century.

Most people, when Roman religion is mentioned, would remember tales like those connected with the Lupercalia: Romulus and Remus suckled by a wolf, Jupiter abducting Ganymede, Diana hunting and killing Actaeon for invading her home in the forest. Roman mythology was as brutal as it was fantastical: there was no hiding from the whims of the gods and goddesses.

The pantheon of divine beings extended far beyond the twelve most well-known figures, headed by Jupiter and Juno. The ancient Roman world was suffused with the divine and their places of worship, from the family gods that cared for a home's hearth to the more communal gods that protected a particular location. Ancient tree groves were often considered sacred, as well as the temples that housed statues and where offerings were made to appease divine wrath. Gods and goddesses from other cultures were frequently imported, sometimes into the heart of Roman religious life, like Cybele, or Magna Mater, an Anatolian goddess. The imperial family were sometimes considered to be, in some way, divine – or, at least, so divinely favoured that they were closer to the gods than any other mortal. Religious calendars detailing all the local and major festivals were a feature of every Roman town. The gods reigned above, on earth, and below, and the lives of every member of the empire, whether free or enslaved, conformed to the rhythm of their worship.

And yet, until very recently, the religion with which Rome was most associated was Christianity. The religion that emerged after a Roman governor had a Nazarene carpenter executed, that developed in secrecy to hide from intermittent but lethal Roman persecution over its first three centuries, that still was not powerful enough in 496 CE for Pope Gelasius I to convince the elites living in Rome to ban their young noblemen from running naked through the streets cracking thongs of goatskin – it is that religion, Christianity, that dominated interpretations of Rome for centuries.

By the time that the city of Rome 'fell' in 476 CE, Christianity was the major – if still not the only – religion in the Roman Empire. Roman emperors by then were Christian and it was churches, not temples, that citizens most commonly frequented and rich patrons donated to. Christian priests were growing in importance and councils on doctrinal issues could have consequences across the empire.

It is Christianity that explains why Greek-speaking, German-speaking, and Russian-speaking rulers could all claim to be Roman.

2

The New Rome

In 476, Rome's ruling elite lived in Constantinople, as they had done for more than a century. They continued to live and rule there until 1453 and, all the time, they called their homeland *Romanía* – Romanland. They maintained the Roman religion, government, and way of life, revering their ancestors as Romans had done for more than a millennium. Central to this identity was their Christianity, which they understood to be the religion of Rome.

These Romans continued to build incredible architecture, create stunning art, fight significant wars, research the world around them, write influential literature, and generally be a major power in the region – all things we associate with their Roman predecessors.

You probably haven't heard them called Roman, though. Theirs is usually called the Byzantine Empire and their religion began to be called Eastern Orthodox Christianity. Understanding them on their own terms is the first step towards seeing Rome in full colour.

Thus it was that the fair city, the common delight and boast of all nations, was laid waste by fire and blackened by soot, taken and emptied of all wealth, public and private, as well as that which was consecrated to God [. . .] On that day on which the city fell, the despoilers took up quarters in the houses spread out in all directions, seized everything inside as plunder, and interrogated their owners as to the whereabouts of their hidden treasures [. . .] They spared nothing and shared none of the belongings with their owners, nor were they willing to share food and house with them; [. . .] they showed them utter disdain and refused to mingle with them, taking them captive while heaping abuse upon them and casting them out [. . .] Gathered into groups, [the citizens of Rome] went forth wrapped in tatters, wasted away from fasting, ashen in complexion, their visages corpse-like, and their eyes bloodshot, shedding more blood than tears.

THE FALL OF ROME IS the type of event that would probably make most timelines of major historical events. After all, Rome was important, wherever or even whenever you lived. Moreover, the history of how later empires have interpreted and claimed the legacy of Rome must surely start with the fall of the original Roman Empire and the end of the last Roman emperor.

So the fourth day of September in the year 476, when Odoacer, a general of Germanic troops, deposed the child emperor Romulus Augustulus and declared he was the ruler of Italy, should be a momentous date.[1] Rome had been conquered and the emperor deposed. This is the obvious starting point for our story.

Of course, it is never that simple.

---

1 This calendar did not exist then – for the Romans, the year was 1229, which was counted from the mythical date of the founding of the city (or *ab urbe condita*, if you like your Latin). A calendar attempting to count from the birth of Jesus like the one now in use throughout much – but not all – of the world, was not invented until forty-nine years later and wasn't much used for another three hundred years after that.

The year 476 is not our starting point. The events described so dramatically in the opening to this chapter *do* recount an attack on the capital of the Roman Empire, but one that took place in 1204, led by Italian-speakers.

This 'fair city', capital of the Roman Empire, was called Nea Rhome in Greek or Nova Roma in Latin. In English, of course, this is New Rome, and the city is commonly known as Constantinople, after the Roman emperor who founded it in 330.

While the city of Rome on the Italian peninsula suffered repeated military defeats and invasions throughout the fifth century, the city where the Roman ruling elite lived was going strong, using its significant tax base to enjoy world-class urban amenities. Constantinople, the Christian city of Constantine the Great, had been the centre of the Roman Empire for more than a century when Rome, the city, 'fell'.

The people who lived and ruled there called themselves Roman, their language and religion that of the Romans. The territories they ruled, from North Africa to the Balkans, called them Roman and so did their allies and enemies to the east. They didn't consider themselves *successors* to Rome or *interpreters* of Rome. As far as they considered, they *were* Roman. They lived in Romanía, or Romanland.

This Christian empire continued for a millennium. For most of that time, it was a dazzlingly glamorous and wealthy one, until it was sacked by European invaders in 1204.

Even then, it carried on, a prestigious city and culture of faded grandeur and major symbolic significance, for 250 more years, before it was finally conquered by a commander who would add 'Caesar' to the list of his own titles and 'Roman' to the description of his own territories.

None of the following empires of this book make sense without the history of Romanland. Instead of the 'fall' of Old Rome, we start with the *foundation* of New Rome and the career of Constantine the Great, the first Christian Roman emperor.

Building (New) Rome: Constantine's career

Constantine I, known to us (but not in his own time) as Constantine the Great, is one of the more famous Roman emperors. He ruled from 306 to 337, he founded the city of Constantinople, and he was the first Roman emperor to convert to Christianity.

Regular readers of Roman history will know there is a lot hidden by that seemingly straightforward set of highlights: he didn't rule alone until 324, a settlement already existed on the site of Constantinople, and both his conversion and his idea of Christianity were quite different from ours.

First of all, at the time Constantine began to rule, in 306, the Roman Empire was enormous and ruling it alone was too big a job for most men (they didn't officially give the women a chance).[2] Things had got so out of hand that the empire itself nearly collapsed on a number of occasions between 235 and 284.

To prevent this from happening again, as we saw earlier, the emperor Diocletian had divided the empire administratively, reviving earlier ideas of collegial rule, like the two consuls of the Republic. One pairing of a senior ruler, the *augustus,* with a junior, a *caesar*, was responsible for the eastern territories in the empire and the other, junior pairing of *augustus* and *caesar* was responsible for the western territories. Collectively these territories remained the Roman Empire.[3] It was an administrative division, nothing more.

---

2 Of course, many elite women had successfully wielded power in the Roman Empire, both before and after this point, as women have throughout history. They were not considered an official option, however, and most sources, written and sponsored by men, tend to represent them rather unfairly. One woman would go on to rule officially, but much later, and with some interesting consequences for us: Empress Eirene, who we will encounter in Chapter 3.

3 For instance, Constantine had been educated in the eastern part and made his name as a military general on Eastern campaigns, before his promotion to *caesar* of the West.

Technically, these positions were to be appointed on merit, not family importance, but this didn't take: Constantine's father, Constantius, was the first *caesar* of the Western territories and, upon his promotion to *augustus*, he immediately nominated his son as his successor.

So Constantine quickly became the *caesar* designated to the western part of the empire. When his father died in 306, Constantine's army declared him *augustus* – the army approving your rule was very important, something that will come up again. Being an ambitious sort, however, he didn't settle for being one of only two *augusti*. By 324, he was the sole ruler of the Roman Empire and his success seemed at least partly connected to his embrace of Christianity.

By any measure, this divided ruling system hadn't lasted long: there were only thirty-one years between Diocletian's formally instigating it and Constantine's sweeping it aside. The idea that the empire could and had been separated, in a meaningful rather than merely administrative way, was to leave a long impression, however (not least for modern historians, for whom the administrative division helps to break down this enormous empire into more analysable units).

Despite being the undisputed sole ruler of the Roman Republic, Constantine was still seemingly quite ambitious to prove himself. In his defence, the bar was quite high: the likes of Julius Caesar, Augustus, Hadrian, and Diocletian, for example, had all contributed to a Roman idea of greatness that involved astonishing military success, good governmental administration, lavish sponsorship of monumental buildings and religious spaces, and the foundation of cities.

This brings us to the second highlight on Constantine the Great's list: founding New Rome.

Technically, a settlement already existed on the Bosphorus strait where Constantine decided to build a new, more Christian capital city for his reinvigorated empire. This place, called Byzantium, was probably almost as old as the original Rome and its history was part of its appeal: Constantine almost immediately celebrated a 1,000-year anniversary for his 'new' city.

How do you found a city on a site where a city already exists? This is actually more straightforward than it seems. In fact, most important cities of the ancient (and, indeed, modern) world were in places where there was some sort of settlement beforehand; otherwise, it was probably an impractical location that wouldn't support a large population. Being the first person to draw up a blueprint didn't necessarily matter: what was important was funding construction on a huge scale, maybe building some new city walls, and having it all recorded in a helpful manner for posterity. Founding a city in the ancient world was almost a form of immortality – arguably the closest way in a pre-Christian world to achieve a semi-divine status. Rulers were falling over themselves to be called 'founder', one way or another.

Part of the confusion is because we are living in quite different societies, speaking literally different languages, many hundreds of years later than the ancient city founders. Translation from one language to another, as any expert will tell you, can never perfectly convey the original meaning because that builds up over time in a different culture and acquires different sets of nuances and associations. You can't capture all of them. The same goes for older versions of a language; the further back you go, the harder it is to 'translate' words, ideas, and values for a modern audience.

This is more than just a scholarly technicality: it helps us think about how far anyone can understand a different society. Latin words like *conditor* and *fundator* have nuances that the English words 'builder' and 'founder' don't quite capture, and the same goes for the ancient Greek words *ktistes* (something close to 'creator') and *oikistes* (akin to 'founder'). There is no need to get into the weeds of translation theory here, thankfully. What matters is that you could be known as the founder of a city even if you weren't the first person to build a house there and Constantine was definitely known as the founder of Constantinople – which is where its new name Konstantinoupolis or 'city of Constantine' came from. This importance meant that cities would quite often re-name themselves after an important political or military leader as a way to gain favour, or 'rediscover' an ancient name that connected them with a prestigious figure in order to compete with a rival city.

Of course, cities change names all the time. The fact that New York City was previously called New Amsterdam is a useful pub quiz fact (though fewer people know it was briefly called New Orange for the same reason: Dutch rule[4]). Saigon is now Ho Chi Minh City. Caesarodunum and Augustonemetum, in France, have long been officially called Tours and Clermont-Ferrand. Between six and seventy cities have claimed a connection with Alexander the Great, with many of them taking his name in some way. Only Alexandria in Egypt has retained the name.[5] Constantinople itself has officially been Istanbul since 1930 and unofficially for a lot longer.[6]

In this case, the various name-changes and new political positions are more than just useful pub quiz facts. They are important clues to the many different interpretations of Rome and the way we imagine Rome today. Emperors in the East and West, Romes in the East and West. Old names, new names, nicknames. Neither Byzantium or Constantinople, however, is the name that Constantine gave his city. Officially, the city was called Nea Rhome (in Greek) or Nova Roma (in Latin).

With Constantine's foundation of New Rome, there was a shift to a different type of Rome: a Christian Rome. This was still a complex

---

4 This name comes from the House of Orange, who are now the royal family of The Netherlands.

5 Although some, like Kandahar in modern Afghanistan, retain traces. Originally Alexandria Arachosia – also Alexandropolis – it might have evolved via Iskander, the Arabic and Persian form of the name Alexander, although other local legends are available, including the role of the Indo-Parthian king Gondophares, a later 'founder'.

6 This official name comes from *eis ten Polin* or "to the City", the nickname from at least as early as the eleventh century.

religious environment of different perspectives and practices. The old gods and goddesses remained for many, alongside or instead of the Christian god, and Christianity in this period was often quite different from what is now often considered mainstream Christianity. The shift towards a Christian Roman empire had, though, started long before Constantine and would continue long after him.

It is with the foundation of his new city, however, that you can start to talk about a Christian Roman empire in both the sense of its power structures and in a way that you can actually *see*, with the construction of major Christian buildings in the imperial capital.

A New, Christian Rome: inspired by Old Rome

The pre-existing settlement of Byzantium had secured a strategic and lucrative location for a city, perched on the Bosphorus strait. Militarily, it was high up and surrounded by water, requiring only one wall to protect it, provided one had naval support. Economically, it controlled trade from all directions, at sea and on land. Despite this, however, it had never been especially important, something that was to change dramatically.

Old Rome was being replaced during the third century by other, more strategically located cities, as military leaders focused on practicalities over prestige. In New Rome, Constantine decided to do both. The location was easy to defend and allowed him to improve his tax base, giving him much-needed funds for the military. It was also situated closer to Persia, Rome's long-standing imperial rival. What was crucial, however, was that it also *looked* like a suitable capital city for the Roman Empire.

Very deliberately, the expanded layout used fourteen regions across seven hills, just like Old Rome. Sculptures, statues, and other artwork, particularly those connected with military successes of the past, were collected from across the empire to decorate the new city's squares in a manner befitting Nova Roma. Temples to the gods – the traditional gods as well as the Christian god – were built and decorated. Four bronze horse statues were repurposed from their original locations elsewhere in the empire to decorate the new Hippodrome, a sporting and social stadium-type structure that was the centre of life in major Roman cities.[7]

This decision to reuse and repurpose decorative items was a deliberate choice, holding a clear meaning for those who viewed it. For a long time, it was seen as indicating that Constantine could not create his own art and architecture and therefore represented a decline from the peak of the Roman Empire. We now know this was the opposite of the case: the Romans had always done this as a way to express continuity with the past. Constantine was demonstrating that he was a worthy and legitimate heir to the likes of Julius Caesar and Augustus, and that his new city was a worthy and legitimate Roman capital.

He didn't stop there. The senatorial families who had made their homes in Old Rome were encouraged to move; many took up the offer, although many more preferred to stay in the symbolic old capital. The grain dole – made famous in the 'bread and circuses' idea of how to keep the citizens of Old Rome happy, complementing the enormous new Hippodrome – was instituted in New Rome. The same political administration and infrastructure was implemented. Craftspeople, merchants, and artists flocked to the city, sensing opportunities and contributing to the sense that this was becoming the new centre of the empire.

The population of Old Rome had declined from around a million at its peak to under 400,000 by the time of Romulus Augustulus in 476 CE. New Rome, in contrast, rapidly expanded, reaching around 500,000 by the same time.

---

7 These ended up in thirteenth-century Venice, stolen during the Fourth Crusade, and re-used as a way for the Venetian Republic to claim Roman-ness.

None of this is to say that Old Rome immediately ceased to matter or that nobody cared about its fate. The sacks of the city in the fourth century caused alarm around the empire and the process by which the balance of power shifted to New Rome was slow. Many of Old Rome's senatorial elite remained, holding power locally and huge wealth more widely. The city was still enormous by the standards of the time and it retained symbolic meaning. By 476, however, New Rome was clearly where the power lay.

It was also, by this point, clearly a Christian city. Just how 'Christian' Constantine was is debated; accounts from the time highlight different elements of his life. It is also difficult, at this distance, to understand what his contemporaries would have understood as an appropriate degree of Christianity. It is often noted he was only baptized on his deathbed but it was then common to postpone baptism until the last possible moment to avoid sinning afterwards, so this doesn't indicate a lack of commitment. In a similar vein, it seems it was also quite normal (albeit not exactly priest-approved) in this period to consider one god to be the highest authority and divinity but not the *only* divinity, so Constantine's reported support for Sol Invictus, the unconquered sun, also does not necessarily mean he did not consider himself Christian.

For our story, it is much more important that he does seem to have made his capital city consciously Christian, setting a precedent for the next 1,100 years. Together with his mother, Helena,[8] who was later made a saint, he supported the building of Christian churches, while his sons supported temples to the traditional Roman gods in Italy. Again, this is what we should probably expect from the first Christian emperors; previous rulers had expressed personal religious preferences

8 Helena was an extraordinary woman who patronized building and art to such a degree that she was sometimes considered a co-founder of Nova Roma. She played an active role in many areas of government, including giving money to the troops and claiming to have discovered the True Cross in Jerusalem, a relic that remains important to a number of Christian denominations to this day.

without banning support of others. Christians had been persecuted by preceding emperors, quite famously, but the problem imperial authorities had with them was their refusal to acknowledge any other religion and express support for the government in the traditional manner and not necessarily a particular opposition to the Christian religion itself.[9]

Whatever the depth of Constantine's personal commitment to Christianity, his actions changed the paths of both the empire and the religion. It also meant that New Rome became an important centre of Christianity. It was not an overnight change and it was not unchecked progress but, before long, Christianity was central to the understanding of Rome in a way that would have been unimaginable a few years previously.

It is difficult to imagine now, when the Italian city of Rome is home to one of the major branches of Christianity and even hosts an independent microstate of which the Pope of the Roman Catholic Church is the official ruler,[10] but Rome was not a major Christian city for some time. Christians seem to have lived there from the mid-first century but there was no Christian church in the forum, a literal and metaphorical way to think about the significance of the religion to the city, until 200 years after Constantine declared New Rome was open for business. A major decline in the population of Old Rome during the following centuries meant that, by the eighth century, Baghdad, capital of the Muslim world, was almost certainly home to more Christians.

---

9 This is complicated but it seems the central issue was that Christians refused to offer sacrifice for the health of the emperor, which they understood as compromising their commitment to monotheism. Imperial authorities understood it as treason, effectively, since to their mind the act of sacrifice was quite compatible with any other religious commitment. Many Christians did offer the required sacrifice, whether because they also felt it could be reconciled with their beliefs or to avoid punishment. Many, famously, did not.

10 Vatican City State is the smallest independent country in the world, by both size and population, and it is entirely surrounded by the city of Rome but it is indeed an independent country. This status is a legacy of medieval Rome, which will be discussed in the next chapter, and Mussolini's rule, which will be discussed in Chapter 7.

Where exactly the centre of Christian authority was located became a centuries-long contest between five bishoprics: Alexandria, Antioch, Constantinople, Jerusalem, and Rome. Eventually, after a lot of changes, this was reduced to two: Constantinople and Rome, New Rome and Old Rome, eastern Rome and western Rome. Which city you considered most important likely depended on where you lived and which variation of Christianity your local priest practised.

It was not clear at first just how important this disagreement was to become and it took a long time to whittle the contest down to the two Romes. But the relationship between Christianity and the idea of Rome, the Roman Empire, and Roman-ness underpins a lot of what follows. From an imperial point of view, that relationship begins in New Rome.

So from 330, there were two cities called Rome. Both were important to the empire and both became important to Christianity. While the repetition of names might seem confusing to us, the same problem does not seem to have plagued contemporary observers. They had a number of names they could deploy to avoid confusion around the cities. New Rome was also known as Roma Constantinopolitana (Latin for 'the Rome of Constantine'), for instance. Most importantly, only one was the capital of the Roman Empire: the one in the East.

It is crucial to stress this: the events of 476 did not mean the Roman Empire had fallen. By far the most important bits of it were still standing, administered from its prestigious capital city, by a man acclaimed by everyone, including the ruler of Italy, as the Roman emperor. It kept going until 1453, almost another millennium. Romans kept living in it, kept practising Roman religion, and kept calling their ruler the Emperor of Rome.

New Rome: a day in the life

What was it like living in New Rome, this fabulously wealthy Christian capital of empire?

Of course, life in the city differed depending on who you were: how wealthy; how educated; your gender and profession; your access to power. As always, we have more insight into the lives of the elite, who tend to leave more evidence and to be the focus of more research. Experiences of the city also changed depending on when you lived there: the city of Theodora and Justinian in the sixth century, for instance, was probably very different from that of Anna Komnene in the twelfth century.

However, one aspect of Romanland's society that is commonly observed is the way in which innovations could be made in art, architecture, religion, and scholarship while sticking staunchly to ancient traditions. As the Romans always had, they found ways to acknowledge the *mos maiorum* or the customs of the ancestors, and still respond to contemporary challenges. This practice allows us to say something about the lives of both the elites and non-elites throughout the history of the city.

If you had walked through the city of New Rome hundreds of years after the rule of Constantine, it would still be filled with monumental buildings, many of them built under his rule. You would still have access to huge public waterworks: aqueducts, cisterns, fountains, and public baths. The Aqueduct of Valens, for instance, built in 368, still supplied the city (and, indeed, is still standing today).

The Forum of Constantine was still a focal point of urban life, where people gathered to do business, to debate, to socialize. The statues Constantine had taken from Old Rome to mark his new city as the centre of the world remained. The huge domes of churches like Hagia Sophia still dominated the skyline. Cities change over time but much remains the same. A visitor to New Rome in the twelfth century would have seen many of the same Roman buildings as someone in the fourth century – although, of course, the temples to the old gods and goddesses were no more; the city was thoroughly Christian now.

Even so, the old gods and goddesses still made the occasional appearance. The literature of the twelfth century, a flourishing intellectual period, made great use of ancient Roman legends. The philosophy of the ancients was still read, studied, debated, and developed: Anna Komnene, writer of one of the great medieval histories and daughter of a Roman emperor, was noted for her command of ancient philosophy, as well as ancient history and theatre. Her history of the period is filled with literary references and flourishes, showing off her intellectualism as so many Romans had delighted in doing before her.

The major theological debates during Anna's lifetime (1083–1153) were frequently conducted in the form of written dialogues, in the manner of second-century Rome and ancient Athens before that, or as part of public debates. They were also often addressed in public letter writing, an approach that the famous ancient Romans like Caesar and Cicero would have recognized. New Rome had a decidedly Christian flavour but it was still recognizably like pre-Christian Rome in many crucial ways.

If life in New Rome, capital of Romanland, was so recognizably Roman, why does anyone talk about the fall of Rome? And why do people refer to 'Byzantium'?

What's in a name: Roman or Greek?

The first thing to know is that, at the time, nobody did talk about the fall of Rome. In both the east and west, it was understood that Rome still existed. It took quite a while before anyone seriously questioned the Roman-ness of New Rome and the Roman Emperor who ruled from there.

The second thing to know is that, when someone finally did start questioning the Roman-ness of Romanland, it was about that religious power struggle between the Old and New Romes.

Old Rome didn't have very much going for it in the sixth and seventh centuries – it was still famous because of its history but its population was dwindling and its hard power had mostly disappeared. Religious and political authority had always been indivisible in Rome and, increasingly, the Christian leaders took over the administration of the city.[11] Their power struggle with New Rome therefore began to become important to the elite in Old Rome and the clergy used all the soft power at their disposal. That included claiming a direct institutional descent from St Peter and attacking both the Christianity and the Roman-ness of the rulers in New Rome.

This wasn't a particularly serious attack on the authority of the Roman emperors, who were a bit too busy with their own concerns, administering a giant empire and fighting major military battles with equally important foreign powers (first Sasanian Persia and then the Muslim Arabs). The bishops of Old Rome writing endless letters and public statements about how they were actually more important didn't usually make the top of anyone's to-do lists in New Rome.

Elsewhere in Europe, as we will see in the following chapter, the kingdoms that emerged from the former western territories of the empire continued to claim connections to Rome, although to differing degrees. The Vandals in North Africa, the Visigoths in south-west France and the Iberian peninsula, the Burgundians in southern France, the Franks in northern France, and the Ostrogoths in Italy all ruled in the Roman tradition – or as much as they could. The same was often true for smaller political entities in places like the British and Irish islands.

In all these areas, Latin was still the common language, Christianity was still the dominant religion, and magnificent rural villas were still

---

11 In general, the idea that temporal and religious power can or should be separated is a very modern concept. Even in the Holy Roman Empire, which the popes claimed was a temporal extension of their religious power, the two could not actually be separated – emperors had to be religious, bishops could lead armies, and the Pope was a head of state.

how the elite differentiated themselves. Politically, economically, and militarily, these kingdoms were no longer integrated the way they had once been under a single emperor but culturally much remained the same. Even as things slowly transformed, their rulers continued to behave in the way they *interpreted* Roman leadership.

Occasionally, some very sniffy members of the old Roman aristocracy left letters and complaints about how much things had changed and, for them, things probably had. For the vast majority, however, the shift in their identity from 'Roman' to 'Visigothic' or 'Burgundian' was quite slow and probably included a great deal of overlap: a Roman *and* local identity had always been possible; choice was only necessary in times of local rebellion.

There was also a brief but significant interruption in many of these regions when they were reconquered by the Emperor Justinian I, who united the former territories in the West with the ongoing empire in the East from 535. Much of these reconquered regions did not remain in Roman hands long after his death in 565, although crucially Old Rome, Ravenna, Sicily, Sardinia, and Corsica all stayed under the political control of Romanland until 717. Notably, Justinian I made Ravenna the capital of the newly reconquered provinces and it remained more important than Old Rome in this period.

By the late eighth century, however, things had noticeably changed in the former Western territories, with local dynasties now meaningful in their own right. The bishops of Old Rome became much more interested in asserting authority in Western affairs than in engaging in theological debates with New Rome. The Franks began to conquer more and more territory in the West, while in Romanland, a woman was ruling – first as a regent and then as the only official sole Empress of Rome – and the Pope sensed an opportunity for a power grab.

All this is discussed in detail in the next chapter. What is important here is that, amongst all these changes, some key western Roman sources stopped acknowledging Romanland as *Roman* and started calling it Greek instead.

This was a conscious and deliberate choice. When they needed something from the emperors of Romanland, their diplomatic language switched, from deliberately insulting and self-aggrandizing to respectful, acknowledging their Roman identity. When they wanted to dismiss their authority, they called them *Graeci* or 'Greeks'. They knew what they were doing and they knew why they were doing it.

'Greek' was not a positive name in this period. Nowadays it is common to think of ancient Greece being as important to Western heritage as Rome, sometimes more so, but this is a very modern understanding. In ancient Latin literature 'Greek' often had connotations of treachery, effeminacy, love of luxury, and cowardice. 'Greek' was unmanly, unvirtuous, unimpressive: the opposite of Roman. Using it to describe a rival empire was deeply insulting; one Roman emperor who received a letter from ambassadors of the Pope addressing him as Greek threw them into prison until he received an apology.

When you look at the literature of Romanland now, it is clear that the language of the empire was Greek, not Latin, a fact which understandably causes some confusion. It was this fact that allowed the papal diplomats who had insulted the emperors of Romanland to save face before changing their terminology. But there are a few really important details.

Firstly, we do not confuse speaking English with being English. English is spoken around the world, as a consequence of the extent of the British Empire and then the cultural dominance of the United States of America. Relatively few English speakers identify as English, and very many of them would be quite offended at the misunderstanding. Many Swiss and Austrians speak German but they are not Germans; many Belgians speak French but are not French, and so on.

Secondly, most people in Romanland called their language Romeika, or the language of the Romans.[12] This is not as contradictory as it seems: much of the reason that ancient Latin used 'Greek' pejoratively was because it was the language of the conquered elite. When the Romans first encountered Greek-speaking cultures,[13] they positioned themselves as rugged and no-nonsense, with strong values and a traditional way of life that was uncorrupted by wealth, in opposition to these fancy foreigners who were more interested in art and philosophy than military matters.

The Romans would very soon adopt many of those same fancy habits they initially scoffed at, including speaking Greek. In fact, an ability to speak Greek soon became an indication that you were a wealthy and sophisticated *Roman*. In New Rome, as with so much else from Old Rome, the elite continued this tradition, surrounded by cities and peoples who also considered Greek the language of the elite – without ever considering it to imply they weren't Roman. In much of Europe, however, the peoples who had moved into Rome's western territories learned Latin and that became their elite language. As a result, the idea of a meaningful distinction between Latin and Greek was revived.

The emperors of Romanland understood exactly what was meant when Western Roman ambassadors addressed them as Greek: that they weren't proper Romans.

There are some clear fault lines emerging here: everyone agreed that to be Roman was important, that Rome meant power. Everyone believed themselves, in meaningful ways, to *be* Roman. However, they all had different ideas of *how to be* Roman. It is a theme that will reappear again and again throughout this book.

---

12 The connection with the modern Pontic Greek dialect is discussed in Chapter 5.

13 'Greece' as a place did not exist in the ancient world. A number of different city states and polities were situated around the Mediterranean, connected by language and culture. There were frequent alliances between some or many of them but states of war existed just as frequently. Their name for themselves was 'Hellenes', not Greeks: that comes from the Latin word *Graeci* to describe them.

These different ideas of what it meant to be Roman and the ways in which they diverged, combined with their desire for authority, began to mean that the rulers in western Rome and Romanland could not recognize the *other* as Roman in the same way that they thought of themselves as being so.

For a time, their shared sense of Christianity kept things to a war of words. Each believed their version of Christianity to be the more correct one, an issue that did greatly fuel the conflict. For much of the time, however, they decided that their differing versions of Christianity gave them more in common with each other than their respective Muslim neighbours.

By this time, the once-Roman, then Visigothic, territories in the Iberian peninsula and south-west France were mostly ruled by Muslim leaders. A Muslim empire held sway across the Levant and North Africa, the economic heartland of the Roman Mediterranean, throughout Persia, Rome's oldest and greatest rival, and into the Arabian peninsula, long part of the Roman world.

The emergence of Islamic empires as superpowers in their own right in the seventh century had meant there was always another possible enemy for the two Romes, and that kept a lid on things, at least for a few centuries. But these Christian and Muslim lands were not always at war; frequently, they maintained diplomatic relationships and occasionally they were even allies. Occasionally the two Romes and their allies even fought together, claiming to defend Christianity.

From words to war: invading New Rome

Eventually, though, after centuries of fighting with words, the two Romes fought with swords. Romanland had been at war with the Christian Normans in Sicily over who had the right to rule there for some time but the Normans were not under the authority of Old Rome and both parties could set aside their differences for the First Crusade in 1096 – in the beginning, at least.

One telling of the First Crusade might highlight the extraordinarily unsuspected success of the fractured, squabbling Christian forces of the former western Roman territories against the fractured, squabbling Muslim forces, on a long, arduous fighting journey that concluded with the violent capture of Jerusalem and the slaughter of its Jewish and Muslim populations.

Another telling might focus on the way that the Roman emperor called for aid from Christians of Old Rome to manage his territories, successfully united their fractured and squabbling leaders under his own authority, received oaths of allegiance from the Christian leaders, and faithfully supplied their armies with the necessary provisions throughout their long fighting journey to make it less arduous, only to be repeatedly betrayed as the Franks saw opportunities for a land grab.[14]

Again, we can see how understanding the differing interpretations of Rome sheds light on major historical events.

The establishment of the Crusader states in the eastern Mediterranean meant that the relationship between the two types of Christianity changed. Whereas previously it had been mostly theoretical, now it was very real. The two Christianities were no longer merely claiming to be allies in a fight against a broadly defined shared enemy in their own specific regions. They were diplomatic and military allies in a shared region against a (mostly) shared regional enemy.

Pilgrimages to Jerusalem had continued despite the Arab conquests and Muslim rulership of the city, usually via Constantinople. The fabulous wealth of Romanland had always been a topic of conversation, talked about by merchants and pilgrims. Now, however, contact

---

14 There were some key participants from the Holy Roman Empire and England but the majority of leaders and military forces in the First Crusade were Franks, or French. The makeup of forces changed during the Second and Third Crusades, although the Crusader forces continued to be referred to as 'Franks' by many of their allies and enemies.

between the two different societies increased and, although there was admiration on both sides for some elements of the other's cultures, there was also tension.

By 1203, these tensions had ramped up. The Italian city states of Genoa, Pisa, and Venice and their formidable navies had begun to dominate international trade and were therefore able to negotiate favourable terms for themselves with Romanland. The Venetians controlled an entire district of the city of Constantinople, where the growing power of the Italians was resented. In much of Europe, the wealth of Romanland was coveted. Meanwhile, the theological differences between the types of Christianity were becoming increasingly clear and another source of tension.[15]

Diplomatic niceties could no longer paper over the cracks and each sought to assert authority over the other.

Venetian shipping power was necessary to transport the forces of the Fourth Crusade but the Venetians had built up their naval and political power through understanding finances and they weren't about to let a religious justification get in the way of being paid. First, they diverted the crusade to attack a Christian city, Zara, in modern Croatia. Then they diverted the crusade still further when Alexios, the nephew of the emperor of Romanland, asked for help overthrowing his uncle and offered very favourable terms. The Venetians happily helped his coup and, when he didn't pay up, besieged the city.[16]

---

15 The Great Schism of 1054 was, in hindsight, a major moment in the diversion of the two forms of Christianity but it did not seem irrevocable at the time. It seems both sides assumed there would be a rapprochement; they were just biding time to make it on their terms – indeed, the First Crusade was an attempt at such a rapprochement. The disagreements between the two included theological matters, such as whether the Holy Spirit proceeded from God the Father alone, as the Eastern Church held, or from the Father and the Son together, as the Western Church proclaimed, but also ones of power and authority, such as which should have primacy in the church leadership and whether the coronation of Charlemagne as Emperor of the Romans in 800, discussed in the following chapter, was legitimate.

16 Not everyone did – many knights walked away before Zara and many more walked away before and during the Siege of Constantinople, disgusted at the turn things had taken.

Eventually, in 1204, they sacked it.

Nearly 900 years after Constantine had founded New Rome, after centuries of fighting the Persian Empire and then a succession of Muslim powers, Rome had fallen – and to a force of Christian, European powers, led by an Italian city state. The mournful description of the sack of an ancient city that opened this chapter was actually written by a man called Niketas Choniates to describe the destruction of Constantinople by its Christian 'allies'.

Damage control: Denying Rome

It is difficult to calculate the damage done to Constantinople in 1204. The wealth lost, looted and burned, was enormous. Fabulous textiles and beautiful manuscripts, gilded paintings and shrines, histories and technologies – all destroyed. Many things made their way to Europe but many more did not. Those four bronze horses that Constantine brought from around the empire to decorate his new capital city and project his authority ended up in Venice, decorating the now famous St Mark's Basilica. They remain to this day, a reminder of the destruction of one Christian city by another.

The political and religious hierarchies of Romanland that survived went into exile; many would return fifty-seven years later to a much-reduced city and find ways not only to survive but frequently to thrive for nearly 200 more years.[17] Meanwhile, the Pope in Rome finally claimed authority over Constantinople and European Catholic Christians claimed the art, libraries, religious relics, and wealth of Romanland for themselves.

Whatever the rivalry between Old and New Rome and between the different Christianities, whatever the diplomatic, political, and cultural

---

17 However, the elites of Romanland were geographically much more fragmented from this point, with various significant centres of power splintered around the eastern Mediterranean and Black Sea sharing a culture, a history, and perhaps dreams of a collective future.

differences between the two societies, such an extraordinary attack did not go unquestioned. Those who had attacked Constantinople and those who had benefited from it had to justify their actions.

The subtle propaganda of the previous centuries against Romanland now went into overdrive. The *Greeks* were treacherous, effeminate, fond of luxury over morality, and cowards, everything the ancient Latin slur had implied. Their political system was unstable and the Europeans were only trying to help. The Greeks had broken their promises. They could not look after their treasures and no longer deserved them. They were barely Christian and they were certainly not Roman.

Both in exile and when they returned to a Constantinople that was now barely more than a city-state, however, these new enemies of Europe continued to call themselves Roman. So did their enemies and allies further east. The successive Muslim Umayyad, Abbasid, Fatimid, Seljuk, and Ottoman dynasties all fought against, and traded with, a place they called Rome. Only in Christian Europe were its people known as Greek.

Even now, nobody was calling them Byzantine.

To get to the bottom of that, you would have to fast forward to the nineteenth century – or Chapters 4 and 5, where the threads of Christian Constantinople are woven into new understandings of Rome.

First, we need to consider the perspective of Old Rome and, before that, it might be useful to pause for a quick recap.

From city-state to empire and back again: a 2,000 year journey

What Rome meant, and where it was understood to be, evolved over time. It began as a city ruled by hereditary kings in Italy, developed into an empire around the Mediterranean ruled by two elected men, then by hereditary emperors, then by four men who divided the territories between them, reverted to a Mediterranean empire ruled by a hereditary emperor, and finally ended as a city-state again. Over this long span of time, it was not just the system at the top that changed but the religion, the elite families, the dominant language, traditions, art, architecture, literature, and much more.

What did not change was the idea that Rome meant power and that to *rule* Rome meant a higher level of authority: militarily, politically, and religiously.

The desire to claim the military, political, and religious authority of Rome made conflict inevitable between the two claimants to Roman-ness, unless one could acknowledge the other as senior. In New Rome, this was fairly straightforward for contemporaries: theirs was very clearly the seat of the senior Roman emperor and the home of the 'authentic' Roman civilization.

In Old Rome, in ways that seem difficult to grasp from a modern perspective, it was much more complicated and meant the employment of varying justifications, linguistic tricks, and denialism to support their case to be understood as the 'real' Rome. This is not to say that the popes and emperors in Old Rome did not genuinely believe they had a right to be called Roman; just that they had to try much harder to convince others.

The methods they employed to do so might not have been terribly successful in New Rome or in the contemporary Muslim empires but they did succeed at home and, as will become clear, they have had an impact up to the modern day.

3

The Holy Roman Empire

A coalition of Germanic peoples and their fragmented Central European territories who, according to Voltaire, were 'neither Holy, nor Roman, nor an Empire' called themselves the (Holy) Roman Empire for a millennium. Sometimes their territories included the city of Rome, sometimes they didn't.

They could call themselves Roman because they were crowned by the head of the Roman Catholic Church, the Pope. To their mind, their Catholic Christianity distinguished them from other claimants, despite the differences in language and history and geography.

The Holy Roman Empire lasted, in one way or another, for just over 1,000 years, and their interpretation of Rome would change much as Rome itself had changed, especially as Protestantism emerged. The ways that ideas of Rome developed and transformed in these territories would have implications for both contemporary and future empires.

In the heart of Rome, on Christmas Day in the year 800, a sacred and momentous ceremony took place. The elites of the city who had gathered to celebrate the birth of Christ were surprised and delighted as Pope Leo III, recognizing that Charles, King of the Franks, was the most pious and powerful of European rulers, spontaneously anointed him with holy oil and crowned him imperator et augustus, emperor of Rome. Charles, stunned and humbled, acknowledged the traditional authority of the pope to select an emperor and graciously accepted the honour. Smoking incense perfumed the air, light danced through the colourful windows and refracted off the mosaics, and music reverberated through the crowd, who sighed with relief. An emperor ruled from Rome again and his new Roman empire, the Holy Roman Empire, would last for more than 1,000 years.

OF COURSE, THIS IS NOT quite accurate.

For one thing, nobody present was stunned – certainly not Charles, who was definitely already angling to become Roman emperor. For another, the empire ruled by Charles (or Charlemagne, as he would come to be known) fragmented on his death and its revival would not be attempted again until 962. It wasn't known as the Holy Roman Empire for centuries. The contemporary sources for the account are quite sparse and give no description, so while the sensory element of this scene is quite likely, there is no evidence for it. Holy oil to anoint a ruler was common by this point in many of the post-Roman kingdoms, but it had never been used before for a Roman ruler, an aspect of the ceremony which caused much confusion in Constantinople.

But, perhaps most importantly, this was the first time a pope had anything to do with selecting a Roman emperor.

In fact, the only element of this event that would have been recognizable to an ancient Roman audience is that a militarily successful leader saw a power vacuum and exploited it to make himself emperor.

This interpretation of Rome as not just a Christian authority, but as a Christian authority specifically conferred by the pope, was an innovation that was convenient at the time rather than anything grounded in Roman history.

It became hugely significant, however, and would have consequences that last until the present day, setting up religious and national identities and conflicts. What it meant to be Christian and what it meant to be Roman underwent a series of twists and turns, interpreted and re-interpreted as people tried to make sense of their world. Germanic Christian rulers based in central Europe contested the right to call themselves Roman with Greek-speaking Christian rulers based in Constantinople. West vs East, Catholic vs Orthodox, Latin vs Greek: by the end of the period covered in this chapter, it was no longer enough to say that Rome meant Christianity.

Then again, Rome had never just meant Christianity. It had always meant power. These differing interpretations of Rome weren't merely academic debates, they were power struggles that defined an era and led to seismic changes that still shape the modern world.

Barbarian or Roman: who decides?

In the last chapter, we saw this divide from the perspective of New Rome, or the city of Constantine, where Romans kept ruling for close to another millennium after the so-called 'fall' of Rome. This chapter considers the other perspective, that of Old Rome, and how some of the former European territories ruled by Rome became the Holy Roman Empire. This time, our starting point is the year 476, when Old Rome was invaded by a foreign commander, Odoacer, and the so-called 'last Roman emperor', Romulus Augustulus, was deposed.

Except, of course, things still aren't that simple.

If you had asked the citizens of Old Rome, the city on the Italian peninsula, just after it 'fell', they would not have been aware of anything significant.[1] In the case of Old Rome, it is not just that people did not realize the long-term significance at the time. After all, Rome had been under attack, successfully and unsuccessfully, many times over the course of its history. People noticed and they left a record.

Rome, the city, simply was not conquered. Romulus Augustulus, 'the last Roman emperor', was, at best, contested as a ruler and certainly not the Roman ruler with the power. Odoacer, the conquering general, was not by any stretch of the imagination 'a foreign conqueror'. Even if we were to insist that Old Rome was the only Rome that mattered, for almost everyone involved nothing really had changed.

Not only was Old Rome no longer the capital of the Roman Empire at this point, it wasn't even the main city in its western territories. It was still important symbolically and much of the elite still liked to spend their time there, but the military leaders who were actually in charge preferred more strategic spots like Milan or Trier – a decision pushed by Old Rome's alarming vulnerability to attack, as demonstrated by the Gothic sack of the city in 410, followed by an even worse attack by the Vandals in 455. Since 408, the preferred choice had been Ravenna, around 350 km to the north-east of Rome on the Adriatic coast.

It was Ravenna where Romulus Augustulus, the young boy who is often called 'the last Roman emperor', lived and from where his father, a military general called Orestes, ruled. Traditionally, the Roman emperor was acknowledged by his army, the Senate, and the people. This trio of approval was considered the golden seal, if you will, with the addition that the junior emperor in Old Rome also needed the recognition of the senior one in New Rome. Romulus only had the support of his father's army.

---

1 This observation applies to many other events that have later been granted historical importance. Most major historical events are only obviously significant in hindsight, even if the locals on the ground are aware of something happening.

At this point, that wasn't so unusual in Old Rome. From 455, when the *augustus* of the West, Valentinian III,[2] had been assassinated, the nominal leader of the western territories was whoever the military tribes had coerced the local Senate in Rome into accepting. They could be and were changed whenever those military tribes were dissatisfied.

In a neat example of how confusing so much of the terminology of this period can be, these military groups were officially known as *foederati*, which technically meant allies. You mostly see them referred to as 'barbarian' and get the impression that they were responsible for the end of Old Rome but they constituted almost the entirety of Roman military forces in the western territories by this stage and were usually Christian. It isn't hard to see why they felt they deserved a say in who was in charge of their military campaigns, especially given the long tradition of what we might euphemistically call 'military involvement' in nominating the emperor. No emperor had ruled for long without the support of the military and a great many had got the job entirely through the military. It isn't hard to see how the *foederati*, many of whom clearly aspired to be Roman, might have thought their position was in fact quite traditional.

The *augustus*, or senior emperor in New Rome, had more pressing matters to deal with than Old Rome's problems and either could not or would not send troops or money to their aid. Finally, around 472, after the latest junior emperor was assassinated, a man named Julius Nepos was granted some military forces, named the junior *augustus*, and encouraged to generally sort things out.

Julius Nepos was surprisingly successful at first, deposing the *foederati*-nominated ruler, getting all the traditional acknowledgements, and working hard to restore some semblance of authority. He managed

---

2 Valentinian III seems to have been a fairly uninspiring sort but his mother, Galla Placidia, was an extraordinary woman who effectively ruled on his behalf for fourteen years. If you visit Ravenna today, you will see much of the results of her investment in glorifying the city.

to negotiate with various former *foederati* leaders who had at this point effectively formed their own states.

This period of success didn't last and yet another *foederati* leader decided to intervene: Orestes. In many ways, he exemplified how entangled Roman and 'foreign' identity were at this stage. He was born into a Roman family but, as his homeland changed hands, became a member of Attila the Hun's court. After the death of Attila in 453, Orestes made his way to Italy and was appointed to a senior military position by Julius Nepos. Very swiftly, he took advantage of this position to march on Ravenna, chase off Nepos, and proclaim his young son Romulus as *augustus*.

Ten months later, this long-running power struggle came to a close. Odoacer, another *foederati* leader, killed Orestes, marched on Ravenna, and suggested that the young emperor consider early retirement. Another branch of the military had taken over.

Odoacer didn't declare Rome over or himself as an independent ruler, however. He sent a polite embassy to New Rome and the senior emperor, reportedly returning the western imperial insignia and saying these territories had no need of their own emperor any more, that in fact they could quite easily share with Zeno, and suggesting that he himself be given a nice title to acknowledge his status.[3] Zeno replied to say that Julius Nepos was still *augustus* and suggested Odoacer talk to him.

This went back and forth for a while but what matters for our purposes is that Odoacer kept ruling in Italy, kept acknowledging that there was an *augustus* in New Rome with superior authority, and kept appointing Roman political positions in the traditional manner. He seemingly never went to the city of Rome in the seventeen years he ruled; but then the city of Rome really wasn't necessarily that important anymore.

---

3 He seems to have suggested *patricius romanorum*, or Patrician of the Romans, an honorary title created by Constantine the Great to distinguish senior juridical and military officers. What Odoacer understood by this title is something a lot of scholars disagree about but the most significant detail is that it seems clear he understood it was less important than *augustus*.

Nothing had really changed.

These events are extremely important, however, in understanding what followed and how two different Roman empires emerged, literally and figuratively speaking, with different languages.

The other one-time *foederati* leaders who had carved out wealthy bits of formerly Roman territories for themselves also continued to behave as much as possible like Roman rulers. The Visigoths, ruling the Iberian peninsula and parts of south-west France, the Vandals in North Africa and southern Italy, the Merovingians in northern France, and the Ostrogoths who later deposed Odoacer in northern Italy, all thought of themselves as Roman and consciously modelled their rule on Rome. They converted to Christianity, hired people to write about them in Latin, wore Roman military cloaks, tried to collect Roman taxes, and acknowledged the senior emperor in New Rome.[4] They understood themselves as Roman.

Inevitably, things slowly changed as the enormous state apparatus that had provided the infrastructure of Rome disappeared. Trade reduced as cities shrank and urban networks fragmented, the numbers of enslaved people fell, tax and coinage systems shifted, military organization adjusted. None of this disappeared entirely but the scale was much smaller and more local.

Sometimes, the *augustus* in Romanland would reconquer a territory and its people would briefly return to the Roman Empire proper and exchange their taxes for some of the infrastructural benefits that came with that.[5] Ordinary people continued about their daily lives, sometimes better and sometimes worse off. The senior emperor remained in Constantinople.

---

4 They often struggled with tax collection, as the wealthy noble families who owned land and still considered themselves Romans were quite often unwilling to hand over their money to men they identified as barbarian foreigners.

5 From the mid-seventh century, many of these territories would be conquered by Arab armies, paying taxes instead for access to the very similar infrastructural benefits of the Muslim caliphate.

Different groups of Germanic peoples rose and fell in power over the following centuries: the Alamanni, the Burgundians, the Franks, the Goths, the Saxons. Consistently, their rulers declared themselves to be Christians and Romans. Where they could, they constructed monumental buildings, had statues erected, minted coins, wrote to bishops, and distributed food: all behaviour they considered Roman. Indeed, bishops in this period had often gained the position by virtue of being from an old Roman noble family.

Romanitas or Roman-ness was essentially being defined among the Germanic peoples by the most powerful ruler (or the one with the best court historian). Christianity and power were two crucial ingredients but the others depended on the time and place. The bishop of Rome, or the pope, was relevant as a symbol of Christianity and a religious leader but had little practical power. Meanwhile, the Roman emperor in Constantinople continued to rule Romanland.

Then, in 797, for the first time, a woman ruled the Roman empire alone.

Negotiating Roman rule

Empress Eirene is known for a few things. She was the first woman to officially rule Rome in her own right.[6] She came to this position after her son had his eyes stabbed out, almost certainly on her orders. She proposed marriage to Charles, king of the Franks. She was overthrown in a palace coup and died in exile.

This is classic Roman imperial drama: scheming, intrigue, violence, high-highs and low-lows. Of course, the drama often takes precedence over the details and the details are very important in this story.

---

6 Many previous empresses had been hugely influential, and often officially acknowledged in some way. Livia, wife of Augustus, Julia Domna, wife of Septimius Severus, and Theodora, wife of Justinian, are all clear examples of women who effectively co-ruled and there are many more that we are still uncovering. None, however, ruled alone.

Eirene was a woman who ruled, in one way or another, for thirty-two years. First, as an official joint ruler with her husband, then as regent for her son, Constantine VI, then again as official joint ruler with her son, and then alone. Sometimes she was a junior partner in these joint-rulerships and sometimes she was the senior partner, but she was always a ruler and always a major player. She was heavily involved in foreign policy and religious policy, essentially the two most important aspects of governing Romanland. And, in those two capacities, she had a lot to do with Charles, king of the Franks, increasingly the most powerful ruler in Latin Christendom.[7]

In 767, as joint ruler with her husband, Eirene began negotiations with Charles for a marriage between their two children. No princess from any of the western, formerly Roman territories had married into the imperial family of Romanland before but Eirene saw the opportunity, took the initiative, and saw it through.

Marriage negotiations for military alliances were common, of course.[8] But this one was much more complex – it was far more than just a military alliance. Over the past 50 years, the papacy had been growing visibly hostile to Romanland. For centuries, the bishops of Rome (otherwise known as the popes) had acknowledged the emperors in New Rome in a number of public ways: remembering the rulers in their official prayers; dating their records according to their reigns; and including imperial portraits in major churches. Since 713, however, they

---

7 Geographical terms for this period can be difficult – Europe did not yet exist as an idea in the way it does today. The Iberian peninsula was ruled by various Muslim kingdoms between 711 and 1492. Sometimes they were allied with other local Christian rulers, sometimes they fought them. Many of their citizens remained Christian and Jewish, and engaged with other Christian and Jewish communities across the continent, but Iberia wasn't part of the collective post-Roman consciousness in the same way. Orthodox Christianity, based in Romanland, had its own increasingly distinct culture. Across the Baltics, much of the British and Irish islands, and Scandinavia, Christianity had not yet made a major impression, although it was increasingly important. So, in this earlier period, we use Latin Christendom to describe the Christian kingdoms on the European continent like the Franks and Lombards.

8 Marriage negotiations for elite women had always been important in Roman history, although previously the alliances would have been for political or financial support *within* the empire.

had withdrawn these public observances of respect, citing concerns about heresy and theological differences.

In 751, Romanland had lost control of the last of its northern Italian territories, centred around Ravenna, to the Lombards. At around the same time, the Franks stepped into the void that was left in terms of protecting the papacy. By the time Pope Adrian I took up the papacy in 772, he felt he could be increasingly hardline about the bishop of Rome's position with respect to Romanland – which is to say, he felt his position deserved more respect from Constantinople and not the other way around. He had not been above asking for military help from Constantinople against the Lombard kings he felt threatened him but, when none was provided, he went back to the Franks for support. With Charles behind him, he could afford to push back against the Roman emperor in Constantinople.

So Eirene's marriage negotiations for her son were much more than an imperial innovation. She was not only seeking to reduce tensions between two potential military rivals but also trying to reverse 50 years of religious dispute with an increasingly assertive papacy that was becoming independent of her authority and was now allied to her possible rival.

It is important to remember that, theoretically, both Charles and Adrian were part of the Roman Empire as it was understood in Romanland. Eirene and her husband were the senior rulers. In the lifetime of Pope Adrian I (he was born in 700 and died aged ninety-five), their predecessors in Constantinople had been officially acknowledged by the papacy and had ruled territories in northern as well as southern Italy. Certainly, there had been some hiccups over the past half-century, but that was a blip in the long, long history of Romanland, the empire of Rome, which stretched back for more than 1,500 years.

At this point, it seems clear that Charles, Adrian, and Adrian's successor, Leo III, all interpreted their respective place in things quite differently. Romanland was still a serious international player, however, and Eirene succeeded in the marriage negotiations. In the 780s, as regent and senior *augustus*, she arranged two major church councils that technically reconciled the churches of Rome and Constantinople. Even though there was an awful lot of pretending some things had not been said, or even written (both sides seem to have told themselves that they had succeeded in their personal aims), maritally-, politically-, and theologically-speaking, the two branches of Rome appeared to be moving back together.

Sometime around this point, Eirene's son, Constantine VI, flexed his imperial muscles and tried to assert himself. It is not quite clear how or why, but the marriage broke down.[9] Possibly as a result of this, military conflict broke out between Romanland and the Franks in southern Italy, which the Franks won. All of Eirene's careful diplomatic work was in tatters. After a brief and difficult period of solo rule, Constantine VI acknowledged he was struggling and re-appointed Eirene as empress and co-ruler in 792. Five years later, she reacted to a series of deeply unpopular decisions made by her son by deposing him, a decision that came with imprisonment and blinding (a brutal but tried-and-tested way in Constantinople to prevent a ruler from returning).

This brings us back to 797, Eirene ruling alone in Romanland, and the situation in Rome's formerly western territories.

One of Eirene's two former major diplomatic connections in Old Rome, Pope Adrian I, had died but Charles, king of the Franks, remained. It seems that Eirene proposed a new marriage to resume their alliance: this time between the two of them, rather than their children. From her perspective, such an arrangement would allow her to continue to rule as the senior emperor in the east, with Charles as her junior colleague in the west – a revival of the Roman tradition. Charles's perspective is unclear but, again, it seems likely he interpreted things a little differently.

---

9 The eastern and western sources contradict each other, where they offer any specifics at all. Indeed, it is possible that it is the engagement that broke down, before the marriage was ever official.

Three Roman perspectives on the events of 800 CE

In fact, it is entirely possible that Charles, with an eye for an opportunity, proposed the marriage himself: the sources from each side offer conflicting accounts. Crucially, however, both Roman rulers seem to have been open to the idea of a union. Charles, moreover, had a trump card in his pocket. Pope Leo III owed him an even bigger favour than his predecessor had, having been personally rescued by the Frankish king after he was violently attacked and chased out of Rome in 799.

The various threads that had been emerging in the west over the past 50 years now came together. The papacy's main supporter was the Franks, not Constantinople. In fact, the bishops of Rome had got used to a certain amount of independence from Constantinople and seemed to have developed a taste for it. Charles, the current Frankish king, was the most powerful yet. He was a Christian ruling increasingly substantial parts of formerly Roman territories, who now had good reason to consider himself a candidate for the title of Roman emperor. The current pope, Leo III, enjoyed no personal connection with Empress Eirene of Romanland and had a desire to push for further independence.

There are three key perspectives on the crowning of a new Roman emperor in Rome on Christmas day in 800: those of Charles, Eirene, and Leo, and the different versions of Christian, Roman rule they represented. Considering this one event in detail allows us to see everything that comes later much more clearly.

For Leo, it was a triumph: he had succeeded in separating himself from Constantinople, he had rewarded his patron, and, crucially, he had set a precedent of papal authority. This latter was an extraordinary innovation: whatever primacy the bishops of Rome had been claiming over other Christian bishops and whatever justification Leo III claimed, the authority to appoint an emperor was entirely new in Roman history. It wasn't clear at the time how momentous it would be but it was certainly a step forward in Leo's claims to authority.

Charles's perspective is a little harder to pin down. Probably, he considered this was, at best, a stepping stone to the more traditional Roman recognition of emperor: that of the senior ruler in Constantinople, his on-off diplomatic ally and military rival, and potential future wife. He may have considered it a form of leverage in the marital negotiations. It is possible that he realized the potential implications of the pope selecting the emperor but, since he was planning to travel to Constantinople to meet Eirene, that would not carry much weight in the end. Leo was simply not as important a player as Charles or Eirene.

The reaction in Romanland seems to have been confused and bewildered: did the Franks not know how a Roman emperor was appointed? Eirene, it seems likely, may have understood the coronation as a power play, or she might have simply thought it was a confused and slightly presumptuous over-reaction to the offer of marriage. Either way, it could be dealt with in marriage negotiations once Charles arrived.

These conflicting interpretations of Rome, the correct way to appoint a Roman emperor, and who was to be the senior colleague, might have been resolved in the negotiations but, by the time Charles arrived in Constantinople, Eirene had been removed from power in a coup and sent into exile. The man who overthrew her was not interested in any sort of marital alliance (although he did negotiate a peace treaty with Charles).

Charles returned to his capital – unmarried and unacknowledged as emperor except on the authority of the pope. During the rest of his life, he used a number of Latin formulations on imperial documents that fudged the issue of his title, using language that allowed him to claim the position of emperor without quite setting himself up directly in opposition to the ruler in Romanland. His heirs did not claim the title of emperor.

Leo died in 816, having found other ways to assert his authority – in the English church and against the Muslim territory of Al-Andalus – that seemed just as likely to be his legacy.

In hindsight, this affair was momentous as the point where different interpretations of Rome went from being interesting and important but not decisive to diverging in a way that would never again be reconcilable. In the early ninth century, though, it probably seemed like a confusing competition of power grabs that didn't quite go anywhere in the lifetimes of the people involved.

Roman-ness re-thought

The next king to assert himself as a Holy Roman Emperor, Otto I, in 962, married his son to a princess of Romanland as a way of legitimizing his own position and improving relations with Constantinople. A few hundred years later, the events of Christmas Day in 800 had become much more significant, as the power of the rulers in the former western territories had increased. In 1157, Frederick I, known as Barbarossa, started using '*imperium sacrum*', or the Holy Empire, in his official documents, and a few decades later he amended that to '*sacrum Romanum Imperium*' to make it the Holy Roman Empire. He officially revived the *Corpus Juris Civilis*, or Code of Justinian from 527, which gave him a number of obligations as well as rights, and strengthened his claim to have revived the Roman Empire. It didn't become the standardized title until 1256 but there was a clear idea under Barbarossa that his empire was a Roman revival.

The dynamics that hindsight allows us to see emerging in 800 were now in full swing. The papacy had become a major player in Christian politics, with the (generally) acknowledged right to promote a king to emperor. The territories that Charles, king of the Franks, had ruled had broken down, reformed, and expanded and were now a (generally) coherent entity. Relations between eastern and western Christianity hadn't completely broken down but it was now (generally) understood that they were different in too many key ways for a reunion to be straightforward.

These three powers, which dominated Christianity in the lands around the Mediterranean and further afield, were sometimes allied with each other and sometimes opposed. It was Christianity that they understood themselves to hold in common, however. The idea of a shared *romanitas* or Roman-ness was too politically fraught.

Romanland continued to define itself as Romanland and this never changed. The papacy had long since brandished the Donation of Constantine – a (forged) document it claimed was written by Constantine the Great, conveniently granting the bishops of Rome the right to rule all the western territories of the empire.[10] Since they could not fight themselves, they had to appoint a king to do the dirty work for them but the senior authority was theirs, a Christianized version of the old Roman system of a senior and junior emperor. The Donation of Constantine was widely believed for centuries (although it was also frequently contested from at least as early as 1001).

The emperors they appointed, meanwhile, were in a tricky spot. They wanted the moral and spiritual authority that came with papal approval and many were deeply religious. They also, however, did not like being told what to do and they frequently pushed back against the papacy – sometimes even going so far as to appoint rival popes. This tension led to a fascinating new interpretation of Rome emerging in the Germanic centre of the Holy Roman Empire.[11]

By the twelfth century, Latin Christendom more broadly (which includes England, Ireland, Scandinavia, and France) knew much more

---

10 It is possible that Leo III used this document, the so-called Donation of Constantine, to justify crowning Charles in 800 CE.

11 At this point, the empire also included some of modern-day Italy, southern France, Switzerland, Luxembourg, Belgium, The Netherlands, southern Denmark, Czechia, Slovakia, and Austria. Collectively, these territories had started to think of themselves as Europa. This, of course, does not map onto the modern geographical understanding of Europe.

about ancient Rome and ancient Roman texts in particular. Their engagement with Al-Andalus, Romanland, and the Abbasid Caliphate in Baghdad had given them access to some Roman scholarship they had previously lacked and monks everywhere had diligently copied, recorded, and built upon the books they acquired.[12]

Increasing access to Roman ideas about themselves and a growing interest in differentiating themselves from the papacy while still remaining Roman combined to produce new ideas among Germanic scholars. One of the most popular was *translatio imperii* and, with that, a particularly Roman interest in Trojan genealogy.

Trojan Romans, Roman Germans

In its simplest form, *translatio imperii* means 'the transfer of power', a way of thinking of legitimacy as linear and inherited. There were numerous versions of this throughout the period, depending on the scholar and their particular context and concerns. One of the most popular and important, for our purposes, is that suggested by Godfrey of Viterbo. This man was a brilliant scholar, a priest, a diplomat, and a man who had professional and personal ties to both the Holy Roman Empire and the papacy. He re-wrote his major life's work multiple times, firstly for Frederick Barbarossa, then for two successive popes. His re-writes make clear the competing interests of the two institutions that patronized him and dominated the Holy Roman Empire and the surrounding Christian territories. It is difficult to imagine a more qualified insight into the time and place.

Godfrey argued for a simple, unbroken series of power transfers: from Troy, to Rome, and then to Frederick Barbarossa. More than

---

12 It is important to note that there was lots of scholarship prior to this period in Latin Christendom: they had access to many ancient texts and were enthusiastic about acquiring more. This is one of the reasons we have access to so many ancient texts ourselves. There was no 'Dark Age' of scholarship. They did, however, have a different focus before the twelfth century.

that, he argued that the Teutons, by which he meant Frederick and, via Charlemagne, his ancestors, were themselves *separately* descended from Troy. One set of refugees had fled to Italy and another to Germany, he insisted. This meant Charlemagne, whose father was Teutonic and whose mother, Godfrey claimed, had Italian lineage, had inherited the authority of both Troy and Rome.

To a modern audience, this claim can seem quite striking, even extraordinary. The Trojans, fierce enemies of the ancient Greeks? Troy, the orientalized city in modern-day Turkey, in territory then ruled by their rival, Romanland? Why put them in the succession of empires at all, never mind in pride of place, *and* assign them as ancestors to Charlemagne? Where did Godfrey get such an idea?

From ancient Rome itself, it turns out. And not just any old Roman.

As ancient Rome shifted from a Republic, run by two annually elected officials, to an empire, ruled by a single dynastic figure, the man responsible for this transition encouraged one of Rome's greatest poets to write a unifying epic about the empire's origins. Publius Vergilius Maro, known as Virgil, composed a story for Augustus that presented the earliest Romans as descendants of Aeneas, a Trojan prince fleeing the most famous war of antiquity.[13]

As we noted in the previous chapter, ancient Greece did not have the cultural cachet that it does now. However *Romanitas* was being interpreted and whoever was doing so, *Graeci* could easily be used as an insult, just as it had been in ancient Rome. Being the enemy of the *Graeci* was easy to turn into a selling point in ancient Rome. Moreover, the Trojan prince Aeneas was the son of Venus – not too coincidentally, the same goddess from whom the first Roman emperors claimed descent.

---

13 The original Augustus, if you will – the first to use the title. He was granted the title 'Augustus' or 'magnificent' as one of many honours to acknowledge that, however discreetly, he was definitely the sole ruler of the empire now.

It was this thread that was picked up by German-speakers keen to differentiate themselves from the papacy in Rome, the city, while maintaining their essential Roman-ness. In fact, it was incredibly common across Latin Christendom, in this period and later, to claim a genealogical connection with Troy. Ancient Rome's interpretation of its own origins was revived, a way for secular rulers to distinguish themselves from both the papacy and Romanland, their religious rivals across the sea. Godfrey's claim, that 'the nobility of the kings and emperors of the Romans and of the Teutons comes from the same root – the king of the Trojans' was, for the period, not that unusual.

Godfrey had a few more diplomatic tricks up his sleeve, however. The papacy might have the Donation of Constantine but Gregory's research showed that Charlemagne, Barbarossa's ancestor, had been descended from the *senior* Trojan line. His Roman mother and Teutonic father meant he united the transfer of power from Troy with a claim that was superior to anyone else's.

In his revised work, which was dedicated to popes instead of emperors, Godfrey tweaked his focus and instead emphasized Charlemagne's role in claiming the senior role over Romanland. He referred to it as 'the kingdom of the Greeks' and suggested the popes inherited its rule in Italy.

Again, at the time, this was not necessarily momentous, although it certainly had an air of audacity. The peoples in the Holy Roman Empire and the surrounding Christian territories had never stopped thinking of themselves as Roman.[14] When the differences between itself and other institutions that thought of themselves as Roman became too clear to ignore, they naturally sought an explanation for those differences in ancient Roman texts about Roman-ness. The explanation was convenient, of course, but it should be understood as an organic development and

14 This was not the *only* aspect of communal identity, far from it. People have always had multiple, overlapping ideas about themselves and their communities.

not an artificial construct. After all, from their perspective, if the ancient Roman emperors were descended from Trojans, why wouldn't the present-day Roman emperors have the same connection?

This increased connection between German-ness, or the Teutonic peoples, and Rome would have major consequences further down the line. They would emerge later in the history of the Holy Roman Empire as the nature of its holiness became contested and ideas of Rome changed again. The work of Godfrey had broadened the possible interpretations and understandings of Rome.

Reforming Roman religion

A few hundred years later, in the sixteenth century, things were very different again. The Black Death had devastated Eurasia, economic systems were changing, ideas of good governorship were shifting, kingdoms and empires had fallen and been replaced. Historians often call this the early modern period, when the contours of the world as we know it started to emerge.

Romanland no longer existed. It had been severely weakened by the Fourth Crusade in 1204, when Constantinople was sacked by military forces from Latin Christendom, supported by the pope. Even so, it staggered on until 1453, when the Ottoman Turks conquered all that remained.

On the Iberian peninsula, Portuguese and Spanish Catholics, claiming a connection with the pre-existing Roman territories, had conquered the various Muslim kingdoms that had ruled there since the eighth century.[15] Not satisfied with their new lands, they had both

---

15 These military campaigns are now commonly called the Reconquista, or 're-conquest' (although they acquired this name more than 400 years later). Iberia had been largely ruled by Muslims since 711 and the final 're-conquest' was in 1492 – so, depending on the territory in question, there had been Muslim rule for roughly four to eight centuries. Prior to that, it had been ruled by Germanic tribes for around 300 years. They were obviously quite different from Portuguese and Spanish-speaking Catholics in the twelfth to fifteenth centuries in many ways. They were Roman and Christian, however, and they had replaced Romans and Christians, and so it was possible for the conquerors to present these religious wars against centuries-old kingdoms as a *return* to something.

immediately begun military campaigns in North Africa and across the Atlantic. At home, the Portuguese and Spanish Inquisitions terrorized anyone suspected of being Jewish, Muslim, or heretical.

Europe as we know it was starting to take shape, a world that would have been unrecognizable in many ways to Frederick Barbarossa and Godfrey of Viterbo, never mind Charles, Eirene, and Leo III.

In the midst of all these changes, Rome remained a source of identity, power, and prestige. But the conflicts over what Rome meant that we could see beginning to emerge in the crowning of Charles at the turn of the ninth century and in the writings of Godfrey of Viterbo in the twelfth century had cracked wide open by the 16th.

The Holy Roman Empire remained. There had been some significant shifts in its territories, its ruling family, and its institutions but it was still a major power and still claimed legitimacy via both Roman Catholicism and its connection with ancient Rome.[16] In many of its territories, however, the legitimacy of Roman Catholicism had been roundly rejected. The emergence of Reformation movements, which eventually became what we would now call Protestantism, had transformed Europe. In 1527, it was the turn of Old Rome to be sacked by European Christians, in the employ of the Holy Roman Emperor, its churches and shrines badly pillaged. Christianity could no longer be counted on to unite different powers, even in Europe.

Crucially, however, as Roman Christianity was being rejected in much of Europe, the city of Old Rome was being figuratively and literally attacked, and people were re-shaping their religion and world, they still looked to ancient Rome for answers.

When Martin Luther attacked the authority of the Roman papacy and Roman Catholicism's role in the identity of German-speakers, he offered

---

16 One of the most famous changes was the emergence of the Italian city states, places like Florence, Genoa, Pisa, and Venice. One of the most significant, however, was the loss of Bohemia – a cultural, economic, intellectual, and religious powerhouse of medieval Europe. Many of the institutional changes in the Holy Roman Empire in this period developed in response to events in Bohemia.

a replacement identity taken straight from the pages of a Roman playbook. The ancient Roman historian Tacitus had described the 'Germani', tribes who had defended their territories against Roman invasion 1,500 years previously, as brave, barbarian, and definitely not Roman. Luther now explicitly identified himself with Hermann, the heroic leader of the Battle of the Teutoburg Forest in 9 CE, one of the worst defeats ever inflicted on the ancient Roman army. A collective German identity, he argued, was just as much in opposition to Rome as Protestant Christianity was. No longer were the Teutons the senior branch of the Roman family tree, as Godfrey had claimed. They were historic enemies.

This new interpretation of Roman-ness, as the opposite of Germanness, gave the Holy Roman Emperors another headache on top of the Protestant Reformation. They claimed their moral authority from the Roman Catholic Pope, an authority that was now roundly rejected in many of their territories.

The incredibly wealthy and important region of Bohemia, for instance, had embraced a reformist type of Christianity well before the Protestant Reformation. The papacy had called for a series of crusades against these reformists between 1419 and 1434, in which they were joined by the Holy Roman Empire. The Bohemians resisted all efforts against them, eventually negotiating the right to practise Christianity the way they believed they should. Understandably, however, they took a fairly dim view of the Catholic Church from this point and refused to pay taxes towards a Catholic endeavour.[17]

Now Lutheran Protestantism had reinforced that same religious opposition to Rome and added a new type of opposition.

17 This episode includes the First Defenestration of Prague, one of three quite famous defenestrations (so far) in the history of Prague. The first event, in 1419, prompted the Hussite Wars against the Holy Roman Empire and the Papacy, supported by other Catholic forces. The second, in 1483, was over an unresolved theological issue from the treaty settling the Hussite Wars. The third and most famous defenestration to happen in Prague, in 1618, led to the Thirty Years' War, one of Europe's worst conflicts. In the events leading to all three defenestrations, the legitimate authority of the Holy Roman Emperor was questioned

In response, the Holy Roman Emperors instituted a series of religious reforms to smooth things over but the hits to their authority kept coming: and these kept being articulated with reference to ancient Roman ideas, practices, and rulers.

Studying the world through Roman textbooks

This was inevitable. The elites across these territories had never stopped being educated as Romans. They read Roman authors, spoke Latin, studied Roman ideas. Rome was the lens through which they saw the world. Even when they stopped thinking of their religion as Roman, even when they stopped thinking of *themselves* as Roman, they couldn't stop looking to Rome. They couldn't help but keep making Rome matter.

At first, this was because most scholars were trained in religious institutions – because those were the only real educational institutions.[18] If you were rich, you might have access to some books at home but, more likely, you had access to a religious institution with the best collection of books and teachers. If you were poor and had received an education, it was almost certainly from a monk, nun, or priest.

And what did these institutions teach? Quite often what a group of educated Roman men that, collectively, we call the Early Church Fathers had recommended. Elite Romans and Christians themselves, they recommended works to educate new elite Romans and Christians. This varied over time and space but would almost always include Roman writers like Cicero and Virgil alongside Christian texts.[19]

As the Renaissance picked up steam, what is now often called a 'Humanist' education emerged, in which the focus was less overtly

---

18 Indeed, much of the papacy's early practical power and influence had come from the way that legal scholars were almost always trained in religious institutions and religious law.

19 Cicero, Virgil, and the Early Church Fathers engaged extensively with Hellenic writings and ideas, which meant, for example, Platonic and Stoic philosophy were also studied in Latin, even when ancient Greek was rarely read.

religious.[20] The collection of texts that were studied was broadening, with increased access to ancient Greek works and contemporary scholarship from Al-Andalus, Baghdad, and Romanland. The core curriculum, however, remained.

An education, any education, in early modern Europe involved ancient Roman authors. Students were taught in Latin – indeed, the reason that so many texts continued to be written, published, and studied in Latin long after it was anyone's native language is that it remained the common language of much of Europe. If you found yourself in a university town like Bologna or Prague and couldn't speak Italian or Czech to ask for directions, you could always try to muddle through with some half-remembered Latin.

Ancient Roman writers like Cicero, Sallust, Seneca, and Tacitus were used by Catholics and Protestants alike because they transcended religious differences, even when they were used to argue for and enhance religious differences. You couldn't discuss tyranny without reference to Seneca or Tacitus, you couldn't think about ethics or law or the duty of the state without considering Cicero. It wasn't just thought that you wouldn't be taken seriously without displaying your familiarity with them, it's that you wouldn't be understood at all. The ideas of those ancient scholars were the framework for everything that followed.

There were other ideas, other scholars, other reference points, of course. Trends came and went, regional variation has always existed. But the works of ancient Rome dominated the education of the men and women who discussed, debated, and documented the intellectual concerns of early modern Europe. They understood everything via Rome.

This was precisely what a German scholar named Hermann Conring pointed out in the 1630s, when he attacked another plank of the Holy Roman Emperor's claim to legitimacy: the maintenance of Roman

20 This itself comes from Cicero and his suggestion for the ideal education, which he called *studia humanitatis*.

law. Conring asked, 'Does the Roman Emperor have the right to rule Germany?' and, in a detailed breakdown of German legal history, he pointed out that the people who *studied* and *wrote* about law in the Holy Roman Empire were rarely the people actually applying it. In fact, the people administering the law were often not basing their decision on Roman law but on local, Germanic traditions. Scholars assumed it was Roman law because, well, of course it was. What else would it be?

Roman law could not justify the rule of a Roman emperor if Roman law had never actually been the law of the land, argued Conring. Ironically, one consequence of this research was that the law of the land began to be implemented as it was studied, bringing it much closer to Roman law. But Conring's point was about legitimacy. He published his research during the Thirty Years' War, a vicious European religious conflict centred around the territories of the Holy Roman Empire and their increasingly different ideas of Christianity, Roman-ness, and German-ness.[21]

This wasn't the end of the Holy Roman Empire and it certainly wasn't the end of Rome as a source of legitimacy.[22] It wasn't even the end of the connection between Christianity and Rome. Conring's interpretation of Roman law and German regional identity and practice wasn't the definitive end point of one interpretation of Rome or the start of another; it's rare that history is so neat and tidy. Christianity was still implicitly relevant to Roman-ness, in a fuzzy, difficult-to-define way.

But, around this point in the seventeenth century, the roads that led to Rome were definitely looking quite different – at least, they did in western Europe. As we shall see, that wasn't the case elsewhere.

---

21 Of course, this long, complex, and convoluted war was also about power – frequently, co-religionists fought against each other while theoretically opposing religious leaders fought side-by-side.

22 Indeed, a member of the Habsburg family, the dynasty that ruled the Holy Roman Empire from 1438 until its collapse in 1806, joked online as recently as 2023 that he had the best legal claim to the title of Roman Emperor.

4

The Third Rome

The imperial Russian title 'Tsar' comes from Caesar. Just like the Ottoman Kaysar and nineteenth-century German Kaiser, imperial Russia reflected an idea of Roman-ness in the title its leader took.

The idea that Russia was 'the Third Rome' emerged in the fourteenth century, when it was clear that Constantinople would soon be conquered by the Ottomans. This claim was grounded in a religious understanding of Rome: that Orthodox Christianity was the true religion of Rome and that, as the remaining major Orthodox Christian power, it fell to Russia to defend the faith. It was a claim cemented by multiple diplomatic marriages between Rus princes and Roman princesses, powerful women who brought with them a visual language of Rome.

The role of the Orthodox Church in the Russian understanding of both Rome and itself casts light on the world today, on Russia's claim to political and religious authority, and on Russia's current imperial wars.

A new Roman ruler, crowned with laurel leaves and garbed in flowing white, stands in the centre of a mighty temple. Above them looms a monumental statue of Themis, goddess of Justice, carved from pale marble, with the scales of law and order in her hands. The petals of poppies burn on a marble altar, a traditional offering to acknowledge this ruler will sacrifice their own rest and concerns in service to the glory of the empire and its subjects. At their feet stands an eagle, symbolic protector of the military, holding an olive branch of peace while guarding the empire's law-codes. Far off, beyond the tall white column, a fleet of ships can be seen, a reminder of Rome's naval power and dominance of the seas.

THE RULER IN QUESTION WAS Catherine the Great, the empire she dedicated her life to was Russia, and she reigned from 1762 to 1796. This scene was painted by the artist Dmitry Levitsky as part of Catherine's attempt to project her authority, legitimacy, and essential *Russian-ness*. To do that, she had herself depicted as a Roman ruler – and not just a Christian Roman ruler, either.

Catherine the Great is often understood as a ruler who embraced so-called western European values, an 'enlightened despot' who married western and eastern traditions to modernize the Russian Empire.[1] Certainly, she had grown up as a member of royalty within the Holy Roman Empire, with all the understandings of Rome that accompanied such an upbringing. Crucially, however, this meant she had to convey to the elites of Russia that she was speaking *their* language to reassure them that they weren't in service to a foreign queen. This was a Russian interpretation of Rome she was using to claim power.

---

1 Fascinatingly, the word 'despot' is a great example of how the context can change meaning because of differing traditions of Rome. Originally, it was a court title in Romanland indicating status, like 'lord'.

And Catherine wasn't just claiming power. She was asserting herself as *Tsarina*, or Empress of all Russia. Born Princess Sophia Augusta Frederica von Anhalt-Zerbst-Dornburg, a Lutheran princess from the Holy Roman Empire, she had converted to Orthodox Christianity and married Peter III, heir to the Russian throne. Six months into her husband's reign, she overthrew him and ruled alone for thirty-four years. Tsarina Yekaterina Alekseyevna, the name she took for herself after her marriage, would be remembered as one of the most famous rulers in Russian history. Part of her success lay in the way she understood Russia's relationship with Rome.

A Roman princess

To make sense of Catherine, we have to go back to another Roman princess named Sophia who married into the Russian monarchy. Sophia Palaiologina was the niece of the last Emperor of Romanland, who died trying to defend Constantinople against the Ottoman Turks, and the daughter of the last recognized heir to the throne. She had also lived in the Holy Roman Empire, this time in the city of Rome itself, under the eye of Pope Paul II.

In 1469, the Pope opened marriage negotiations with Ivan III, Grand Prince of Muscovy, the Russian ruler who had recently united the varying semi-independent Russian principalities under his own rule.[2] The arrangements would take three years of careful diplomacy – the marriage of the last princess of Rome was a major geopolitical event.

This display of international statesmanship came on the back of another set of major geopolitical negotiations. From 1431 to 1449, prompted by the rise of the anti-Catholic Hussite rebellion in

---

2 It is difficult to sum up the nature of the principalities of Rus before this point but, much like elsewhere, a shared culture, language, and eventually religion did not necessarily make them a coherent entity. Although they often recognized one overall leader, it wasn't a formalized long-term arrangement. It is only with the reign of Ivan III that most historians think of them collectively as 'Russia'.

Bohemia and the clearly unstoppable advance of the Ottoman Turks on Constantinople, Old Rome and New Rome had come together to try to work out their differences. Serious theological scholars from both the Catholic and Orthodox Churches, now two quite distinct strands of Christianity, along with imperial representatives from the Holy Roman Empire and Romanland, and many other members of the clergy gathered to find common ground on four key issues: faith, peace, reform, and 'common concerns'.

Desperate for military aid against the Ottomans, after nearly two decades of discussion (and nearly a millennium of disagreement), the delegates from Constantinople finally agreed at the Council of Florence to call themselves a united church under the superior religious authority of the Pope in Rome. The rulers of Romanland and the Orthodox Church of Constantinople had always considered themselves to be the senior authority, it was central to their identities. Meanwhile, the bishops of Rome and the Holy Roman Emperors had spent most of their existence trying to become the senior authority. This was no small matter, it was a major diplomatic agreement – or it would have been, had it lasted. The agreement was met with jubilation in Old Rome and dismay in New Rome, especially when no military aid was forthcoming. In 1453, Constantinople fell. The Catholic and Orthodox Churches never did unite.

One of the major diplomats of these councils, an Orthodox monk named Bessarion, encountered such hostility in Constantinople for his attempts to reconcile the two rivals that he emigrated to the Papal States in Italy, where the Pope promptly made him a Catholic Cardinal in 1439. He spent the rest of his life on diplomatic missions for the papacy and as a leader of Renaissance scholarship, sharing the expertise of Romanland in ancient Greek scholarship. In 1465, when Sophia and her siblings were adopted by the Pope after the death of their parents, it was Cardinal Bessarion who oversaw their care.

Daughter of the last rightful heir to Romanland and living in Rome under the care of popes and a Catholic cardinal who had formerly been an Orthodox diplomat partly responsible for the (theoretical) unification of the two churches, Sophia was right in the centre of the contest over what it meant to be Roman. With her marriage and role as Grand Princess of Russia, she would help transform that contest.

Rome in the eyes of the Rus

The principalities of Rus had long looked to Constantinople, which they called Tsargrad or the 'City of the Emperor'.[3] It was a place of trade, wealth, opportunities, and religion. Treaties had been made between the Rus and Romans as early as 907, and possibly even earlier.

Since at least the late tenth century, when Vladimir I (c.958–1015) converted to Christianity, the rulers of the Rus had also connected themselves with Romanland. Vladimir's conversion was explicitly compared with that of Constantine the Great and his grandmother, Olga, was compared with Constantine's Christian mother, Helena. Both pairs were presented in Russian literature as converting, on their own, the populations they ruled to Christianity.[4]

Vladimir was the first leader of the Rus to marry a Roman princess. Needing military aid, Emperor Basil II had proposed a new alliance between Romanland and the Rus, cemented by the marriage between his sister, Anna Porphyrogenita, and Vladimir in 989. It seems likely that the timing of Vladimir's conversion was to facilitate this alliance and wedding.

---

3 It was far from their only reference point and it is unlikely it was the most important in the earlier periods. The Rus were deeply engaged with Arabic, Slavic, Turkic, and Viking traditions and often made reference to those as well as Romanland to project their own power. The importance of Christianity and Romanland is inevitably increased in hindsight, as these other traditions became less significant.

4 In both cases it is clear that Christianity was already prevalent. It was by no means certain that Christianity would become the dominant religion of these territories but its popularity was increasing. In this case, however, it is how the process was *presented* for posterity that matters.

Later reports suggested that a conversion to Catholic Christianity had been an option but Vladimir refused to submit to the authority of the Pope. It is impossible to know whether or not this is true but it reflects the Russian understanding of the tension between the two competing claims to Christian authority. This triangular power dynamic of the Roman Papacy, Romanland, and a marriage negotiation is a recurring theme of this period and a reminder of how significant an imperial wedding could be.

Anna Porphyrogenita brought with her architects and artisans to construct and decorate churches that symbolized the new official religion of the Rus, in the style of a true Roman ruler. Together, the two of them set the principalities of Rus on a new course.

Five hundred years later, when marriage negotiations opened between Pope Paul II, Sophia Palaiologina, and Grand Prince Ivan III, the power dynamics had shifted. Romanland was no more, and the City of the Emperor had fallen to the Muslim Ottoman Turks. The Orthodox Church might not, in practice, acknowledge the senior authority of the Papacy in Rome but there was no doubt that the latter was now a major player. And the Rus were no longer a collection of principalities or defined by Mongol rule; they were now a rising power of Eurasia, under the rule of a single Grand Prince.

Pope Paul II saw an opportunity to convert Orthodox Russia to Catholic Christianity and bring it under the religious authority of Rome, finally cementing the promise of the Council of Florence and dramatically enhancing his prestige. Grand Prince Ivan III saw an opportunity not just to marry into the Roman imperial family as part of an alliance but to inherit Roman imperial authority, dramatically enhancing *his* prestige.

Perhaps nobody asked Sophia what her goals were throughout the three years of diplomatic negotiations over her marriage but it seems she had also identified an opportunity for herself. After a high-profile, glamorous wedding, she immediately re-converted to Orthodox Christianity.[5] The representative of the papacy who accompanied her to Moscow was not permitted to triumphantly enter the city carrying the Latin cross, a symbol of Catholic authority, as planned. Moreover, it seems she took a large number of valuable books, pieces of art, and sacred relics with her, tangible pieces of her Roman inheritance with which to build a new life for herself, as well as artists, architects, artisans, and dignitaries to create more.

Throughout the fifteenth century, as it became increasingly clear that Tsargrad would not hold out against the Ottomans, various elite figures in Russia had suggested that they should build on the long-standing connection between the two and assume the responsibility of leading the Orthodox Church. Moscow, the capital of Russia, it was suggested, should become the *Third* Rome. Both Ivan and Sophia, it seems, understood their marriage in this light. The papacy, it is clear, did not.

Sophia set about rebuilding her life and worked with her husband to establish her new country as the heir to her homeland. With the help of the entourage she brought with her, she built major Russian buildings like the Kremlin, the Cathedral of the Assumption, and the Cathedral of the Archangels, combining the styles of medieval Russia, Renaissance Italy, and late Romanland to project the new identity of Russia. She patronized churches and artists, parented eleven children, and is also credited by later sources with a key role in international affairs, internal religious disputes, and courtly politics. She also passed on her Romanland inheritance: future rulers would be crowned not just Grand Prince but Tsar, or Emperor, of the Rus.

Russia had claimed the title of the Third Rome and its rulers claimed the lineage of the caesars. Neither was possible without Sophia Palaiologina.

---

5 It's at this point she took the official name Sophia; prior to this she was known as Zoe Palaiologina. Name-changes like this were the traditional practice of the imperial family in Constantinople.

Successive Romes

At the time of the first Rus-Romanland marriage, between Anna and Vladimir in the tenth century, there were very different and specific ideas of Rome. Everyone agreed that Rome meant Christianity and power but *how to be* Roman was up for debate.[6]

In the Holy Roman Empire, the focus was on speaking and reading Latin, for instance. Vernacular languages developed all over Latin Christendom throughout this period, but Latin was the language of the educated. Interestingly, there are a number of sources where scholars obsess over the 'correctness' of the Latin being spoken and written, as though it is nearly as essential to their identity as the 'correctness' of the Christianity they practised. To them, Latin was self-evidently the language of the Roman Empire. In Romanland, it was equally evident that Greek was *also* the language of the Roman Empire. After all, speaking Greek had been a marker of elite status since Alexander the Great had conquered as much of the known world as he could manage. The art, literature, and scholarship of the Greek-speaking world had been part of the Latin-speaking world too.

It is tempting to choose sides here, to decide that one interpretation of Rome is better than the other, that one just makes more sense. Different interpretations are all well and good but, if you look at all the evidence dispassionately, surely an answer will emerge? But, of course, markers of culture and identity are too fluid for this sort of approach – for the 1,000 years of Roman history, the idea of monotheism would have seemed alien to nearly any Roman. Christianity had been understood as anti-Roman by many Roman emperors for hundreds of

---

6 These changes could increasingly be seen in religious practices, and what were slowly being defined as Catholic and Orthodox Christianity. Theological differences like those discussed at the various joint religious councils can seem obscure to modern eyes but the finicky language hides issues of authority and identity. The average Christian perhaps didn't think too deeply about the precise nuances of Jesus' body, mind, and soul, for instance. But they did know which language their church service was in and how that connected them with their fellow Christians.

years. Empires change, just like people change. Whatever element we prioritize, the other 'side' would be able to make a good rebuttal.

What is most important is that none of the institutions we are discussing – the Holy Roman Empire, the Roman Catholic Church, Romanland and the Orthodox Church – thought of themselves as *interpreting* or *recreating* the historical, long-gone Roman Empire. They simply thought they *were* Roman, as they always had been. And, therefore, their way of doing things was Roman by virtue of the fact it was being done by Romans.

Among the Rus, however, we can start to see Rome being more consciously interpreted and in ways that changed over time. In the first place, like Old and New Rome, they understood Rome as *power* – or, more accurately, legitimate power. There was no distinction between religious and temporal power in this period, no separation of Church and State. You ruled by divine right. Religious authority *was* power.

For instance, before Ivan III had united the rival principalities of Rus, various competing rulers had compared themselves both to Roman rulers *and* Biblical rulers to legitimize their authority. They used the same word 'tsar' to refer to both Roman and Biblical rulers: Tsar Augustus and Tsar Solomon, for instance. In fact, throughout the periods discussed in this chapter, Muscovy (now Moscow) much more frequently framed itself as 'a new Israel' or 'a new Jerusalem' to the same end – claiming legitimate power. In this, as with claims to Rome, they were like many other European powers of the same period. Although Solomon and Augustus had reigned before Jesus died, their successful rule was understood to have been ordained by the Christian God, who had always existed. Correct rule was necessarily Christian – and therefore incorrect Christianity was necessarily incorrect rule.

By this time, the Rus understood the ultimate example of correct rule to be that based in Tsargrad, or Romanland. They were not disconnected from the various kingdoms in Latin Christendom in this period, far from it. As well as Tsargrad, they understood the city of Rome as being Roman in some sense. However, perhaps accustomed to seeing Constantinople as the senior seat of Roman-ness, perhaps simply because of a much greater degree of contact, they understood *how to be Roman* primarily through the lens of Romanland.

The 'fall of Rome' in the West, as they understood it, did not date to 476 but 1054, when the Latin (subsequently Catholic) and Greek (subsequently Orthodox) denominations of Christianity formally separated.[7] The split left the Popes, in the view of New Rome, as heretics and meant Old Rome, or Catholicism, no longer had legitimate power. When New Rome, or the Orthodox Church of Romanland, accepted the Latin religious position in 1449 at the Council of Florence, they too lost legitimate power and 'fell'. The subsequent conquest by the Ottomans was viewed as the inevitable consequence of their heresy, rather than the fall itself.

Finally, it was understood in Russia that Rome, in some form, had to continue to exist before the Day of Judgement.[8] This was connected to the theory of *translatio imperii*, which we encountered in the previous chapter, and the idea that legitimate rule was transferred rather than lost. A Christian, Roman empire was needed to ward off the Apocalypse. As the remaining correctly Christian power, it naturally fell to the Rus to lead as the Third Rome.[9]

---

7   This is usually referred to as the Great Schism of the Christian Church, although, as with so many major historical events, its importance was only clear in hindsight.

8   Dostoevsky would, much later, express this concept by saying, 'a fourth Rome there shall not be', and 'the world cannot do without Rome'.

9   This might strike us as quite convenient but, firstly, it is no less relevant or significant an interpretation with long-lasting consequences for that. Secondly, the Russian interpretation, crucially, would have been recognized by both Old and New Rome as it pertained to the *other* Rome, just not – of course – themselves. It also appears to have been understood in Russia as a warning. Failure to rule correctly would lead to the fall of the Third Rome, just as it had previously.

It was not enough, however, to assert Russia's religious claim to be considered the Third Rome.[10] They had to show it, to rule in the manner of Romans.

By 1453, while Old and New Rome had increasingly diverged in religious behaviour, they were much closer in cultural matters than they had been when the first Rus prince had married a Roman princess. Despite the rulers and church leaders growing further apart, contact between the rest of the two societies had been quite consistent. Constantinople had ruled some areas in the Italian peninsula until 1071 and the Crusader states of the twelfth and thirteenth century were effectively next-door to Romanland. Finally, the events of the Fourth Crusade in 1204 meant looted art, books, and other treasures made their way from Constantinople to western Europe, followed by scholars in exile who were eager to rebuild their cultural and intellectual communities.

Renaissance artists in the Italian city states may have claimed to be reviving a true Roman style, in contrast to that of the 'Greeks' in Constantinople but, just as they also drew on innovations and trends in the German-speaking parts of the Holy Roman Empire, so they were also inspired by the art and scholarship of Romanland (and, for that matter, of the Muslim-ruled states in Al-Andalus). In fact, many of them were not just inspired by the art of Romanland but trained by artists from Constantinople.

So, when Sophia Palaiologina arrived in Moscow, ready to use her experience and entourage to help the city and its ruler realize the ambition of becoming the Third Rome, the First and Second Romes were both dramatically different and yet very similar. The art and architecture of all three, for instance, took skill to combine but were more like three branches of one tradition than three separate trees. And, while in the

10   Just as it is not enough to write a nice letter saying you are the legitimate heir to the throne – you have to get yourself *on* the throne and then rule successfully.

earlier centuries of the Holy Roman Empire the focus had mainly been on Latin art and learning, Greek scholars were back in fashion by the fifteenth century, as they had always been in Constantinople.[11]

There seemed no plausible way for the different Romes to unite politically after all the disagreements and betrayals but, in Russia, the idea of a third Rome as a cultural and religious successor to Romanland meant there was still some common ground that capable rulers might be able to exploit to speak to multiple audiences.

Sophia Palaiologina was one such capable ruler. Catherine the Great would be another.

Roman expressions for Russian rule

It would seem, in 1762, that the stage was set for the idea of Moscow as the Third Rome to fulfil the potential opened up by the efforts of Roman-born, Russian-ruling princesses like Anna Porphyrogenita and Sophia Palaiologina. Princess Sophia Augusta, now Tsarina Yekaterina Alekseyevna, needed to legitimize her authority at home and abroad. Both her upbringing in the Holy Roman Empire and her commitment to Russian Orthodoxy suggest that 'the Third Rome' would be the ideal answer to her predicament.

Yet there is no official record of this idea being referred to during her reign.

Although Ivan IV (r. 1547-1584),[12] grandson of Sophia Palaiologina and Ivan III, had used the idea of Moscow as the Third Rome in his wars against 'Muslim unbelievers' and 'the Catholic enemy of Christianity', it had since become unfashionable as a specific expression of Russian power.[13]

---

11 Of course, in Russia there were other major traditions that had to be included in a successful projection of power but they are not, however fascinating, the focus of this particular book.

12 Ivan IV is often known as Ivan the Terrible, although this is something of a mistranslation of the Russian грозный (grozny), which means something closer to 'terrifyingly powerful'. An overview of some key events of his reign suggest both might be reasonable descriptions, in fact.

13 This was particularly so because it was associated with heretical beliefs and the Great Schism in the Russian Orthodox Church, in 1652.

And yet it is probably under Catherine the Great that we can most clearly *see* Russia using interpretations of Rome to project power. It wasn't just in paintings of her as ruler, although she patronized and collected art on a massive scale, attracting artists from across Eurasia. Like Anna and Sophia before her, she understood how to *project* power and identity visually and she drew on every tool available to her.

She sponsored a major building programme across Russian cities, inspired by ancient Greek and Roman architecture (or, at least, ancient Greek and Roman architecture as they were then being interpreted, in what is now called the neoclassical style). Catherine even 're-founded' the important city of Tver after it was destroyed by a fire in 1763, rebuilding it completely in the latest fashion. She decorated those cities with monumental statues like the Bronze Horseman, which depicts Peter the Great in the style of a famous Roman statue of the emperor Marcus Aurelius.

These art and architectural projects, which were hugely expensive, are often understood as an indication of Catherine's 'Western' preferences, and of her attempts to 'modernize' Russia, and impress fellow European monarchs and Enlightenment thinkers like her pen-pal, Voltaire. It is certainly true that this is how her actions were perceived in Europe. She would have gone further, this line of thinking suggests, but there was a limit to how much Russia could be 'Westernized'.

Such an interpretation does Catherine, an extraordinarily capable ruler, a disservice and misunderstands Russia in this period.

Catherine's husband, Peter III, had ruled for only six months. Like Catherine, Peter had grown up at a German-speaking court and had converted to Russian Orthodoxy only on being made heir to the Russian throne. Unlike Catherine, however, he seems to have made little effort to learn the Russian language, engage with the Russian church, or make friends at the Russian court. On succeeding to the throne, he immediately involved himself with military matters in the German-speaking world and instituted military changes in the manner of his hero, King Frederick II of Prussia, a major Russian rival. Catherine had been able to depose her husband, the grandson of Peter the Great, with minimal fuss because she could present him as too German, too western, in comparison with her: a true Russian.

The main danger to Catherine's power was not that she was a woman. In fact, since the death of Peter the Great in 1725, Russia had been ruled by women for twenty-three of the thirty-seven years before Catherine deposed her husband. Three previous empresses had set a clear precedent for her rule, the first appointed by Peter the Great himself. The main danger to Catherine's power was being seen as not sufficiently Russian, like her husband.

Catherine ruled for thirty-four years, 1762–1796, despite her son turning eighteen in 1772 and thus providing a viable alternative, if she was not considered appropriate (indeed, her son frequently and unsuccessfully tried to encourage people to promote him in her place). However the elites of Europe understood Catherine's behaviour, it is clear that, in Russia, she was understood as exercising power as a Russian monarch was supposed to.

How is it that Catherine's behaviour could be understood as 'Western' by European monarchs and thinkers and appropriately Russian at home? Partly this is simply because she was an incredibly clever ruler, capable of presenting herself to multiple different audiences in the way each wanted to see her. Partly it is because the many different ideas of Rome present at the time gave her a language of power that she could use to communicate to those many different audiences. The phrase 'the Third Rome' might have fallen out of fashion in Russia but the symbolism of Rome as *power* had never gone away.

One of the clearest ways to see this is in Catherine's coronation. Peter III had not bothered to arrange a ceremony, perhaps thinking such affairs frivolous and a distraction from the important business of playing soldiers.[14] Catherine, however, understood this as a major opportunity to communicate to her subjects that she was *Russian*. She ordered a new crown to be made, inspired by those from Constantinople (in contrast to her predecessors, who had worn crowns in the styles of current fashions in western Europe). The crown consisted of two separate gold and silver spheres to represent the eastern and western parts of Rome and the diamonds that decorated the surface were arranged in patterns of laurel and oak wreaths, ancient Roman symbols of power. Just as the emperors of Romanland had, Catherine placed the crown on her own head (unlike the Holy Roman Emperors, who had to be crowned by the pope, as we saw in Chapter 3).

The art and architecture that Catherine sponsored, the founding of classical gymnasia (schools based on those in Constantinople, with a curriculum like that of ancient Greece and Rome), and the intellectual scholarship she engaged in and promoted could be recognized as the right way for a monarch to exercise power in both Russia and its rival powers in Europe because everyone understood Rome as power, consciously or not.[15]

Catherine could encourage poets to write in a classical style, in French or Russian, comparing her to Roman heroines like Dido, and saying, 'All the glory of all the heroes presented by Rome / All the glory of those men embodied in you' because Russian rulers had portrayed themselves as descendants of Roman rulers for centuries, just as her fellow monarchs around Europe had. The Enlightenment thinkers

---

14 There are many stories about Peter's interest in playing with soldiers, some undoubtedly spread by Catherine herself to discredit him. For instance, he apparently often dressed up as a general and ordered his servants to dress as soldiers and play with him and he loved to watch his actual soldiers perform their military drills. Perhaps the most famous story about him is that he had a rat court-martialled and hung on a tiny set of gallows because it chewed the head off one of his toy soldiers.

15 One of the Roman connections she promoted was with the emperor Justinian, just as Frederick Barbarossa had in the Holy Roman Empire 500 years previously. A connection with Justinian meant monumental building, legal reform, military success, and correct religion – all areas Catherine pursued.

who praised her interest in the ancient world might not recognize this was the case but Catherine did and she used it to her advantage, at home and abroad.

Roman Rulers of Russia

Perhaps the most famous of the Russians who had ruled before Catherine and drawn on Rome to symbolize their power was Peter the Great. Like Catherine, he had collected art to decorate Russian cities and palaces and he also encouraged Russian scholarship on Rome, particularly on military texts like Caesar's *Gallic Wars*, and Frontinus' *Strategemata*. Peter called himself *pater patriae* (Latin for 'Father of the Fatherland') and *imperator* (Latin for 'general') and held 'triumphs' for himself, all ways to celebrate his military successes in the manner of Roman generals.[16] To reward one of his most valued generals, Peter granted him the title князь-кесарь (*knyaz-kesar*) or 'Prince-Caesar', a junior ruler to his *augustus* in the ancient Roman way. In fact, Peter the Great originally ruled as a co-tsar, and the junior partner to his half-brother, just like the system that had long been used in Rome. He also appointed his wife, Catherine I, to be empress after his death, formalizing a system whereby the emperor could select the best successor during their reign rather than rely on an appropriate child – again, just like the system that had long been used in Rome.

Again, this behaviour is often interpreted as Peter's engagement with 'Western' ideals and it is clear he had a great interest in the behaviour and practices of other European monarchs and how Russia might benefit from them, but we should not forget that Rome was always part of Russian understandings of power. Whether that was conveyed through

---

16 The word 'emperor', of course, comes from *imperator*, which initially meant something more like 'successful general', and 'triumph' comes from *triumphus*, a sacred procession of ancient Rome to acknowledge and protect military victories.

religion, imperial titles, official ideologies, or the visual language of monarchs, the example of Romanland was a key reference point.[17]

Peter is perhaps most famous for his imperial ambitions and the great reforms of the Russian military and navy that he put in place to achieve them. Two of his major imperial rivals were the Ottoman Turks, who had been one of Russia's major foreign policy concerns since they had conquered Constantinople in 1453, and the Safavid Empire in Persia.[18] These imperial rivalries did not go away and Catherine's approach to the Ottomans brought the three Romes back together in a revealing policy: the so-called Greek Project (Греческий проект or *Grecheskiy proyekt*).[19]

Together with the Holy Roman Empire (now based primarily in Austria, which shared a border with the Ottoman Empire), Catherine planned to defeat the Ottomans entirely and split their imperial territories between the two. Russia would take Constantinople and her grandson, Constantine (a deliberate name choice that she was responsible for), would rule a revived Orthodox Christian Roman empire, allied with – and junior to – the Orthodox Christian Russian empire. The plan never came to fruition but, during the fifteen years it was an active policy, Catherine's army was compared to Jason and his Argonauts and other heroes of ancient Greece, all connected through the Orthodox Christian tradition of Rome.

---

17 It is important to stress again that it was not the *only* way to understand power in this context or any of the other chapters of this book – just like Rome itself, different rulers drew on multiple different ways to symbolize and express power, depending on their personal context, needs, and preferences.

18 It is tempting to connect these imperial rivalries with their ancient Roman precedents: Sasanian Persia was the great imperial rival of ancient Rome and, of course, the Ottomans had been the rivals that finally overthrew Romanland. It certainly seems likely that a Christian empire fighting Muslim rivals was part of Russia's understanding of appropriate imperial behaviour, especially in the case of the Ottoman Empire, with its substantial number of Orthodox citizens. However, in this case it is also important to remember geography and the simple fact that the three were neighbours and therefore always likely to compete for territory and power.

19 Although Russians understood Tsargrad or Constantinople as a New Rome and thus Romanland as Roman, they primarily referred to its inhabitants as Greeks, referring to the language they spoke. There doesn't seem to have been any pejorative connotation in this from their perspective.

The significance of Russian engagement with the idea of itself as 'the Third Rome' has often been over-emphasized. There is very little suggestion that it directly informed much of Russia's imperial policy over time, for instance. The phrase itself was little used until the nineteenth and early twentieth centuries – and, even then, it did not dominate Russian intellectual thinking. However, there are other ways to see Roman influence. So much of Catherine the Great's activity is considered engagement with 'Western' ideals and traditions, without considering how important it was for her to convey to her Russian subjects at court, in the church, and beyond, that she was unimpeachably *Russian* like them and unlike her deposed, half-German husband. Her rule is often described as combining *opposing* traditions or pushing her Enlightenment, Western ideas as much as possible in the Russian context, forgetting both the background to her reign and Russia's own long-standing engagement with Ancient Greek and Roman traditions, via its connection to Romanland.

By this time, western Europe had moved away from understanding Rome as essentially Christian and the new interpretation of Rome complicated their view (as it still does today). Catherine, however, seems to have understood both interpretations of Rome and been able to use them to present herself as a powerful and worthy ruler at home and abroad.

Of course, it is much harder to see how, where, and why Rome has influenced Russia over the centuries because of the tradition of describing Romanland as 'Byzantium'. Insisting that the people who lived in Romanland, who called themselves the Roman people, and practised what they understood as the correct Roman religion were somehow not Roman makes it harder to see what is right in front of us.

In Russia, the language around Romanland may have changed (they too now refer to Byzantium) but the essential connection between Roman-ness and religion has never changed – as we can see in the present.

The Third Rome revived

On 22 June 2020, seventy-five years after Nazi Germany invaded the Soviet Union, the Resurrection of Christ Cathedral in Moscow was opened to the public. Dedicated to the Russian armed forces, this church is a monument to the Soviet victory in the Second World War and its construction reflects that, with some of the main building measurements corresponding to key numbers of the victory.[20] The inside is decorated, according to tradition, with wall murals and mosaics. The subject of many of these, however, are historical military heroes of Russia.

Originally, it was reported in Russian media that they would include Vladimir Putin and a number of current high-ranking figures from politics, the military, and the FSB (the successor agency to the KGB), as well as references to the recent military occupation of Crimea. Images of the mosaics circulated widely shortly before the cathedral was scheduled to open and caused a great deal of discussion. Eventually, the mosaics were removed from display, reportedly according to the wish of Putin himself.

This trilogy of religion, military, and politics helps us see how the idea of Russia as 'the Third Rome' is understood today. In the post-Soviet era, as Russia seeks to define itself with reference to its pre-Soviet past, the Russian Orthodox Church has emerged as a key element of modern Russian identity and, with it, a revival of 'the Third Rome' doctrine. Justinian (r. 527–565), one of the most famous Roman emperors, favoured a concept called *symphonia*, the perfect harmony of church and state: the state as the body, the church as the soul. Under

---

20 The diameter of the drum under the main dome measures 19.45 metres, for example, and the 'Road of Memory' has 1,418 steps, the same as the number of days the Soviet Union fought.

Putin, the church is once again understood as essential to Russian identity, indivisible from politics and the military.[21]

The importance of Romanland (or 'Byzantium'), its legacy, and Russia's moral duty as its heir can be seen across the modern Russian intellectual, political, and religious elite since the 2000s. Former FSB Director Nikolai Patrushev, for instance, has claimed that Russia's history of state security can be traced back to the time of Ivan III and Sophia Palaiologina, who '[herself] paid close attention to questions of security'.

He is not alone among the FSB in seeking to connect current policy with the Byzantine past – or an interpretation of it. Most modern scholars of Romanland, or Byzantium, highlight the cultural complexity, the flourishing artistic and intellectual movements, and the diplomatic expertise of this long-standing empire. Diversity of gender, race, and sexuality are major areas of research, as is the role of women at all levels of society. The focus among the FSB, however, tends to be on Byzantium as a beacon of religiously conservative morality, besieged on all sides throughout its history, and betrayed by the West.

The clearest expression of this position comes from Aleksandr Dugin, a Russian philosopher and media figure who is popular among the conservative Russian elite, and has written:

> *Our formula: the West is evil, Byzantium is good. Everything bad that is written about Byzantium is a lie . . . In the Russian historical tradition, Byzantium is often negatively treated, repeating the insinuations made by the West. Every Russian should know that*

---

21 There are many examples of military heroes in Romanland becoming saints in the Orthodox Church, for instance. The connection between the Russian Orthodox Church and the Russian military would probably not have seemed strange to early Roman Christians, inhabitants of the Holy Roman Empire, or people living in Romanland – there are many examples of important military saints across the various Christian traditions, including St George, St Maurice, and St Theodore.

Byzantium is pure goodness. Anyone who claims otherwise is an enemy . . . If you criticize Byzantium, you are the enemy of the Russian people. Such should be our firm policy.

Fascinatingly, he uses Византия, Byzantium, rather than Rome or Romanland, a tradition that emerged in English and French scholarship in the nineteenth century to deny both the Roman and Greek heritage of Romanland, just as those two traditions were emerging as central to Western ideas of identity and heritage. For Russia, as well as the West, it is now helpful to divorce the Second Rome from its origins and identity.[22]

This new interpretation of Russia as the Third Rome reverts to the understanding that fifteenth-century Orthodox monks presented to Ivan III: that a correctly Christian Roman empire is necessary to keep the Apocalypse at bay and Russia is that correct Christian empire. It also connects with Catherine the Great's imperial ideas from the eighteenth century. When Russia invaded and annexed the Crimea in 2014, it was praised among conservative Russian circles as a reclamation of territory that was once Byzantine as well as Russian and further evidence that Russia was a legitimate claimant to the title 'the Third Rome'. It was also suggested that this action might revive Catherine the Great's Greek Plan and the possibility of a Russian Constantinople.

And yet, the idea of Moscow as 'the Third Rome' and Russia as a new Roman empire is also distinctly different under Putin than previously in Russian history. And, fascinatingly, it is different in ways that directly reflect interpretations of Rome in the West. Gone are the references to pre-Christian Roman rulers or pre-Christian gods, philosophers, and

---

22 Dugin was once the Chief Editor of Tsargrad TV, a channel launched in 2015 that is known for its support for the Kremlin, the international far right, and conservative Russian Orthodoxy. It is named after the Russian name for Constantinople and it has produced a number of documentaries about the history of 'Byzantium' and its connection to Russia, past and present.

scholars. As the West has moved away from understanding Christianity as central to Rome, Russia has correspondingly moved away from any other element of Roman identity. This interpretation allows Russia to claim the inheritance of Rome while opposing anyone else's claim.

It is, however, still an interpretation that is grounded in some key elements of Roman identity. As we have seen in the previous two chapters, what Rome meant and how that was expressed changed over time. An institution as long-lasting and diverse as the Roman Empire, which regularly reinvented itself to continue to thrive, offers endless opportunities for interpretation and reinterpretation.

Moreover, these different later interpretations have always been in contact and conversation with each other.

One way to see this is in the phrase *Russkiy Mir* or, in Latin, *Pax Russica*.

Famous Roman writers of the first century CE, like Seneca, Lucan, and Tacitus, referred to the Roman Empire and its areas of influence as *pax Romana*, the peace of Rome. They most likely did so satirically, a way to subtly critique the Roman emperors who now held the power of life and death over men who, 100 years previously, would have been their peers.[23] This was never an official phrase but it was picked up and popularized in eighteenth-century Europe as a way to (non-satirically) describe the glories of empire and cultural influence of European colonial powers, directly connecting European imperialism with the Roman Empire.

Now it is back in vogue in Russia. Both *Russkiy Mir* and *Pax Russica* present Russia and Russian culture at the heart of a new world order, one that opposes American, Western liberalism. Aleksandr Dugin, to promote his International Eurasian Movement, another interpretation of the same idea, gives interviews in an office draped in Russian flags that

---

23 Such critiques of empire were probably a little less concerned with the mass conquest, death, and exploitation of others that the Roman Empire also entailed.

bear the slogan *Pax Russica*. This interpretation of Rome is grounded both in the Romanland culture that influenced the Rus from the tenth century *and* later, western European interpretations that Russia now finds itself in opposition to.[24]

Whereas previously, these two different interpretations of Rome were connected enough that Catherine the Great could exploit them to present herself as Roman in a way that made her appear both sufficiently Russian at home and plausibly European abroad, now they have been developed in a way that makes them seem incompatible.

Much of this development is entangled with other empires who claimed an inheritance of Rome for themselves, as we see next.

---

24 Russia's relationship to Romanland, or Byzantium, has often been stressed in Western scholarship as a way to present Russia as intrinsically different from the West, an 'Oriental' power, whose so-called love of autocracy can be explained through its connection with the corrupted version of Rome found in Romanland.

PART TWO
EMPIRE

Soldiers march and generals strategize, relentlessly pushing the borders of the empire ever outward, while leading politicians in the Roman government catalogue the people, places, and property that now fall under their control. Food supplies are taken from the provinces to feed the capital city, jostling for harbour space with ships that groan under the weight of looted goods and newly enslaved people. The funds of conquest pay for monumental buildings to rise at home and abroad, reinforcing the identity, power, and wealth of Rome. Across the city, the diverse gods, languages, and traditions of the empire can be found alongside one another: traded in crowded marketplaces, studied in quiet academies, and debated at elite dinner parties. Peace, prosperity, and progress spread across the conquered territories and beyond. Allies are reassured, rebels are crushed, rivals are intimidated, and, everywhere Roman citizens travel, they know they are kept safe by the might of the empire.

Throughout its long history, Rome was ruled by hereditary kings, elected consuls, and discreetly (or not-so discreetly) elevated emperors. It wasn't always an empire – at both its start and end, Rome could not really be described as anything other than a city-state.

How Rome was understood by the people who ruled it and the people who were ruled *by* it, never mind the people around it, changed over time – as with any empire. How any individual felt about Rome would likely differ depending on where and when in the empire they lived, whether they were free or enslaved, rich or poor, in power or without. Political, philosophical, and religious beliefs might influence their feelings or they might be entirely separate; there were as many different ways to respond to Rome as there were people to do so.

There is always a problem of evidence for historians: who leaves it, who finds it, who interprets it. There is no perfect source – how could there be? Everyone who lived in or near the imperial territories would probably have had their lives impacted by Roman rule at some point, and not just by armies marching past or against them. Trends in the capital could affect trade, the whims of a new local governor could affect law and order, pollution from silver-mining could affect the air you inhaled.[1] Small farmers in rural areas might be asked to contribute to the grain requisition and nomadic communities might be recruited for military service.

Of these many different ways to experience the Roman Empire, however, the evidence available for us to interpret is skewed. The people who left written records of the Roman Empire were almost exclusively elite men, although they did not always think of themselves as primarily or even at all Roman. Their main focus was often on the behaviour of elite men like them, Roman or not.

The archaeological record offers the potential for a much broader perspective. Most people don't leave an archive of writing about their lives but we all leave material traces, strange as it may sometimes be to consider how the contents of our homes might be interpreted if they were frozen in time and discovered centuries later, as with Pompeii and Herculaneum.

These two Roman cities, famously destroyed by an eruption of Mount Vesuvius in 79 CE, were 'rediscovered' a millennium after

---

1 Ice-cores as far away as Greenland show traces of pollution from lead-silver ores mined in Roman provinces.

the death of their inhabitants and have been officially excavated and explored since the eighteenth century.[2] The 'discoveries' prompted a frenzy of interest across Europe and North America in the lives of the 'ordinary' people who lived there, caught at the most extra-ordinary moment.

For a long time, however, most of the people *conducting* archaeology were from the elites of their own societies and they were primarily concerned with the elites of the society they were exploring, so the focus was often much more on artefacts with aesthetic value that would look good in a museum or a stately home, rather than on, say, anti-Roman graffiti. Even when it wasn't, their perspective on the evidence left by 'ordinary people' was heavily influenced by their own experiences and prejudices.

This is always a problem in trying to learn about a past society. Historians are forever working with an incomplete jigsaw set, trying to fit the few pieces they have together according to a picture that only really exists in their imagination. In the case of Rome, this is perhaps even more complicated because of how dominant ideas about it have been, ever since it first started to conquer the lands in and around the Mediterranean, and how contested the idea of a Roman 'legacy' was and still is today.

The word 'empire' itself comes from the Latin word *imperium* – the meaning of which inevitably changed over time, depending on the context. It always meant something connected with power, however.

The Romans themselves thought about *imperium*, their power over other peoples and places. They discussed and debated legal connotations, moral implications, and practical considerations. They described their own power and critiqued the power of others, sometimes in their own words and sometimes in words they assigned to others.

---

2 They were consistently known to locals, who unofficially excavated and explored them before they became famous.

Those words have frequently been used by the men and women who came after the Romans to discuss the nature of power, the correct uses of it, and ways to resist it. Time and again, people who read Cicero, Seneca, and Tacitus for their education returned to those words to understand the empires of their own worlds.

These men were all citizens of Rome, a privilege that, in their lifetimes, was reserved for a minority of men. Moreover, they were part of the ruling class, men with access to power. The ideas they voiced for and against empire, however, have been taken up by both the ruled and ruling since, and are therefore worth an introduction.

Cicero was a famous Republican politician whose rhetorical skill was so impressive that his letters, speeches, and studies have been preserved for two millennia. He prosecuted some of his peers for abuses of power in the law courts and argued against them in Senate debates. In one such case, which made his name as a lawyer, he accused a Roman governor of the province of Sicily of exploitation, saying:

> . . . and you [. . .] seized and stole these [pieces of art] through fear, by your power and the official signs of your authority, from that man, whom, along with the rest of our allies in that country, the Roman people had entrusted not only to your power, but also to your upright exercise of it.

Cicero's ideas about power and the appropriate use of it changed over time, partly in response to the huge growth of Roman economic, military, and political influence abroad over his lifetime and partly in response to the ever-changing political situation at home – and who his allies were. He left a huge body of work for later thinkers to refer to.

Reading the works of a man like Seneca the Younger, who lived around 100 years later, gives us a different insight into Roman ideas of power. Rome was no longer a Republic, ruled by a collection of men who were elected by citizens of the city. It was now a hereditary monarchy, if one that politely observed some Republican niceties. The memory of the Republic as an ideal remained, however, particularly among elite men. Stoic philosophy became increasingly popular among such men, as they sought to find meaning in a life that could be transformed or ended by one-man rule. In his version of *Medea*, Seneca's lead character claims 'unjust rule never lasts' as she fights for an alternative future for herself.

A little later still, when the historian Tacitus was writing, it was clear there was no going back. One of the most famous critiques of empire comes from a speech Tacitus described a British rebel leader giving to inspire his troops against Rome:

> *Robbers of the world, having by their universal plunder exhausted the land, they rifle the deep. If the enemy be rich, they are rapacious; if he be poor, they lust for dominion; neither the east nor the west has been able to satisfy them. Alone among men they covet with equal eagerness poverty and riches. To robbery, slaughter, plunder, they give the lying name of empire; they make a wasteland and call it peace.*

Tacitus certainly had a flair for the dramatic but no less a source than Augustus, in the official record of his actions as the first sole-ruler of the Roman Empire, had claimed after his death in 14 CE:

> *When foreign peoples could safely be pardoned, I preferred to preserve rather than destroy them.*

In the same record, called the *Res Gestae Divi Augusti*, he listed the peoples and places he had conquered, the booty he had claimed and re-distributed, the number of men who had served him personally, the official titles he had been granted, the extraordinary buildings and lavish entertainments he paid for, and the 'peace' he had established. Tacitus's critique of Roman power can easily be read as a different interpretation of Augustus's boast.

Empire can mean many things; there is no single fixed definition. But Augustus's listing of his accomplishments makes a good starting point: conquest and booty, the accumulation of titles, massive state expenditure, and the suggestion that conquered peoples should be grateful for the benefits of empire.

How rulers tried to promote and maintain the power of their empires, and how the people they ruled tried to navigate that power and their own place in it, are the themes of the next three chapters.

5

Conquering Rome:
the Ottoman Empire

After 800 years of trying, a Muslim ruler finally conquered the city of Constantinople – or, as they knew it, Rome. Immediately, despite the history of religious, political, and military opposition between the two powers, Mehmed II, Sultan of the Ottomans, added 'Caesar of the Romans' to his list of titles.

Moreover, the leader of the Eastern Orthodox Church in Constantinople, the Patriarch, acknowledged his claim. The right to the title came with the successful conquest of what they *both* called Rome, the city of Constantinople and the rule of the people who still lived there.

Throughout Ottoman rule, different groups of subjects found ways to navigate their identities and negotiate a place within, or without, the empire. The last Ottoman Sultan was deposed in 1922 and his claim to be 'Caesar of the Romans', never the most important of his titles, disappeared with him. The ways in which Rome was interpreted and understood by both the rulers and the ruled throughout the long history of the Ottoman Empire helped shape the modern world.

The mighty city, so long considered impregnable, loomed large, the last hold-out of the enemy. In the distance, having already slowly surrounded the rival capital and cut off its supply chains, the brilliant young military commander surveyed his forces. For more than a month, they had relentlessly gone about their work. His camps, meticulously organized to maximize efficiency, remained alive with activity. From across the empire, the renowned cavalry and elite infantry troops applied pressure, refusing to accept they could be beaten by the famous fortifications of this ancient city. Now, as his siege equipment continued to harass the defenders, he ordered his engineering experts to execute his latest ingenious plan to get through the monumental walls. Through the smoke and deafening cries of battle, he turned to face the ranks of his soldiers, to prepare them for their final assault.

THE BRILLIANT YOUNG COMMANDER WAS Mehmed II, ruler of the Ottoman Turks, and the formidable city he finally conquered was Constantinople, city of Constantine the Great, capital of Romanland. His success allowed him to add two titles to his already impressive collection: *Fatih*, the Conqueror, and *Kayser-i Rum*, Caesar of Rome.

The Ottomans were already established as an important regional power by this time, ruling almost all of Anatolia and Rumeli (the 'land of the Romans'). Their current capital was the former Roman city Edirne in Rumeli (originally named for the Roman Emperor Hadrian). Constantinople had been surrounded and cut off from its allies for decades. The emperor of Romanland had been paying a financial tribute to the Ottomans for more than a century. At times, they had even acknowledged Ottoman rulers as a regional overlord. The city's walls, however, had held out.

The conquest of Constantinople is often seen as inevitable. Impoverished, abandoned by its allies, depleted by plagues, and left with perhaps as few as 7,000 people to defend it against a far larger force, what chance could it have?

This narrative forgets a number of things: the defences of the city of Constantine were justifiably famous. To overcome them, Mehmed had to go to extraordinary lengths. Firstly, he constructed a brand new fortress to cut off the city from any support by sea, support which had previously been essential to its survival.

Secondly, he found a way around the Great Chain of the Golden Horn, which blocked access to the city's harbour. Unable to break the chain and approach the city by water, Mehmed ordered his engineers to erect gigantic, greased wooden beams along the land. His men then attached enormous cables to sixty ships and hauled them by hand up and then down the steep hill that lay alongside the city's harbour.

Finally, he bombarded the city's walls with a cannon, the first time such technology had been used in this way. This cannon was so large it reportedly required ninety oxen and 400 men to move it, so powerful that the heat generated meant it had to be soaked in warm oil regularly to cool it down and could only be fired three times a day, and so expensive that Constantine XI, last emperor of Romanland, had not been able to afford to accept the offer of the engineer to make it for him instead of his enemies. It could fire a cannonball of approximately 540 kg at a distance of around 1.6 km, allowing the Ottomans to smash through the city walls while standing well out of range of the defenders.

Still, it took fifty-three days and a military force ten times the size of that defending Constantinople for Mehmed to finally succeed in his aim and declare victory. In doing so, he announced himself and his people as a major new power.

A Renaissance rival

As *Kayser-i Rum* and the ruler of a Mediterranean empire, Fatih Mehmed and his successors were key participants in Europe's ongoing power plays. They fought, negotiated, and traded – all while they worked to expand their territories and influence. At various times and for various reasons, they maintained alliances with Dutch, English, French, Genoese, and Venetian rulers. Once, the Papacy in Rome sent a request for help from the Ottomans; later, it organized a coalition of partners to attack them.

Territorially, the Ottomans' main European rivals were the Habsburg rulers of the Holy Roman Empire and, later, the Russian Empire: three rival successors to Rome competing for authority. It was not always explicitly framed as such but, as we have seen, there were always traces of Rome in these rivalries. The Ottomans also maintained significant rivalries and on-off alliances with the maritime republic of Venice, the Portuguese, and the Polish-Lithuanian Commonwealth, among others.

These were not the only or even, frequently, the most important foreign relations of the Ottoman rulers, whose territories would expand to include the Arabian peninsula, much of North Africa, and what is presently Iraq. Their rivalries with the Mughal rulers of south Asia and the Safavid rulers of Persia were incredibly important, as were their claims to the titles of *Khalifa* ('successor' to the Muslim prophet Muhammad) and *Khan* ('ruler', a title that connected them with the previous great Mongol dynasties). The Ottomans were adept at speaking to different audiences inside and outside of their diverse empire to present themselves as legitimate and powerful rulers. However, it is their many Christian audiences, both their own subjects and those of their European rivals, that concern us here.

Fatih Mehmed absolutely knew how to present himself to his fellow European rulers (he may not have considered them his *peers*, as we will see later, but they were certainly a relevant audience for him). He commissioned the Venetian Renaissance master Gentile Bellini to paint a portrait of him in the fashionable style in 1480, flanked by traditional columns supporting an arch. Below the left column is an inscription that includes the Latin phrase *victor orbis*, or 'conqueror of the World'. On the top right and left of the painting are three stacked crowns, possibly to symbolize that Mehmed II was the ruler of Rumeli, Anatolia, and western Asia.

He sponsored brilliant artists and artisans, built on a monumental scale, promoted Constantinople as a centre of scholarship, and arranged a trip to what was thought to be the site of Troy to show off his historical knowledge. European visitors to Mehmed II's court would find libraries filled with books in Arabic, Armenian, Coptic, Hebrew, Greek, Persian, Syriac, and more. They could browse copies of ancient classics like Homer's *Iliad* or more recent, famed scholarly works like those of Ibn Sina and Maimonides. The new *Kayser-i Rum* read widely, reportedly passionate about the latest military manuals and medicinal texts; treatises on law, natural science, and philosophy; as well as epic poetry of various traditions.

In doing so, he ruled in a way that drew on the traditions of ancient Roman emperors, just as the leading Christian and Muslim courts of Europe, west Asia, and North Africa did. Fatih Mehmed ruled this way because it was how Muslim leaders had always ruled, rather than in an attempt to be understood as European; although he was aware that many of these traditions also effectively presented him to his European rivals. Just as we saw with Catherine the Great in the previous chapter, the shared legacy of Rome across different contexts could be exploited by capable rulers to speak to many different audiences at once.

Mehmed II and many of his heirs showed themselves to be incredibly capable rulers. The small Anatolian principality founded by Osman I, a Turkic warrior, in 1299 had become a transcontinental empire even before the conquest of Constantinople. It would expand further and play a major role in international affairs until 1922. Whether as an ally or a rival, an inspiration or a threat, an enemy or a peer, the Ottomans could not be ignored.

A new great power ruled from the ancient city of Constantine the Great.

Expanding the empire

Fatih Mehmed died in 1481, as he planned a campaign to conquer territories in southern Italy. He was succeeded by his son Bayezid II, who continued many of his father's policies. He drew on the experienced administrative class of the Rum (the collective name of the Orthodox Christians who had remained in Constantinople after the conquest), he patronized scholarship, and he played an active role in the diplomatic entanglements of his rivals to both the east and west.

In 1492, when the joint Catholic rulers in Iberia, Isabella I of Castile and Ferdinand II of Aragon, expelled their Jewish and Muslim subjects, Bayezid II sent his navy to help evacuate them safely and bring them to Ottoman territories to be resettled. He publicly announced their welcome under his rule and scorned Ferdinand as someone who 'has impoverished his own country and enriched mine'.

In 1512, Bayezid II was deposed by one of his sons, Selim I, who would focus on military expansion, primarily against his Muslim rivals in Safavid Persia and Mamluk Egypt. In his public relations against his rivals, Selim claimed he combined the wisdom of Solomon and the military prowess of Alexander.[1] A contemporary historian described the Ottoman ruler to Charles V, Holy Roman Emperor, as a great admirer of Julius Caesar's military leadership.

Selim I was succeeded by perhaps the most famous of the Ottoman rulers, Suleyman I, known in Europe as 'the Magnificent'. For forty-six years, Suleyman was one of the most powerful men in the world. Helped by his extraordinarily capable wife, Hürrem Sultan, also

---

1 While neither Solomon nor Alexander was Roman, they were two of the most iconic rulers in the Roman traditions, as well as the Arabian and Persian.

known as Roxelana, he expanded Ottoman influence diplomatically, economically, and militarily. At home and abroad, the empire was transformed.

His reign involved a dizzying number of diplomatic and military rivalries across the three continents his rule reached. In the last ten years or so of his rule alone, the Ottomans agreed the Peace of Amasya with the Safavid Persian Empire, gaining a number of new territories; defeated an alliance of Christian naval forces off the coast of Tunisia to assert their naval dominance of the Mediterranean; repressed a Slavonic Christian rebellion in north Macedonia; besieged (unsuccessfully) the Knights Hospitaller on Malta; assisted the defence of Aceh, Indonesia, against the Portuguese; and besieged (successfully) the Habsburg fortress of Szigetvár in Hungary.

With so many rivals abroad and such a diverse range of subjects at home, Suleyman was deeply conscious of the importance of his public image and what we might call 'soft power', as well as successful bureaucratic, military, and religious leadership. When it came to his major European rivals, the Habsburg rulers of the Holy Roman Empire, he pulled out all the stops.

A Roman triumph

Kayser-i Rum was never the most important title of any Ottoman ruler. However, since their major imperial rival dynasty, the Habsburgs, also claimed to be Roman emperors, it was often a powerful card for them to play. Suleyman, in particular, seems to have been irritated by Charles V's use of the title. In the early 1530s, he was determined to prove his claim to Roman authority to be the superior one.

A heavily rumoured joint campaign with the French, assisted by the Venetians, against both Charles V and his ally, the pope, in Italy, never materialized, although the rumours certainly had Pope Clement VII worried. Instead, Suleyman requested his Grand Vizier and closest friend, Ibrahim Pasha, to work on a new project. The new Kayser-i Rum was going to recreate a traditional Roman *triumph* – but rather than celebrating a successful military campaign, it would form part of the campaign itself.

During the Roman Republic (*c.*509–27 BCE), a triumph had functioned as an official recognition of extraordinary military accomplishments. They were strictly governed by both civic and religious laws and could only be granted by the Roman Senate. In a system that resolutely refused to allow its rulers to behave like kings, a triumph was the closest thing.

The triumphing general laid down his legal authority to command an army at the city walls, while his soldiers laid down their weapons. Then, wearing specific regalia to acknowledge his elevated accomplishments and divine favour, including a crown of laurel leaves, the general would ride through the city from the walls to the centre, followed by his army, his prisoners of war, and any booty they had taken. At the end of the parade, the general would make an offering to Jupiter Optimus Maximus, Rome's highest divinity.

As public relations opportunities went, there was no equal in the Roman Republic. Over time, as the Republican city-state became an empire and the spoils of conquest increased, the right to a triumph became part of the competitive infighting that led to the imperial system of one-man rule. The triumph – the iconic celebration of military success, divine favour, and service to Rome – became the prerogative of the imperial family. Over time, especially under Christian emperors, its form changed somewhat, but its usefulness as a public projection of power never did.

By the sixteenth century, the idea and iconography of a Roman triumph was popular in the Holy Roman Empire and its neighbours so, when Charles V won an important victory against Suleyman in Tunis in 1535, he took the opportunity to stage one for himself in Rome, helped by Pope Clement VII. When Suleyman heard about it, he was determined to upstage his rival.

Ibrahim Pasha was sent to organize the commission of a number of extravagant pieces of regalia in Venice for Suleyman's own triumph – and to do so ostentatiously. The sultan wanted the rumour mill in Europe to go into overdrive. The centre-piece of the regalia was a golden 'Roman-style' helmet topped by four crowns, similar to the papal tiara but much grander. The invoice (settled in a manner approvingly noted by the rumour mill) described the crowned helmet's decoration as including fifty diamonds, forty-nine pearls, forty-seven rubies, twenty-seven emeralds, and a large turquoise. It was topped by a giant plume, also thought to be in the Roman style.

Additionally, there was a golden chain so heavy that Suleyman needed help moving around, a jewel-encrusted golden sceptre, and a golden throne. The artist who made these items reportedly showed the jewels to Pope Clement VII, likely encouraged by Ibrahim Pasha. Suleyman, on campaign towards the Hungarian territories of Charles V's brother, Ferdinand, stopped repeatedly en route in Ottoman cities like Belgrade, where he paraded under classical-style arches he had ordered to be constructed. His horse and courtiers were similarly dressed in lavish attire, the details of which were breathlessly reported around other European nations.

All the while, the Habsburgs were attempting to slow Suleyman's military progress with peace negotiations. In Niš, in present-day Serbia, the Habsburg envoys were made to watch from a minaret as Suleyman paraded through more arches decorating the streets. Eventually they were ordered to meet him at a carefully stage-managed scene so dripping with gold and jewels that the Habsburg ambassadors turned into 'speechless corpses', according to a (hardly unbiased) Venetian report.

The French envoys, keen to embarrass their Habsburg rivals, also gleefully supplied details of the Ottoman's Roman triumphal processions to be repeated in the popular media of contemporary Europe: news pamphlets, plays, and songs. The French political theorist Jean Bodin wrote specifically about the contested claim to Roman authority, siding with the Ottoman ruler: he was wealthier, ruled more impressive territories, and had the better army. Moreover, Bodin observed, he ruled more formerly Roman territories than the Habsburgs did.

Suleyman got what he wanted: a peace treaty, recognition of overlordship in Hungary from Charles's brother, Ferdinand, and a reputation in Europe for magnificence that outlasted his reign.

That this big-budget display was designed for his European audience only is made clear by Suleyman's later actions. The dramatic four-crowned golden helmet, which had no symbolic usefulness to Suleyman's other audiences, was seemingly melted down and the jewels re-used. He returned to Constantinople and pivoted to a new language of power, more appropriate for the Muslim audiences he wanted to win over in his competition with the Safavid Shah of Persia.

With the same eye for reputation management, he publicly reversed his controversial decision to display several ancient Roman statues captured while on campaign, which were decorating several of the monumental columns in the city by the ancient Roman Hippodrome, just as Constantine had once adorned the city. Ibrahim Pasha was blamed and Suleyman moved on to the next stage of his reign, secure in his title as the senior Caesar.

What's in a name? Ruler edition

It is tempting to see re-enactments of this sort as frivolous: over-privileged rulers playing fancy dress as they compete for the most impressive title among peers. But this kind of spectacle is often essential. The power to do something is often not enough, everyone needs to *know* what you can do.

Suleyman was showing the rulers of Europe that he could spare the enormous resources required to afford and arrange such an event, even while also undertaking a major military campaign. He was showing the Holy Roman Emperor that he had allies in Europe who were willing to help his reputation management as well as his wars. He was showing the emperor's Protestant enemies that Roman-ness was possible without the papacy. Crucially, he was doing all this in a visual language that his audience understood.

The Ottoman rulers would also do this in verbal and written form, with the language of titles. With themselves, their allies, and their enemies, they were incredibly precise about the titles they used – and always conscious of their audience.

As a Turkic people, the title of *Khan* was always important to them; as Muslims, so was the title of *Khalifa*. The pre-Islamic Persian title of *Shah* and its variant *Padishah* also held significance for them. Just as we saw in the previous chapters, these titles were deployed to convey to fellow rulers their place. The Ottomans' French allies, for instance, might receive the valued title of *padishah* but the Habsburgs were consistently denied the honour and instead referred to as merely 'kings' (and reduced to 'king of Vienna' or 'king of Spain' to boot, rather than any acknowledgement of their claim to be Roman, for instance).

The audience was always a relevant factor in the choice of title. Sometimes the deciding factor could be geographic, such as the inscription in one of Suleyman's fortresses that uses the traditional title of each region, declaring him 'the Shah of Baghdad and Iraq, the Caesar of Rome, and the Sultan of Egypt' or the titulature used by Mehmed IV (r. 1648-87), which described him as 'the one who issues orders to the Roman, Arab, and Persian kingdoms'. Sometimes a reference would be made to a historical figure that transcended the geographical range of territories, such as Alexander the Great.

Often, the language of the document naming the Ottoman ruler seems to have determined the title choice – a literal act of translation helped by the shared Roman origin of many of the different terms. Ottoman documents in Serbian, for instance, used *tsar*, the Slavic derivation of the Latin title Caesar. By the time Mehmed II conquered Constantinople, the term used for the Greek-speaking ruler had shifted to *basileus* and, when official documents were written in Greek, as they often were for Venetian ambassadors, this was the term used. If Latin were used, to the Ottomans' Catholic subjects, for instance, or to their Polish allies, the title used was the Latin *imperator*.

These usages and their understood meanings shifted over time. Moreover, as the Ottoman rulers' interest in communicating their power to certain audiences changed, they ceased to issue official documents in languages other than Turkish and Arabic and their use of titles adapted. However, they show clearly the Ottoman awareness of their multiple audiences with their differing understandings of power and the Ottoman's willingness – or later, their lack of willingness – to speak to those audiences.

We can also see this understanding in the communications between Elizabeth I of England (r. 1558-1603) and Safiye Sultan. First as *Haseki Sultan* – the official title of the principal consort – then *Valide Sultan* – the official title of the mother of the ruler – and finally as the grandmother of two rulers, Safiye Sultan was another powerful woman at the heart of Ottoman rule, following in the tradition Hürrem Sultan had established. She lived in Constantinople during the reigns of seven sultans: Suleyman the Magnificent, Selim II, Murad III, Mehmed III, Ahmed I, Mustafa I and Osman II, from *c.*1563 to *c.*1619.

As part of her diplomatic role, she corresponded with Elizabeth I, the Protestant queen of England. The letters that remain to us (only three of what seems likely to have been many) are often noted for their consciously feminine language and their discussion of gender roles and beauty products, as these two powerful but culturally very different women tried to establish some common footing on which to base their diplomatic relationship.

In one of the letters that remains, Safiye gently broaches the idea that they have other things in common, too: that, as Turks and Britons, they are both genealogical heirs to the Trojans. Before doing so, she invokes other shared reference points that she must have known would be familiar to her audience: the Ottoman claim to rule the Romans, and comparisons between the Sultan and Alexander the Great, and then with Mars, the Roman god of war. Just as Suleyman had done before her, Safiye was drawing on specific elements of Ottoman identity to speak the language of her audience, build a connection, and project power.

As rulers of Anatolia, having conquered its Greek-speaking rulers, a connection with Troy seems like a straightforward claim for the Ottomans. Fascinatingly, however, the link long pre-dated their presence in the region. In fact, the many efforts across Latin Christendom to make a genealogical connection to the Trojans had also linked the peoples of central Asia, specifically the Turkic peoples, with Troy. These peoples, it was claimed from around the seventh century, were descended from Hector's son, Astyanax, also known as Francio. As the name suggests, this was also a connection the Franks, or French, claimed, a connection that was very useful in the Franco-Ottoman alliance.

By this time, the interest in Trojan heritage that had previously existed in much of Latin Christendom as part of their Roman identity had faded. Increasingly, the ancient Greek-speaking city states were drafted into an idea of shared European-ness that was now often used to exclude the Turkish-speaking Ottoman rulers of Romanland instead of their Greek-speaking predecessors.

Among the Tudor rulers of England and Wales, however, it remained popular. Their rule, they claimed, had been founded from the ashes of Troy, just like Roman rule. Elizabeth herself was frequently cast in literature and paintings as a descendent of Paris, the Trojan prince. Safiye had done her homework.

We do not have a letter in response from Elizabeth, although we cannot know if it simply does not remain to us. We do know, however, that Elizabeth sent a magnificent gift to Constantinople for the then Ottoman ruler, Mehmed III. A musical organ and clock that automatically played music four times a day, this expensive present followed in a long-standing tradition of *automata*, charming and complex feats of technical accomplishment for which Constantinople had traditionally been famous. Such was its complexity that the clock-maker had to travel with it and assemble the device at the Ottoman court. The organ and its maker, a man named Thomas Dallam, travelled from England to Constantinople on the merchant ship *Hector*, named after the crown prince of Troy and the city's greatest warrior.

It is possible, of course, that the choice of ship was coincidental rather than deliberate. After all, Trojan themes were hugely popular in Tudor England. If so, it would indicate that Safiye Sultan had judged her audience correctly when she tried to deepen their relationship with reference to their shared claims to Trojan heritage. In the subtle language of international diplomacy, however, where two intelligent women could invest recommendations of certain beauty creams with significance, it is very possible that Elizabeth selected the ship she sent with a view to her own audience.

We cannot say. In 1603, Elizabeth died and Ahmed I took the Ottoman throne and turned his attention to different audiences, different priorities. An Anglo-Ottoman relationship was no longer a concern.

Changing Romes: inventing Byzantium

While the Ottoman rulers were claiming Roman titles and using Roman imagery to project their power to rivals in Europe, their subjects were developing new ideas about Roman-ness, interpreting their past differently through the lens of their present.

In many ways, the Ottomans had continued the governing infrastructure of the Roman Empire they conquered. One of the most powerful men in Ottoman administration after the conquest was a man named Mesih Pasha, who was the nephew of Constantine XI Palaiologos, the childless last Roman emperor of Constantinople – a man who might in other circumstances have had a claim to the throne. Many other members of the old Roman aristocracy joined him in the imperial government, making the best of their new situation.

The city of Constantine was repopulated, encouraged back to its former glory as one of the major cities of the Mediterranean, and Mehmed II funded an extensive building programme. Before Fatih's conquest, it had been popular among the Christian aristocracy of Romanland to wear kaftans and turbans, a style that was also popular among elite Ottomans. The majority of the population in the city and empire remained Christian. Some things changed but many stayed the same.

Inevitably, as time went on, things did change: sometimes slowly, sometimes quickly. As the Ottoman elite increasingly identified themselves as *Rum* or Roman, to denote themselves as the new elites of the Roman geographical space, the former elites of the city seem to have begun in contrast to emphasize their Orthodox Christian religion and Greek language as identity markers more than their Roman history, inside and out of government. Their tripartite Roman-Greek-Christian heritage remained, but the focus now lay less on the Roman-ness that their conquerors also claimed. This shift was nudged further as the Orthodox Christian Church negotiated an increasingly formal role for itself in the imperial administration of its community and, over a long stretch of time, '*Rum*' fell out of fashion among the Ottoman elite.

Ottoman relationships with the other European powers also changed in ways that affected their subjects. In particular, Orthodox Russia's claim to responsibility for the Greek-speaking Orthodox Christians of the Ottoman Empire became part of their ongoing imperial rivalry, as we saw in the previous chapter. Catherine the Great's 'Greek Plan' never came to fruition but, in 1774, the Treaty of Küçük Kaynarca had granted concessions that would lead to formal Russian protection of Orthodox Ottoman Christians.

At the same time, across Europe and the newly founded United States of America, people were increasingly connecting themselves to ancient Greek city-states as well as Rome, drawing on interpretations about the period of ancient Athenian democratic government to call for revolution and changing forms of representation.

Amidst this swirl of change, the Greek-speaking Orthodox Christians of the Ottoman Empire tried to navigate their own identity and carve out a place for themselves in their world. In hindsight, we can see this inevitably building towards the Greek Revolution of 1821–32 and the founding of the modern nation state of Greece. Hindsight always emphasizes the road taken, however, and there were other roads at the time that seemed just as likely to be followed.

As Christianity and Greekness became more relevant and increasingly well-articulated elements of their identity, the Roman-ness of this community also re-emerged. The official Ottoman name for Greek-speaking Orthodox Christians became Rum, and the Orthodox Church gained official religious leadership over Orthodox Christians in the Balkan region, once part of Romanland. These Greek-speaking, Orthodox Christian Romans were increasingly influential in the Ottoman economy and government. As the Greek Revolution approached, Roman-ness was also back in fashion.

In this case, however, the road that led to Rome was not taken.

Partly, this was chance: a case of which voices emerged most clearly from the debates over identity. Partly, it came out of the logic of contemporary nationalism, which demanded clear, narrow parameters of identity. Partly, it stemmed from the need to garner international support: Greekness was no longer understood as an orientalized, untrustworthy rival to authority but a westernized, philosophical tradition that was fashionable among the powers willing to support a rebellion against the Ottomans – powers that had their own, very specific interpretations of Rome.

It is here, after all this time, that Romanland, the Roman empire that had ruled from the city of Constantine the Great until 1453, received its new name.

Britain, France, and Russia were more than willing to fragment Ottoman authority and protect a Christian community of Greek-speakers, one increasingly understood as 'European', in a rebellion. They were not, however, willing to upset the careful balance of power they had established by introducing another imperial power, never mind one that could claim the prestige of Romanland and might have ambitions to reconquer Constantinople.

Part of the agreement these powers negotiated with the Ottomans for an independent Greek state specified that its monarch could not be from the ruling houses of any of their own monarchies. They selected Otto, the second son of the king of Bavaria, a Germanic kingdom that had emerged from the destruction of the Holy Roman Empire. Otto was seventeen, a Roman Catholic classical scholar who was descended from two former ruling dynasties of Romanland, and crucially, no threat to anyone.

At around the same time, Anglophone and Francophone scholarship began to use the idea of 'Byzantium' much more expansively. Once an occasional, and quite academic way to refer to the city of Constantinople, emphasizing its antiquity and pre-Constantinian roots, this now increasingly began to refer to the entire Romanland empire and its history. Of course, nobody could quite agree when this empire stopped being *Roman* and started being *Byzantine* because it was never a term anyone inside or outside the empire had previously used.

The name Byzantium, however, meant that nobody could really claim it as their own national heritage: an empire that combined Christian, Greek, and Roman traditions and ruled from the Bosphorus strait that connected the European and Asian parts of the continent now became a historical curiosity that officially seemed to belong to none of those traditions.

This was neither a coincidence nor a conspiracy; it was indicative of the cultural and intellectual climate of the nineteenth century, which we will encounter again in the following chapters. All around the world, communal identities were shifting in response to the challenges of the various European empires; geography, language, and religion competed for importance as people searched the past to find respective 'national' histories that would help to define them.

Communities had re-defined themselves in such a way before, of course; many are currently doing so, many more will in the future. However, the unprecedented level of connectedness across the globe in the nineteenth century, and the manner in which European colonial empires united and divided peoples around the world meant that these searches for new communal identities were also connected.

Enough Greek-speakers found a stronger identity in their language and pre-Roman history to forge a new nation state. In doing so, they navigated the same intellectual currents that would invent the Byzantine Empire and forget Romanland.

Remnants of Rome

That is not quite the end of Rome in this part of the world, however. Remnants can be found, clues to a mostly forgotten history.

The Greek Revolution and establishment of the nation state of Greece was not the end of the conflict between occupants of former Romanland. Territories changed hands, identities and allegiances continued to shift in response to local and global events. Mediterranean islands like Crete and Cyprus, which have been nodes in cross-continental networks of exchange for thousands of years, became caught up in on-going demands to define Eastern vs Western, Asian vs European, Christian vs Muslim.

Part of this conflict was the way in which Rome was now increasingly being seen as Western and European, a part of the so-called classical antiquity that ran from democratic Athens, via the Roman Empire, though to the Renaissance, and then on to the Enlightenment and 'modern' world. This was the heritage of the West, it was claimed.

This narrative simplifies and skips over both geography and history in favour of a straightforward origin story. Eurasia is one continent, geographically. Throughout their histories, the ancient Greek-speaking city-states were part of the communities and cultures of the Mediterranean, a sea that hosted one set of the many connections between Eurasia and Africa. The Roman Empire, throughout its history, had exploited and then dominated those connections, in the tradition of Eurasian powers.

One way to see this complexity is to return to Troy. Legends of a fabulous city-state on the coast of Anatolia had long been part of the oral storytelling traditions of ancient Mediterranean communities, and tales of its destruction were broken down and retold in thousands of different ways.

In Greek-speaking city-states, Homer's *Iliad*, the now-famous version of the story, likely came together alongside and as part of the formation of a collective identity in opposition to the Persian Empire. Troy is, in some sense, a proxy for an 'eastern' enemy. Except that, throughout the narrative, the Trojans are shown to be just the same as the men who fight them. Theirs is an enmity created through the machinations of the gods, not a civilizational divide. The Trojans still have heroes, still have families, still honour the same gods. Literally and metaphorically, these two sides speak languages that the other understands.

The Roman interpretation of Troy not only saw them as peers but as ancestors. We saw in Chapter 3 that, when the ancient Romans were required to navigate their own identity crisis, as the Republican system of government shifted to an imperial one, they looked to Troy for inspiration to hold them together. Rome's fascination with Troy was returned to again and again as people looked to define themselves in connection with and relation to Rome.

Greek-speakers, Latin-speakers, German-speakers, English-speakers, and Turkish-speakers – who had all claimed some sort of Roman-ness – had all looked to Troy, a city on the coast of Anatolia, to create shared identities. Now that same coast of Anatolia, rather than being a central point in a shared world, was the focal point of a divide between worlds.

This contest was sometimes over claims to ideas of heritage, like the debate over the origins of Homer, the legendary (and probably imaginary) poet who sang of gods and men and the wrath of Achilles. Sometimes it was over claims to material pieces of heritage, archaeological finds from ancient Troy, Greece, and Rome. Sometimes it was over claims to places, like the catastrophic fight over Smyrna, modern-day İzmir.[2] Frequently, it was over claims to people themselves.

These contested claims repeatedly had devastating consequences for those caught up in them. Throughout and after the First World War, individuals, families, and entire communities were murdered on suspicion of being on the other side, from localized violence to wholesale ethnic cleansing and genocide.

After the Ottoman Empire had dissolved, the Lausanne Treaty of 1923 formally recognized the Republic of Turkey and decided on

2 This ancient city on the Aegean coast of Anatolia was arguably one of the most famous in the Mediterranean for more than two millennia. It was contested and occupied during the Greco-Turkish War (1919–1922), at the end of which much of the city was destroyed in the Great Fire of Smyrna.

a formal exchange of populations between the two nation states of Greece and Turkey: determined only by religion. Any and all Muslim Greek nationals in Greek territory were to be 'exchanged' with any and all Orthodox Christian Turkish nationals in Turkish territory. People whose families had lived and died in one place for centuries, often more, were forcibly moved from their homes, irrespective of their language or personal sense of belonging and community.

It was a traumatizing attempt to impose a simple answer to the complex question of identity, enforcing a single difference over many similarities.

Other population migrations were formally encouraged in bilateral agreements across the former territories of the Roman and Ottoman empires: between Romania and Turkey from 1936, and Yugoslavia and Turkey from 1938.[3] The ongoing conflict between Greek- and Turkish-identifying Cypriot communities since 1974 and the genocide and ethnic cleansing in Bosnia-Herzegovina and Kosovo in the 1990s are both legacies of the same, very modern approach to narrowly defining identity.

These legacies remind us of the complexity of identity and ancient histories, which cannot be argued or imagined away. Many remains of the Roman past might be catalogued and displayed behind glass in national museums, scrubbed of colour and nuance and presented with a clear narrative, but they are also all around us, prompts for a different interpretation.

One such clue is the Romeyka language spoken by an estimated 4–8,000 Muslims in the Trabzon region of northern Türkiye, on the Black Sea. This language, named for its Roman speakers, is closer to

---

3 Forced population movement is a common feature of empires throughout history, as rulers seek to impose 'stable' conditions for government. It was particularly common during the twentieth century, as imperial governments both fought to continue their rule and also came to violent ends around the world.

the ancient Greek language than the modern version, having developed separately. In Romeyka, the threads of Greek and Roman traditions that have been separated from both each other and Ottoman history remain woven together.

6

Pax Romana, Pax Britannica

The men who conquered and administered the territories of the British Empire were educated in Roman language, literature, economy, engineering, history, law, warfare, religion, and culture. The empire they created and ran consciously modelled itself on what they understood to be Rome, claiming its legacy as an economic and military superpower.

From as early as 1576, England and then Britain used Roman imagery, language, and tactics to project its imperial might around the world. So successful was it at promoting the relevance of the Roman Empire that many of its colonies would themselves use Roman literature and philosophy to resist Britain, from India to Ireland.

Many popular current interpretations of Rome come from the men who participated in the British Empire, who saw themselves in Rome and Rome in themselves. However, the peoples they conquered and the peoples they rivalled didn't always agree and frequently offered competing interpretations that cast light on ancient Rome, the British Empire, and the modern world.

A mighty goddess rests on a lonely rock, serenely gazing out across the surrounding waves. In one hand, she holds Neptune's trident, pointing high into the skies. In the other hand sits an imposing rounded shield, a spike protruding out from the centre. Her robe, belted at the waist, flows down under her embossed breastplate to her sandalled feet. Crowning her hair is a warrior's helmet, topped by a large crest of horsehair. Here, at the edge of the known world, the goddess triumphantly surveys the seas and defends her realms.

By the end of the nineteenth century, Britannia ruled the waves. Representations of the British Empire in the form of a Roman goddess had spread around the world. This personification of the collection of islands in the North Atlantic as a goddess figure dates back to the Roman conquest of the region in the first century, when it began to appear on Roman coins around the empire. This Britain was an exotic, distant place, the conquest of which symbolized just how far Roman power reached.

Nearly two millennia later, Britannia was back – and she was everywhere. She appeared once again on coins but also on statues, paintings, satirical sketches, and more. By 1672, Charles II was using the image of Britannia on the coinage, reflecting his support for imperial expansion. She has featured in some way on official British coins ever since. Depictions of Britannia varied but she was almost always shown in Roman dress, with a variety of Roman accessories. She connected British rule in the present with Roman rule in the past, suggesting a direct link between these two great empires.

Of course, a lot had happened between Roman rule in the province of Britannia ending in 410 and the eventual emergence of England (and later Britain) as a colonial power under Elizabeth I. The identities, languages, political systems, and religious beliefs of the peoples inhabiting these islands had undergone many significant changes over that time – in conversation and conflict with each other.

Rome, in the form of the Catholic Church, had played a major role in those negotiations of identity during the sixteenth century, most often appearing in the part of the villain. As first the Tudors and then the Stuarts tried to form imperial identities of their own, however, Rome returned as an inspiration – this time, in the form of the ancient empire that, long ago, had ruled those shores.

This idea of Rome, the ancient empire, is the one that had developed across Europe, formalized by the Italian Renaissance. It did not include Romanland, or the Holy Roman Empire, both of which were now seen as sorts of successor states to Rome, if they were acknowledged as Roman at all.

Moreover, unlike in the empires we have previously considered, the English (and later the British) did not really consider themselves to have inherited the rule of the Roman Empire, either by right of religion or conquest. They did, however, use it as a model for their own.

Sometimes this approach drew on the historical connection between the two but it didn't need to: Rome was a natural reference point for European empires. As we saw in Chapter 3, the elites of Europe were educated in what was considered to be the ancient Roman style. Rome was the framework for how they understood the world. That was supplemented by Christian theology, local traditions, and, increasingly, ideas about ancient Greeks, particularly Athenians and Spartans. When it came to empire, however, Rome was the blueprint.

Educated for empire

This education was not just a relic of tradition, unquestioningly passed on. It was a conscious and clearly articulated choice, repeatedly made.

In the 1850s, the imperial administration of India (by far Britain's most lucrative imperial province) was reformed and the Imperial Civil Service was created. Instead of the men who ran the empire being appointed according to who they knew, they would now theoretically be selected on merit. Any subject of the British Empire between eighteen and twenty-three was eligible to take the examinations for entry.[1] Those who were successful would be trained for the role before being assigned to the potentially lucrative positions.

By this time, there were multiple options for a university degree and an increasing range of institutions in which to acquire one. However, the vast majority of those who passed the Imperial Civil Service exam from its establishment until the First World War were men who had studied *Literae Humaniores*, commonly known as Classics, at the University of Oxford.

At the height of the British Empire's global reach and power, the decision-makers were primarily men who had studied the ancient Greek and Latin languages,[2] and the art, history, literature, politics, and philosophy of the elites of Ancient Greek and Roman societies – at least, as they were then understood and taught at Oxford, as 'the classics'.[3]

This should perhaps not be too surprising: the exams were designed by men who had studied Classics at Oxford, who felt that the best people to follow in their footsteps were likely to be men who had been educated in the same manner. It helped that leading professors of Classics at Oxford, also convinced of the superiority of their own experiences, could lobby the men responsible for updating the exams – men who were frequently former university peers or students – and remind them

1 Queens as well as kings presided over the imperial expansion of first England, and then Britain, demanding, funding, and ruling the provinces that were conquered as well as spending the money extracted from those provinces. Women were not, however, eligible to formally administer the empire.

2 Increasingly, ancient Greece and Rome were twinned together, a development that is traced in the previous and following chapters.

3 Despite the fact that we know many of their ideas were quite simply wrong, Victorian scholarship on ancient Greece and Rome remains hugely influential to this day. The colour (or lack of colour) of statues and buildings is one such example.

of the greater suitability of their degrees as a test for merit.[4]

Sir Stanley Mordaunt Leathes, the First Civil Service Commissioner from 1910 to 1927, had studied Classics at the University of Cambridge. He responded to questions about the role of this degree in the civil service exam by arguing, 'the nearest approach to the ideal education for administrators in the Empire was in Classics and History'. It just happened to be the case, he claimed, that these were subjects studied by a much higher proportion of undergraduates at Oxford than elsewhere.[5] After all, so the thinking of Leathes and his peers went, the civilizations of ancient Greece and Rome were the foundation of European culture, the cornerstone of Western superiority. Britain had inherited that cultural legacy, combined it with an Anglican Christianity, and produced the men who had *conquered* the world. Within this framework, it seemed only reasonable to assume that the same background would produce the men most suited to running the world they had conquered.

To have a chance of passing this prestigious exam, then, you had to have studied a certain amount of these 'classic' societies and, ideally, studied them as recommended by Oxford dons. Ambitious men from around the empire knew that if they wanted to amount to anything, they had to be proficient in ancient Greek and Latin, had to understand the fundamentals of ancient philosophy and history, and would benefit from reading Julius Caesar's war manuals and Seneca's ideas of statesmanship. There might be other ways but there weren't many and, if you did succeed by means of an alternative route, you would still spend your life working with – and for – men who made jokes in Latin and expected you to understand their references to

4 Whatever the public claims about these exams being merit-based, a repeated refrain of the private correspondence about these exams was the need to make sure that the *right* sort of person passed them: English gentlemen rather than 'wild Irishmen', the 'middle-class', or 'natives'.

5 Although Leathes was a Cambridge classicist, Mathematics was considerably more popular at Cambridge in this period and the greater number of Oxford students than Cambridge, never mind any other university, was often questioned.

Cicero and Homer.[6]

This circular system had a number of consequences. As intended, it further encouraged classical education generally and ensured that the civil servants of the British Empire were educated to some degree about the cultures of ancient Greece and Rome. It also reinforced the ideas that were communicated as part of that education: that these were the pre-eminent cultures humanity had produced throughout all of human history, the most worthy of study. These were 'the classics'.

There were many brilliant and influential scholars who argued for other languages, cultures, and literatures to be considered worthy of study: it was frequently suggested that Persian and Sanskrit were sufficiently ancient and impressive to have some merit, for instance. Mandarin and Arabic might be considered, should one have a flair for the unusual, and there were even some who made the case for plain old English. The 'antiquity' of a language was always a point in its favour, in these calculations. Indeed, there were many European scholars who argued that, given the antiquity of Sanskrit as a language and the epic texts written in it, Indian culture might be considered, as the French historian Jules Michelet argued, 'the womb of the world'.

Many people did specialize in these languages and the study of the associated cultures, histories, and literatures. It was almost unheard of, however, to do so without first studying ancient Greek and Latin – the foundation of education, the lens through which any other culture was viewed and the standard they were held up against.

Even when people argued against this idea, which many did, it was hard to escape the framework of civilizational hierarchies that it set up. This framework went hand in hand with theories of racial supremacy and religious difference: the idea that some groups of people were

6 Many men who did not receive a formal classical education recognized the value of one in such a system and taught themselves, embracing the idea of Ancient Greece and Rome as superior civilizations as much as anyone else. Two such examples are Thomas Babington Macaulay and Evelyn Baring, Lord Cromer, who both feature in this chapter.

simply better in a meaningful, measurable way and were thus destined to rule. Much of the scholarship in this period, across all disciplines, was produced in this same framework: that everything could – and should – be categorized and ranked. Top of the rankings, always, were Europeans: the inheritors of Rome, the world's greatest pre-modern empire, and the current rulers of the world's modern empires.

The calculation was quite simple, to their minds: no other place had produced a civilization superior to Europe, and particularly to Britain; if they had, they would not have been conquered by the British.

Educated *by* empire

Scholarship and empire were intimately connected and constantly self-reinforcing: academic research studied and assessed which civilizations were better, bestowing a superiority that granted people from certain places the right to rule everyone else. Huge donations were made to the universities from the profits of empire, many of them directed towards further study of the regions from which the wealth had been ruthlessly extracted. Those who ruled were trained and assessed according to this system; many of them continued their research as part of their imperial postings or returned to academic studies later, drawing on their experiences of running the empire. The men who reformed the Indian Civil Service weren't just conscious of this element, they explicitly argued for it as a benefit of the system: the universities would benefit from empire and empire would benefit from the universities

One way we can see this connection is in popular contemporary scholarship about the rise and fall of the Roman Empire: that it had 'accidentally' acquired an empire by protecting its trading concerns, an argument that was also being made about the British Empire at the time, and that the Romans had been 'corrupted' by exposure to Eastern luxuries, which reflected a repeatedly expressed worry about the British in India.

The phrase 'pax Britannica', meaning 'the peace of Britain' in Latin, directly played on 'pax Romana'. These were euphemisms for empire that suggested imperial rule created peace and prosperity in the territories that were ruled – a key theme of scholarship in this period. Fascinatingly, this argument in favour of empire is one that we have already seen critiqued by a Roman at the height of empire, a critique he suggested had been expressed by a British rebel against Roman rule. Tacitus was widely studied in imperial Britain but his specific criticisms were frequently interpreted differently.

Another way we can see the connection between empire and scholarship is in the career of Thomas Babington Macaulay. In the 1830s, Macaulay worked for the Governor-General of India's Supreme Council and, in his spare time, taught himself about ancient Greece and Rome and wrote a collection of poems called *Lays of Ancient Rome*. Macaulay intended to recount Roman legends, as well as two recent European religious conflicts, in a style directly inspired by Roman literature.[7] The texts were accompanied by a scholarly discussion of the legends. The collection was hugely popular, then and later. Prime Minister William Gladstone was reportedly reading a copy as he ordered British troops to occupy Egypt in 1882;[8] Winston Churchill won an award at school for his ability to recite the entire text.

On his return from India, Macaulay became an MP and served as Secretary of War and later as Paymaster General. When he lost his seat, he became Rector of the University of Glasgow, before returning to parliament and playing a major role in the Imperial Civil Service reforms of the 1850s. In his later life, he wrote hugely influential histories of England. In Macaulay's life, we can see the entangled connections of imperial administration, scholarship, and British government.

7 These were, respectively, a Protestant French victory against Catholic forces in 1590 and the English defence against the Spanish armada in 1588.

8 There were five Oxford classicists in Gladstone's first cabinet, in addition to himself, and two further men who had studied Classics at Cambridge.

Finally, of course, the role of classics in the examination system that men like Macaulay created meant that these specific ancient societies became the *ideal* reference point for imperial administration. After all, you had to know about them to pass the exam. You assessed the needs of the situation, decided which of the two ancient cultures understood as 'classical' was most appropriate, and proceeded from there.

Interpretations of the ancient Greek political ideas and their colonies were much more fashionable when it came to the relationships between the various leaders of the white settler colonies of Australia, Canada, New Zealand, and South Africa, and the 'home' government in London because they acknowledged equality within the racial and religious hierarchies that European empires constructed and enforced.[9] This allowed the white settlers to negotiate greater degrees of self-rule for their own societies, while allowing governments in Britain to still insist on a degree of moral, cultural, and political authority.

However, when it came to the British *ruling*, which was the fate of everyone else, Rome was the more likely reference point. Charles Prestwood Lucas, who had studied Classics at Oxford, made this clear in his book *Greater Rome and Greater Britain* in 1912, which explicitly compared and contrasted the two empires. He argued that Britain had two spheres of empire: areas of white settlement, which he suggested aimed to run only themselves, and the spheres of rule: 'tropical lands and coloured races [. . . where] the English have come, not to settle, but to administer and rule wholly alien peoples'.

There was some overlap between these spheres, Lucas acknowledged – including the existence of indigenous peoples in the white settler territories. The sphere of rule, however, was much more comparable to the provinces of the Roman Empire. They required absolute rule,

9 These ideas of ancient Greek-speaking colonization practices have since been challenged in scholarship and we now have a much more complex, nuanced picture of the processes and relationships involved than those which were invoked by white settler societies.

he argued, by a different and superior civilization, and to be brought slowly (if at all) to a position where self-rule might be considered. In these territories, most particularly in India, Rome was the most appropriate reference point. In fact, the imperialist Cecil Rhodes was reportedly fond of saying, 'Remember always that you are a Roman' as advice for imperial governance.

Thus the 'merit-based' system for selecting the men who would run the empire trained them to make decisions, consciously or unconsciously, based on the Romans.

Ruling like a Roman

It is one thing to observe how much ideas about Rome were absorbed by those who administered the British Empire, or even to observe the Roman-inspired architecture and statues that marked the landscape of British rule (and frequently remain to this day).[10] It is somewhat more difficult to discern just how much those ideas actively influenced their decision-making. Quite often, however, they told us themselves. One of the most famous examples is a speech by Lord Palmerston, a leading British politician from 1830 to 1865 and twice Prime Minister. In a speech to the British Parliament in 1850, he declared that Britain's foreign policy should ensure that, 'as the Roman, in days of old, held himself free from indignity, when he could say *Civis Romanus sum* [I am a Roman citizen]; so also a British subject, in whatever land he may be, shall feel confident that the watchful eye and the strong arm of England will protect him against injustice and wrong.'[11]

---

10 Many examples of classically-inspired British imperial architecture have been cleverly re-purposed in the modern day to reflect independence narratives and the stories communities wished to tell about themselves, rather than the ones that had been told about them. One such example is Rashtrapati Bhavan in Delhi, now the official residence of the President of India. This twentieth-century, 19,000 m² mansion combines neoclassical elements with some of the many south Asian architectural traditions.

11 Palmerston was enthusiastic about using military force to intervene on behalf of wronged British citizens – or, rather, about using the idea of wronged British citizens as a justification for using military force to expand British influence.

Palmerston was not alone. In India, in Egypt, and in western Asia, leading men of the empire recorded drawing inspiration from the Romans in their policies for imperial rule. Macaulay, for instance, did not just write poetry inspired by Rome while in India or shape the Imperial Civil Service exams. He also heavily influenced the education policy imposed on India, in which an 'English' education was delivered in English, rather than local languages. In his words, this was necessary 'to form a class who may be interpreters between us and the millions whom we govern; a class of persons Indian in blood and colour, but English in tastes, in opinions, in morals, and in intellect.'

His brother-in-law, Charles Trevelyan,[12] was explicit about the basis of this policy, saying: 'The Indians will, I hope soon stand in the same position towards us in which we once stood towards the Romans. Tacitus informs us, that it was the policy of [the Romans] to instruct the sons of the leading men among the Britons in the literature and science of Rome, and to give them a taste for the refinements of Roman civilization. We all know how well this plan answered. From being obstinate enemies, the Britons soon became attached and confiding friends; and they made more strenuous efforts to retain the Romans, than their ancestors had done to resist their invasion.'

In the same way, it was hoped by such men, Indian subjects of the empire might learn to be grateful for British rule as they learned Shakespeare and Anglican Christianity. The British aimed to influence their subjects just as the Romans had. Naturally, most people did not appreciate being governed without their consent or having their culture, language, and history belittled, so the policy was ultimately unsuccessful.

12 Trevelyan is better known for his role in cancelling relief programmes that provided food for the millions of Irish people who starved during the Great Hunger of 1845–1852, reducing and limiting other aid programmes, and blaming the catastrophic loss of life on the "defective part of the national character".

These education reforms, in theory, should have allowed Indian students to compete on an equal footing with British students in the Imperial Civil Service examinations that opened a few decades later. In practice, the odds were stacked against them in several ways and the number of Indians eligible to take up positions of government in their own country was extremely low for some time, according to the British system. When this situation changed, it was openly expressed as a problem, as we shall see.

Evelyn Baring, Lord Cromer, was a military man and another self-taught classicist who served as Controller-General of Egypt in 1879 and then, after the 1882 Anglo-Egyptian War, was promoted to Consul-General of Egypt until 1907. In these two high-ranking positions, he had a huge influence on British policy in Egypt. After he resigned in 1907, he wrote a book, *Modern Egypt*, which outlined his impressions of Egypt, his actions, and his justifications.

The book is littered with classical references and quotations (never translated because, of course, his audience would not require ancient Greek or Latin to be translated). He explicitly compares himself to a Roman proconsul, quotes a late Roman poet in his closing advice to his successors,[13] and compares Ismail Pasha, his Ottoman predecessor, with Gaius Verres, the Roman governor notorious for abuses of power who was prosecuted by Cicero.

The idea that only the British could be trusted with Egypt's finances and the rule of law was central to all of Baring's policy decisions as presented in *Modern Egypt*. He doesn't just insult Ismail Pasha by calling him 'the Egyptian Verres', he quotes some of the legal charges that Cicero brought against Verres in 70 BCE (in Latin, of course), and

---

13 The quote he uses is *quod regnas minus est quam quod regnare mereris*, from Rutilius Claudius Namatianus, a fifth-century Roman. In English, it can be translated as 'that (which) you rule is less than that (which) you deserve to rule' and is taken from a wider section that argues Rome deserved her empire more than any previous power because it was more moral, a popular argument among contemporaries for the British Empire.

adds 'There is certainly a somewhat close analogy between Verres and Ismail Pasha'.[14]

The specific charges he referenced were those that accused Verres of abandoning both legal protections and common rights, allowing the greediest and strongest men to exploit weaker members of society; of torture and murder; of exposing cities and ports to pirates; and of generally bringing Roman rule into such disrepute that it was difficult to justify it continuing. In this way, Baring presented Ottoman rule as illegitimate and British rule as the best thing for the 'natives' of Egypt. All of *his* decisions are implicitly positioned as within the tradition of good Roman rule, whereas his predecessor's actions are explicitly like those the Romans themselves had critiqued.[15]

Baring also spent a great deal of time in the book discussing the *fellahin*, the Egyptian peasant class. He made sweeping generalizations and disparaging remarks about their irredeemable attitude, including examples that he claimed dated back to the Roman rule of Egypt. These generalizations and his understanding of history informed his policy on tax and military service for the *fellahin*, although he expressed disappointment that his benevolent rule was unlikely to be met with gratitude.

---

14 This case was a famous articulation of what some Romans in the first century BCE had considered to be fair and unfair imperial rule. The full list of accusations that Baring refers to is, 'While this man was governor, the Sicilians enjoyed neither their own laws, nor the degrees of our senate, nor the common rights of every nation. Everyone in Sicily only has left that which either escaped the notice or was disregarded by the satiety of that greediest and most depraved man. For three years, no legal decision was given except as he decreed; no property was secure to any man, even if it had descended to him from his father and grandfather, but he was deprived of it at the governor's command; enormous sums of money were extracted from the property of the cultivators of the soil by a new and nefarious system.'

15 Of course, it should be noted that, although Cicero criticized Verres and a jury of their peers condemned his behaviour, Roman rule was hardly welcomed by those they imposed their ideas of good governance upon – the conquered understandably felt very differently about what might be understood as ideal rule. Indeed, Tacitus records many of the same critiques of the Roman Empire two centuries later.

'Bequeathed to us by the Romans'

Perhaps one of the most explicit examples of Rome being taken as a model, even an inheritance, for British imperial rule can be seen in the twentieth-century 'Mandate' territories of Palestine, Transjordan, and Mesopotamia (modern Iraq).

At the Treaty of Versailles in 1919, the empires and nations that had succeeded in the First World War declared that some of the former territories of the defeated empires and nations were not 'able to stand by themselves under the strenuous conditions of the modern world [. . . so for their] well-being and development [. . . needed to be] entrusted to advanced nations who by reason of their resources, their experience or their geographical position can best undertake this responsibility'. In theory, these were not imperial colonies; in practice, as many of the people living in them observed, there was little significant difference.

Many of these 'Mandates' were formerly part of the Ottoman Empire. Before that, they had been part of Safavid Iran or Mamluk Egypt, further back the Abbasid and the Umayyad Caliphates, and, prior to that, the Roman Empire. Some of the oldest and most storied cities in human history, such as Amman, Baghdad, and Jerusalem, were now placed under British supervision.[16] Communities who had been building and living meaningful lives for centuries, carefully managing their resources within the demands of external imperial rule, creating beautiful art and literature and knowledge, were now the 'responsibility' of the British Empire.[17] Among these communities,

---

16 Interestingly, in such cities, the British often drew on what they understood to be Ottoman, Abbasid, and Christian (sometimes Roman) precedents. Urban settlements were approached in a very different framework than the desert zones of the Mandate territories.

17 We could trace these histories much further back, of course; western Asia is one of the longest-standing inhabited regions of the world. Moreover, while the empires are the focus of this book, there have been numerous other forms of rule in the region throughout history.

the Bedouins in particular were seen as primitive, dangerous, and desperately in need of European guidance.[18]

Of the many examples the new rulers might have taken inspiration from, it was neither the peoples themselves nor the other previous empires, but the Romans.

This was especially the case in the desert regions, which the British misunderstood as having been abandoned since the time of Roman control. Rather than recognizing how the Bedouin had maintained and cared for the Arabian deserts in a way that allowed both settled and pastoral communities to live sustainably in the surrounding areas, the British noted 'the extensive remains of water storage bequeathed to us by the Romans [...] the neglect and decay of [which] drove the boundary of cultivation many miles further back, turning the surrounding country into grazing deserts.'

The nomadic Arab conquerors who had defeated the Roman Empire were 'quite unable to maintain those Roman irrigation works, and so the Negeb was left derelict and became the wilderness of today', argued Theodore Zissu, a British officer and Zionist activist in Palestine. 'This desolate state is due solely to human neglect since no change in the climate or the soil has ever occurred – it is the work of man alone and consequently could be remedied by him once more. The great task of the present age is to try to revive the productivity of all these lands.'

The British, as the only 'responsible' imperial power in the region since the Romans, claimed they would bring back 'civilization' to the region. The Roman policies and, specifically, their irrigation works, would be revived. In fact, British officers and the archaeologists who assisted them in Palestine frequently mistook existing Bedouin

18 Intriguingly, when British administrators in the Mandate territories presented their work to a British audience, they would often compare the Bedouin to Scottish Highlanders as a way of explaining the Bedouin to an unfamiliar audience: the implication was that they were 'savages', despite being surrounded by the opportunities of 'civilization'.

groundwater and rainwater storage and management for Roman infrastructure, unable or unwilling to imagine the alternative.[19]

In the Transjordan and Iraq Mandates, Roman water cisterns were reclaimed and guarded by local police forces in order to bring about a 'return' to perceived Roman methods of agriculture and, not accidentally, sideline the traditional Bedouin way of life. In Iraq, in fact, the Benu Huchaim, which consisted of nomadic, semi-nomadic, and sedentary groups, were blamed for constructing 'unauthorized dams' and other water systems to support themselves. The water infrastructure was destroyed and the villages and pastoral encampments bombed to 'develop' them into a more European, modern way of life.

These policies can seem confusing, contradictory, or inconsistent but they reflect the world-view of the administrators. In a framework that ranked civilizations and placed all things Roman and European at the top of that hierarchy, anything that was Roman (or perceived as Roman) or British was necessarily better and anything else was inevitably worse. Not everyone fully bought into this framework, of course, but it was a world-view that was difficult to entirely escape.[20]

It is not surprising then, that we also find interpretations of and references to Rome in the resistance to the British Empire.

A Roman response

Across the empire, the people ruled by the British were repeatedly taught that British and classical civilizations were simply better and that, in part, they were ruled *because* of this difference. Unsurprisingly, men and women across the empire who were taught that the ultimate

---

19 Their attempts to create what they understood to be a productive, forested space have consequences to this day: forest fires are common among the non-indigenous plants that the British imagined would transform the land into what they deemed useful.

20 For example, while alternative traditions were frequently acknowledged, their respective merits were identified according to the standards put forward by European scholars. Additionally, they were often presented as being *better* rather than different and equally worthwhile – the hierarchical framework was difficult to escape.

example was Roman began to look to Rome for a blueprint of how to demonstrate their right to rule themselves. In the Caribbean, Egypt, India, Ireland, and West Africa, people found new ways to resist and respond to imperial domination of Britain by combining Rome with their own traditions. Of course, there had always been resistance to the British Empire, like any empire in history. Rome was just one method among many, in a long tradition of resistance.

In Ireland, nobody needed to be introduced to classical traditions, especially not Roman. Ireland had been a centre of Roman Catholic culture and learning from perhaps as early as the fifth century and was the home of people who understood themselves to be descended genetically and linguistically from the ancient Celtic peoples who fought both against and alongside Rome. The level of classical education across Ireland was often extraordinarily high, frequently irrespective of wealth.

Part of the British justification for their rule in Ireland was Irish Catholicism, a connection to Rome that a few centuries previously was understood as positive but was now very clearly framed by Protestant Britons as problematic, backward, and in need of correction. Quite often, ancient Roman texts about the Celtic peoples they encountered militarily were used by the British to demonstrate that the Irish had always been 'barbarian'.[21] Frequently, this position led to leading Irish figures connecting their resistance to imperial rule with Celtic traditions.

Often, however, Irish men and women rejected the British framing and positioned themselves as inheritors of Rome, or sometimes even as a historical influence on ancient Rome, such as George Sigerson in the

---

21 As we have seen frequently throughout this book, claims to Rome were always contested: in Wales, opponents of English rule have often argued that they had a better claim to both Roman-ness and British-ness, as well as connecting themselves with Celtic traditions of opposition to both. This should not be seen as incoherent but as part of the process of identity construction, reflecting the multiple different strands of history and identity that develop over time.

late nineteenth and early twentieth centuries. A scholar and politician, Sigerson refused to accept the Roman or British framing of imperial cultures, re-translating the Latin *barbara* as 'free nations' rather than the more common 'barbarians'. He argued that no culture develops in isolation, especially imperial cultures, and acknowledged the many debts Roman life owed to other peoples and places, both within and without its empire. It is a debt that the Romans themselves frequently acknowledged, whether explicitly or implicitly, in numerous texts that remain to us. Egyptian, Etruscan, Greek, Persian and Phoenician are just some of the other cultures commonly acknowledged by Romans to have influenced themselves.

A civilizational model that ranked peoples according to hierarchies would not allow for Celtic influence on Romans, he noted, but it was clear that contact had existed and thus it was reasonable to assume influence had gone both ways. Connections to Celtic poetic traditions could be made between, for instance, the great writer Cicero and Diviciacus, a Celtic ally of Rome, as well as later Latin literature (we now tend to link Celtic culture, language, and tradition with parts of the British and Irish Isles, but in Cicero's time, they were predominantly associated with central Europe).

In making this argument, Sigerson pushed back against the British narrative in a number of ways. His theoretical approach rejected the hierarchical framework of civilizations and thus the modern logic of empire in general. Moreover, the examples he used presented a problem for anyone unwilling to accept his theory. After all, if Celtic culture had influenced Roman literature, then it should not be seen as 'inferior' and in need of civilizing – by anyone.

In India, as in Ireland, many Indians were unwilling to accept that their own cultural traditions were inferior to anyone else's and repeatedly found ways to assert their own identity and history.[22] This was particularly the case when it came to the Imperial Civil Service exams: there was regular, sustained pushback about the assumptions that underpinned the 'merit-based' exam. Occasionally, there were slight adjustments to the exams to take account of the reasonable suggestions that Arabic and Sanskrit might be of some use in India. Classics remained the dominant part of the exam, however. In response, despite the fact that the British funded-education system in India did not provide much of the education it argued was so superior, many Indian students studied and passed the exam to demonstrate their merit to rule their own country.

By the turn of the century, they were successful enough to cause concern to Lord Curzon, Viceroy of India from 1899 to 1905. He wrote to George Hamilton, then Secretary of State for India, in 1900, that 'Some day I must address you about the extreme danger of the system under which every year an increasing number of the 900 and odd higher posts that were meant, and ought to have been exclusively and specifically reserved, for Europeans, are being filched away by the superior wits of the Native in the English examinations. I believe it to be the greatest peril with which our administration is confronted.'

For all the claims that Britain, like Rome, was benevolently ruling its provinces until they could be trusted to rule themselves, by introducing them to superior cultures, evidence that the claimed mission was succeeding on its own terms provoked alarm.

Many who had taken the time to acquire the much-vaunted classical education were dismissive of its merits. Jawaharlal Nehru, the leading nationalist and India's first Prime Minister, researched and wrote his *Glimpses of World History* during one of the many periods of the early-

---

22 Where they did engage with 'classical' traditions, the British self-identification with Rome meant that scholarly engagement with ancient Greek traditions was more common than Latin texts in India.

to-mid twentieth century that he was imprisoned for resisting British rule. In it, he assessed the claim that Roman culture was superior, and dismissed it.

All empires were exploitative and thus to be resisted, he argued, but Rome's greed and reliance on enslaved labour made them particularly bad. Their individual emperors had mostly been poor examples of rulers and their greatest general, Julius Caesar, was 'petty' in comparison with Genghis Khan, who he argued was the greatest Asian general. Nehru was particularly interested in ideas of statehood and he analysed various models of empire. There was nothing special about Rome, he concluded, and many other empires had a greater claim to superiority.

When it came to the claimed connections between Britain and Rome, Nehru was also sneering. He traced the history of titles based on the name of Caesar, noting tsar and the various Kaisers, and observed it was amusing that George V, king of England (officially also called 'Kaisar-i-Hind', meaning emperor of India) 'alone today should remain to bear the name or title of the Julius Caesar, who conquered Britain for Rome'.[23] Finally, he observed, there was one 'strong resemblance between the Romans and the English people [. . . for they are both . . .] Smug and self-satisfied, and convinced that the world was made specially for their benefit.' Nothing about either British-ness or Roman-ness, he observed, should stop the Indians fighting for independence.

On the other side of the globe, the great Barbadian-Canadian writer Austin Clarke recalled the way he and fellow students would adapt the Roman histories and literature they read in Latin at school to find new ways to see themselves in the world. This classical education and engagement with it were sufficiently common across the British colonies in the Caribbean that Eric Williams, the historian and leader

---

23 Fascinatingly, the British adopted 'Kaiser' to denote their rule in India not directly from Caesar but because the previous rulers of much of the Indian subcontinent, the Mughals, had some-times used it as one of their titles, adapted from Ottoman usage.

of Trinidad and Tobago's independence movement, was able to leverage classical ideas in public debates to delegitimize British rule.

In West Africa, Frederick Lugard, who governed Nigeria in various roles from 1912 to 1919, had argued that, 'As Roman imperialism . . . led the wild barbarians of these islands of Britain along the path of progress, so in Africa today we are repaying the debt, and bringing to the dark places of the earth . . . the torch of culture and progress.' Again and again, the men and women that the British dismissed and exploited under colonial rule found ways to adapt to the traditions imposed upon them, articulate a place for themselves both inside and out of those traditions, and deploy them against the British.

James Africanus Beale Horton, a surgeon, classical scholar, and nationalist from Sierra Leone, adopted the Latin-name 'Africanus' to advertise both his mastery of classical traditions and his pride in his heritage. In one of his pieces of scholarship, *West African Countries and Peoples*, written in 1868, he pushed back against British ideas of racism and racial superiority, using Caesar and Cicero's writings about the ancient Britons. They were famously 'very barbarous', he noted, and were considered unworthy even to be enslaved, as they could not learn to read and write.

Like Irish and Indian scholars, he was also able to demonstrate the antiquity of African traditions and their long-standing engagement with those of the 'classical world' and assert the many intellectual contributions peoples and societies across the African continent had made throughout history. He relentlessly turned the arguments of British imperialists against them to demonstrate their own unfitness to govern and to demand self-rule.

Everywhere the British insisted on the superiority of classical traditions and the connection between the Roman and British empires to legitimize their right to rule, people found responses to and critiques of empire in those same traditions and connections. In popular culture, especially art and literature, as well as political debate and scholarship, over and over, Rome was used to delegitimize British rule, as part of the wider repertoire of resistance.

In Egypt, the flourishing theatrical scene in Cairo provided numerous opportunities to make implicit or explicit critiques of British rule. Ancient Greek and Latin plays were adapted and performed in their own right and, as with many other plays, used as inspiration for the creation of new literature. An Arabic translation of Euripides' *Oedipus Rex*, an ancient Greek exploration and critique of tyranny, was particularly popular in the early twentieth century, as Egyptians pushed for the right to rule themselves.

The Death of Cleopatra, written by poet and nationalist Ahmed Shawqi in 1929, riffed on Shakespeare's famous *Antony and Cleopatra* but cleverly re-worked it to critique Rome and, by implication, the British. Instead of showing Cleopatra as a corrupting influence on Roman virtue, he wrote her as a heroic leader of resistance, articulating the dangers of Roman rule and defending Egypt's right to sovereignty, ultimately sacrificing herself for the cause.

Fatima Rushdi, one of the most celebrated actresses of the day and founder of her own theatrical troupe, starred as Cleopatra. This casting cleverly exploited one of Fatima's previous famous roles: as Mark Antony in Shakespeare's *Julius Caesar*, a performance that had been censored because of its political implications. Not only did *The Death of Cleopatra* openly critique past Roman imperialism and thus, implicitly, present British imperialism, it also ended with a prediction that the Roman Empire would meet its end in Egypt. The play was hugely popular, helping to cement the reputations of both its author and star.

'Unjust rule never lasts'

Of course, as we have seen, many Romans critiqued their own empire. Indeed, many British subjects at home as well as abroad objected to the idea and reality of the empire. For every argument made in favour of empire, for every reference to Rome made to justify British rule and project power, opposing arguments could be found.

The particular emphasis around the empire on a 'civilizing' education that was seen as connecting Britain to Rome left a significant amount of evidence of the way these ideas permeated society, from schoolchildren to prime ministers. Perhaps more than any other empire considered in this book, we have an unusual degree of insight into the many different ways Rome was interpreted and understood in the British Empire. We do not need to speculate or imagine: over and over, the rulers and ruled left us accounts of their interpretations in their own words.

When General Napier conquered the territory of Sindh (in modern-day Pakistan) in 1843, the famous Victorian satirical magazine, *Punch*, joked that he had sent a telegram to his seniors in Westminster with a single word written in Latin: 'peccavi', which translates as 'I have sinned'. The pun presumably seemed witty to their audience but it also reflected the way he, his peers, and the wider British elite understood their place in the world. Educated in Roman language, literature, economy, engineering, history, law, warfare, religion, and culture, they understood themselves as having *the right* to conquer places just as the Romans had, as well as the ability to make jokes in Latin. That education was carefully chosen to equip them to rule an empire that consciously modelled itself on what it understood to be Rome and claimed its legacy as a global superpower.

One of the great promoters of this type of education for the imperial elite of Britain was Benjamin Jowett, Master of Balliol College, Oxford. More than any other Oxford college, his students were famous for their prominent roles in the British Empire. Perhaps the most famous classicist from Balliol College in the modern day is former British prime minister Boris Johnson: a man with an acute understanding of the enduring power of both the Roman and British empires in the popular imagination and how that could be used, as well as a man who loves to display his classical learning. Johnson's father explicitly argued his son's classical education made him suited to government; as mayor of London, Johnson himself supported efforts to reintroduce Latin to more state schools to improve social mobility.

Johnson's career is not the only way we can see the enduring influence of the interpretations of Rome that were popular in the scholarship undertaken during the British Empire, scholarship that was frequently inextricably linked with the violent reality of that empire. The idea of Rome as a peaceful economic region maintained by trade and threatened by 'foreign' incursions, for instance, was partly developed in this period and underpins many of the arguments *for* the European Union and *against* immigration, in Europe and elsewhere in the West. We can find contrary interpretations of this idea written in Latin by Romans like Seneca and Tacitus, the very same places where scholars who rejected British rule found opposing interpretations of empire.

It was not only the scholarship and governing class of the British Empire who promoted the ideas we have seen here, however, nor was the only pushback in the territories they ruled. They were popular across much of Europe and North America in this period. It is those interpretations, and their influence on the world today, that we turn to next.

7

Roman Fasces, European Fascism

The fascist movement that exploded across Europe in the early twentieth century originated in the European conversations and cultures of the previous centuries, twisted into a new interpretation. It directly connected itself with ancient Rome: ideologically, visually, and in its very name. The word *fascism* comes directly from the Latin word *fasces*, symbols of authority that doubled as weapons and could legally be wielded by senior Roman politicians to inflict corporal or even capital violence without a trial. A very particular idea of Rome was now formed: autocratic, racially superior, explicitly violent – a re-interpretation of an ancient empire repurposed for the modern world.

Fascism was not unique to Germany and Italy in this period, nor were the ideas that underpinned their interpretations of Rome. However, the extreme uses of these ideas, language, and symbolism connected with Rome in these two empires – and those that resisted them – are the clearest expression and the ones that most affect the present day.

Ancient stone columns reach up into an azure blue sky, bleached by the endless gaze of the sun. Huge blocks of stone, worn smooth by the winds of time, rest calmly on the abandoned soil. Through a triple archway gate, stone steps are still visible at the end of a long, partially paved road. Further back, a monumental fountain stands, its damaged nymphs serenely surveying the empty landscape, its water-spouts long dry. Nature's campaign to reclaim the remains creeps forward, green shoots emerging everywhere from the cracks, grass slowly overtaking monumental stone.

NINETEENTH-CENTURY EUROPE UNDERSTOOD ITSELF TO be thoroughly modern – an idea that was inseparable from a specific idea of its past.

Around the world, people had been slowly forming national identities for themselves in response to their experience of imperial rule, forging paths to what they hoped would be self-determined futures. They found new ways to unite themselves in broader communities and distinguish those communities from others by re-analysing what they understood to be their pasts.

These conversations responded to the massive changes brought about by industrialization: new technologies demanded ever more resources to fuel the machinery and ever more people to work them. New cities emerged and old cities expanded as a huge population shift took place. People and places became better connected by railways, newspaper distribution broadened, literacy rates went up, and languages were increasingly standardized. Culture, ethnicity, folk tradition, heritage, language, and religion were all debated as markers of identity, as people constructed new frameworks to understand their place in this rapidly changing world. In some places, these frameworks were quite expansive; in others, they were much more narrow.

The Holy Roman Empire had officially been demolished in 1806 by Napoleon, when he forced Emperor Francis II to abdicate and release all the remaining states of the empire from their oaths of allegiance. By some people, this was seen as an apocalyptic event, an inconceivable event. Some simply refused to believe it. In fact, in many places, things did not change very much.[1] Francis continued as the first Emperor of Austria, as well as remaining the king of Bohemia, Croatia, and Hungary.[2] These territories eventually formed what is known as the Austro-Hungarian Empire, which continued until 1918. The title changed and the role of the papacy was removed but the ruling family remained the same. It was no longer officially Roman, although its religion remained officially Roman Catholic.

Many people, however, saw an opportunity to build new nation states, based on different shared ideas than Roman Catholicism. Slowly, Germany and Italy emerged as two of these over the course of the nineteenth century. Immediately, as so many other European states had done, they looked to carve out overseas empires for themselves. It was probably inevitable that they would look to Rome for an example. Even if Germany and Italy had no historical connection with Rome in any way, pursuing their own empires during this time would have meant engaging with contemporary ideas of Rome. It was the main language of power in Europe.

By this time, the ideas of Rome that were popular in Europe were something much closer to common ideas today – precisely because much of the present day remains influenced by that world of European empires. Neither the Holy Roman Empire nor Romanland existed any more and with them had gone the idea of Rome as a specifically Christian

---

1 It is famously very difficult to capture all the nuances of the Holy Roman Empire and its governing structures. For the very elite, many of these things mattered a great deal. For most people, however, the changes were probably a lot less significant.

2 Somewhat confusingly, he became Francis I in the process, as he was the first occupier of the newly created position.

empire or a contemporary entity.[3] In fact, religion was now frequently treated with suspicion and considered an impediment to enlightenment.

Instead, Rome was now understood as an *ancient* empire and a European one; it was the ancestor of the European empires. The intervening centuries had been re-cast as the 'Middle Age', a backwards time when the progress made by Roman civilization had been abandoned in favour of religious superstition. That march towards progress had been picked up by modern Europe, it was claimed, which was returning to the glory of ancient Rome and developing it as it should have been.

In Chapter 3, we saw that fifth-century leaders across Europe had shared an idea of how to rule based on what they understood the Romans to have done: monumental building, erecting statues, minting coins, supporting bishops, distributing food. By the nineteenth century, a new ideal had emerged: it was still a mark of good rule to construct grand buildings and statues but it was now also important to be seen as supporting scientific research and encouraging technological progress – and not just at home. The Enlightenment thinkers had argued that their ideas were universal. Good rule, therefore, also meant bringing 'civilization' to 'savage peoples', helping them from a 'medieval' stage of primitive ignorance to a 'modern' age of reason and progress.

Previously, similar distinctions had been drawn between societies to justify conquest but they had primarily been articulated in terms of religious difference. Now, however, it was about history and heritage: did you have the monumental remains and great literature of your ancestors, as Europeans did?[4] If not, you would benefit from European rule, which had inherited the greatest civilization of all. This was a

---

3 In Russia, as we have seen, this idea remained and was later revived but it is now expressed in the language of 'Byzantium' rather than 'Rome', making it more difficult for many audiences to perceive.

4 As we will see, having the monumental remains and great literature of Rome *outside* of Europe was not considered the same; only Europeans were the descendants of Rome.

very specific understanding of time, one where a direct connection was made between the past and the likelihood of success in the future.

As we saw in Chapter 3, some of these ideas had been developed in German-speaking regions as Protestants struggled to disconnect themselves from Roman Catholicism while retaining a sense of Roman-ness. Many others had been pushed forward during the Italian Renaissance. In both Germany and Italy, there was an idea that they had only joined the 'modern' era when they had come together as nation-states. The Holy Roman Empire and the Italian city states and regions had been irrational, medieval mistakes, hampered by religion, that had clung on long after more advanced nations had begun to usher in eras of progress. In order to catch up, both nations had to look once more to their ancient past.

A new sense of time

The kingdom of Italy, which was formally proclaimed in 1861, immediately faced a number of questions with regards to its identity: despite the success of the Risorgimento in uniting the Italian peninsula, the regional traditions that had developed over the previous millennium were now very strong. Moreover, the Catholic papacy refused to recognize the authority of the new kings of Italy, meaning that arguably the most unifying feature of the people living in the new state was not an option to anchor a new national identity.[5]

However, the idea of Rome as a glorious ancient past was, understandably, strongest in Italy. Indeed, the idea of a 'middle age' that had been a backward, barbaric failure had first emerged during the Italian Renaissance, which sought to remind people across Europe and the Mediterranean how much better things had been when they had been united under the leadership of Rome.

---

5 This didn't change until 1929, when the Vatican City was declared a sovereign microstate by Benito Mussolini.

This new sense of time across Europe presented the infant kingdom of Italy with a clear solution to its problem: by looking far enough back to the past, before the emergence of the papacy and regional differences, they could forge a united identity for themselves to move into the future. Moreover, that identity was Roman, now widely considered to be the most prestigious empire of European history. They immediately began to define themselves and their hoped-for position in the world with reference to Rome.

The city of Rome was made the Italian capital and re-built to more closely resemble the way the governing elite believed it must have looked before the papacy interfered. Convents and monasteries were torn down to build broader roads and enormous monuments like the Vittoriano, a gigantic neoclassical building that dominates the centre of the city. It combines an altar to the ancient goddess Roma with a fountain that represents the two seas surrounding Italy and a monument of Victor Emmanuel II, the first king of a unified Italy. The building gleams white in the Italian sun and is a perfect example of the way Rome was now being interpreted across Europe: ancient, grand, pre-Christian, and inseparable from modern imperial ambitions.[6]

There were some particular elements to this process that were specific to Italy because of its geography.[7] However, because of the changing interpretations of Roman-ness throughout Europe, many of the ways in which Italy now referenced Rome were strikingly similar to the ways that many other European nation states were behaving.

6 The Italian kings also demanded huge financial support to develop a massive navy so they could attempt to conquer an empire around the Mediterranean that would give them a level of global authority like Britain and France. It was pointed out that such investment was to the detriment of any other reform that might have improved the lives of new Italian citizens, a problem successful kings believed would be solved by extracting wealth from the colonies conquered with the help of the navy.

7 Fascinatingly, the discussion over geography and Italy's literal place in the world *in* Italy in this period reveals something about ancient Rome and its supposed European-ness: there was a common saying in northern Italy that Garibaldi had divided Africa rather than uniting Italy, suggesting that the southern part of the Italian peninsula was more African than European.

In the German Empire, which formally emerged in 1871 from a confederation of German-speaking states, Roman-ness was more complicated. The former Holy Roman Empire was now more of a problem for Germany's rulers than a benefit. There were some who still believed that Francis II had ruled the same Roman Empire first created by Augustus in 27 BCE, and that Germany was in some way intrinsically Roman, but they were increasingly few and far between. Most people, both inside and outside of Germany, believed that the Holy Roman Empire had been something fundamentally quite different – even if they couldn't quite put their finger on how or why.

Moreover, the idea that being German was somehow *opposed* to Rome, that we saw Luther draw on in Chapter 3, was now widespread. It was a feeling exacerbated by Napoleon Bonaparte's claims to Roman-ness and the enmity towards him in Germany at this time. There were a number of competing ideas as to what German-ness might mean, just as there had been about Roman-ness, but there was no doubt that it was now important.[8] While the popularity of Rome as an imperial reference point meant that the new German rulers had to use it to show they were a serious empire, they also needed to distinguish themselves. This meant a careful weaving of the so-called separate 'traditions', both German and Roman.

Of course, they often could not be separated, even artificially – German and Roman history had been shared for far too long. An interesting example is the title 'Kaiser', the German word for emperor. Like 'tsar' and 'kayser', the titles we saw used in earlier chapters, this is simply the local pronunciation of 'Caesar'. It wasn't adopted as a specific reference to Rome by the new German emperors, however; by then, it was simply the local word for emperor.

---

8 One famous attempt to contribute a coherent idea of 'German-ness' in this period was the project of the Brothers Grimm, who collected and edited folktales they felt somehow reflected a coherent common German psyche. These were a hugely popular interpretation of German-ness and their success, as well as their virulent anti-semitism, made them particularly popular with the Nazi regime.

As with Italy, the solution for Germany lay in looking further back in time, to a pre-Christian Rome.

Inheriting Rome, collecting antiquities

This new emphasis on Rome as an *ancient* empire gave European states a sense of a shared 'European' heritage as people who had once been Roman but it also caused problems for anyone who wanted to combine these ideas of Roman-ness with local identities that differentiated them from their neighbours. In Germany, this was accentuated by the development of the idea that German-ness was necessarily opposed to Roman-ness but it exemplified a wider issue. If you looked closely, membership to this club required you to have been *conquered* by Rome – unable to defend yourselves and remain independent, a less than glorious membership (and an idea, moreover, that would exclude a sizeable amount of the continent).

One way to navigate this difficulty, popular across Europe, was to focus on the idea of *inheriting* Rome, as though conquest was a type of selection and could be displayed on the national equivalent of the mantlepiece.

A common ancient Roman practice had been for generals to strip conquered territories of art and monuments along with food, other booty, and enslaved people and take them back to Rome.[9] They would be displayed as part of the general's 'triumph', the sacred procession throughout the city that acknowledged his accomplishments, and then either sold, with the profits donated to the public treasury, or used as a trophy to commemorate the victory. Larger foreign trophies might be displayed in public squares, such as the many gigantic obelisks taken from Egypt, whereas smaller ones might be incorporated into existing buildings or stored in temples. The result was an acknowl-

9 It was, in fact, a common practice of empires across the ancient world, and can be traced back long before the emergence of Rome.

edgement of Roman superiority and also a way to incorporate these material expressions of conquered nations' identities into the fabric of Roman society.

This approach was revived and reversed: now the formerly conquered nations presented their superiority and incorporated Rome into their own identities by displaying material remains of the ancient empire in their own cities. New distinctions were drawn: civilized peoples protected Roman history, barbarians neglected it. More than that, the so-called true heirs of Rome 'discovered' these remains, preserved them, and researched them, passing on this heritage to future generations.

This was only possible because Rome was now understood as being in the *past*: Rome, *ancient* Rome, was now seen as ruined monuments and fragments of artistic accomplishments, scattered pieces of a jigsaw puzzle that allowed its so-called heirs across Europe to fill in the gaps. Archaeology, art history, and anthropology emerged as academic disciplines through which the material evidence of the past was interpreted. Funding such research was now a major component of the wider European language of power and it permeated elite life.

This idea inevitably expanded as the European empires expanded: if Europe's present could be explained by studying the physical remnants of its past, so could everyone else's. Visit any European capital city now and you will find a museum filled with such 'antiquities', collected into categories of time and space, usually contained in glass cases, with a brief description provided to give the viewer an insight into what they represent.[10]

---

10 This approach emerged partly from the Grand Tour tradition, where elite Europeans travelled around major European cities and ruins as the final stage of their education. On their way, they collected art, both contemporary representations of the sites and ancient material remains. Sometimes this might be no more than a small trinket for the mantelpiece but others formed huge private collections that would become the basis of scholarship and future museum collections. Gradually, the role of 'collectors' was acquired by states – although many individual collectors remained.

Another important consequence of the focus on Rome as an *ancient* empire was that it could be merrily bundled together with ancient Greece as the 'classic' European civilizations. While Romanland existed, ancient Greece and Rome had been considered incompatible cultures, languages, and identities. Indeed, this was also true in the new nation state of Greece, where their connection threatened the interests of others and so the focus was primarily on pre-Roman Greek antiquity. At a safe distance from the present, however, the long-standing shared connections between the two cultures could be acknowledged and presented as 'classical antiquity', the origin story of Europe. That many of these ruins were then to be found in the Ottoman Empire was not seen as an indication that the Ottomans could be considered European, or Roman, or that Rome should be considered as something other than European; rather it meant that European nations had an obligation to reclaim them and put them on display for their citizens, the true inheritors of such items.

The new German Empire embraced this approach with gusto, financing archaeological excavations at home, around the Mediterranean, and further abroad. They specialized in Biblical and Islamic archaeology as well as Greek and Roman, and negotiated the 'return' of various ruins from the Ottoman Empire. The results were added to existing private collections and displayed for public viewing in magnificent buildings, sometimes purpose-built, sometimes former municipal buildings, or even palaces. The German Empire's investment in archaeology gave its national museums international reputations. Two particularly famous examples that remain in Berlin are the Pergamon Altar and Miletus Gate. Fragments from each were 'saved' from local reuse,[11] excavated, and shipped to Berlin, where they

11 It was common practice in many places before, during, and after the ancient Roman Empire to reuse monumental sites as building materials for new constructions. This practice had been maintained in this region but it horrified European visitors who now felt the material remains of the past must be preserved rather than recycled.

were 'reconstructed' and displayed as part of the antiquities collection in a new museum, publicly demonstrating the German Empire's connection with – and protection of – the past.[12]

As the nineteenth century turned into the twentieth century, both Germany and Italy competed with their European imperial rivals in hard and soft power: they used their respective militaries to impose (or try to impose) their rule on peoples abroad, extracting resources for their own economies and creating markets for export. Meanwhile, at home, scholars and museums kept reproducing the hierarchical ideas that condemned some peoples and places to exploitation and subjugation based on the past. In the previous chapter, we saw how the idea that Britain had 'inherited' the literature and culture of Rome dominated the scholarship, elite culture, and administration of the empire; here we can see the same approach in the German and Italian empires exemplified in material culture – although this is purely a division of content. Across all the European empires, scholarship focused on both materials and texts of the past and indigenous peoples found ways to engage with and push back against the narratives imposed on them. Power politics and scholarship were entwined: the German Empire's diplomatic and military alliance with the Ottoman Empire, for instance, allowed Germany to pursue oil and archaeological interests simultaneously.[13] Their alliance was commemorated by a German-built monumental fountain, in a late Roman style, erected in the former Roman hippodrome of Constantinople. It can still be seen to this day, a memorial to many layers of Roman-ness.

Meanwhile, the Kingdom of Italy worked hard to conquer territory for what it saw as its rightful empire, its inheritance. In particular, Italian leaders wanted to acquire some of the Ottoman territories for themselves:

12 This museum was explicitly framed as a rival to the British Museum, which had opened in 1753.

13 The German Archaeological Institute is still part of the Auswärtiges Amt, or German Federal Foreign Office, a position that acknowledges its importance in Germany's international relations.

after all, had these areas not once been under Roman control?[14] The Italians managed to gain control of some parts of Albania, fourteen of the fifteen Dodecanese islands in the Aegean, and Cyrenaica and Tripolitania in Libya, in addition to their colonies in Eritrea and Somaliland, but remained dissatisfied. Their frequent appeals to the so-called Great Powers of Austro-Hungary, Britain, France, and Germany to support Italian imperial efforts had, they felt, little to show for it (although the people living in the Italian colonies felt they had far too much to show for it, consistently resisting Italian imperial rule).

This increasing competition between European powers for empire and its economic benefits, combined with nationalism, militarism, and new technologies, led to the First World War, a disastrous and vicious global conflict from 1914 to 1918 that destroyed lives, lands, and economies. It resulted in the victorious empires of Britain, France, Japan, Italy, and the USA carving up and redistributing the territories of the defeated empires of Austro-Hungary, Germany, and the Ottomans.[15]

Speeding up the future

After 1918, Italy still felt it was not being taken seriously as an imperial power, an anxiety exploited by Benito Mussolini's Fascist Party. Mussolini openly promised to revive the ancient Roman Empire, using the Latin *mare nostrum* or 'our sea' to describe the Mediterranean, as well as promising an end to the economic difficulties the country was struggling with. Italy could modernize faster and make progress quicker, he insisted, by taking *more* inspiration from the past – a past that made them superior to everyone else. He would not just build a

---

14 This was explicit: the attempted invasion of Ethiopia in 1896 was justified at the time by the idea of returning to *Romanità*, or Roman-ness, although Ethiopia (or its predecessors, Aksum and Meroe) were never under Roman control.

15 The Kingdom of Bulgaria also fought and lost, with some of its territories confiscated in the aftermath.

new Roman empire and restore Italy to its rightful position as a major power, he would do so by returning to *Romanitá*, or Roman-ness. The Roman *fasces*, physical symbols of authority that linked the ancient kings of the Roman city-state to the Roman Republic, and the Roman Empire, was revived to link modern Italy with its past[16] – as well as justify autocratic, dictatorial rule.[17]

In 1922, the Fascist party marched on Rome and besieged the city to demand Mussolini's rule. King Victor Emmanuel III assented and, within the framework of the Italian Constitution, invited Mussolini to form a government as prime minister. The Fascists moved quickly. One of their first actions was to increase the military efforts of the previous regime in North Africa, brutally wiping out indigenous and regional resistance to Italian rule there. In the Aegean, the Balkans and in East Africa, Italian military forces were dispatched to push for more power, supposedly to restore the ancient Roman Empire for the glory of modern Italy.

Mussolini's understanding of *Romanitá* or Roman-ness hadn't emerged in a vacuum, however, so reviving Rome meant more than military conquest or the visual symbols that often spring to mind when thinking of Mussolini: the fasces and the so-called Roman salute, using an outstretched right arm. Ideas about Rome permeated fascist ideology and we can see them in archaeology, architecture, and education, all of which were also used to connect Fascist Italy with ancient Rome.

The Fascist government funded archaeological work in Italy, claiming that the 'liberation' of formerly Roman sites such as Herculaneum would benefit 'scholars of all nations'. In Rome, the work of bulldozing

---

16 A version of the *fasces* had continued, of course, into Romanland and is attested as late as the fourteenth century. In fact, the symbol was used by a number of revolutions in the eighteenth and nineteenth centuries to symbolize collective unity and a supposedly Roman idea of liberty.

17 The word 'dictator' comes from Latin and originally was a neutral title, describing a limited, six-month period of one-man rule, elected by the Senate, in an agreed-upon emergency. The negative connotations developed after abuse of the role in the first century BCE, first by Lucius Cornelius Sulla and then by Gaius Julius Caesar.

down the medieval city to 'restore' the ancient one that had begun in the 1870s was intensified. These word choices were deliberate, part of an approach to presenting actions and decisions that we can see elsewhere. The mausoleum of Augustus, which had been re-used as, among other things, a bullfighting arena and an opera house since the death of Rome's first emperor, was now also restored and connected with Italy's new leader.

Across the city, pale white buildings were constructed that supposedly looked like Roman originals. Mussolini ordered a new forum built in his honour, just like ancient emperors did, but with statues depicting modern war and sports – he hoped to host the 1940 Olympic Games there. It remains to this day, with its giant obelisk that imitates the ancient Roman obelisks taken from ancient Egypt. Buried underneath this obelisk is a time capsule that contains the Codex Fori Mussolini, an account of the Fascist rise to power written in Latin by an Italian academic.

Latin was deliberately revived as a language for the Fascist party.[18] It was encouraged as a subject in schools and a textbook on Italian history (according to the Fascist narrative) was produced in Latin. Mussolini had some of his most famous speeches translated into Latin to record them for posterity, and a translation committee was instructed to create new words for modern ideas that could be used in Latin, bringing the ancient language into the modern world. Many of the Latin inscriptions you can see across the city of Rome date from the twentieth century, not the first.

We can see all these strands come together in one example. On 23 September 1937, at the same time as the Italian military was invading East and North Africa, Mussolini inaugurated the *Mostra Augustea della Romanità,* an exhibition to mark the 2,000th anniversary of the

---

18 At this time, the language was almost entirely associated with the Catholic Church, although it was also quite common for poets in Italy to use it.

birth of Augustus.[19] A temporary façade in a 'Roman' style was built to house a massive collection of Roman archaeological remains that were organized chronologically to show the history of the city, from the legendary kings of the seventh century BCE all the way through to Mussolini's rule. Cities like Algerian Timgad and Syrian Palmyra were highlighted as once belonging to the Roman Empire, implicitly connecting the exhibition with Italy's present empire-building efforts in the Mediterranean. A number of Latin texts that articulated Roman patriotism and its imperial ambitions to civilize the world were placed in key areas of the exhibition, translated into Italian, to imply that Fascist ideology was inseparable from ancient Rome.

Just the year before, having invaded Ethiopia,[20] Mussolini had announced: 'Italy finally has its empire. It is a fascist empire, an empire of peace, an empire of civilization and humanity.' Tacitus would have recognized this vision of empire, reminiscent of his own words: 'To robbery, slaughter, plunder, they give the lying name of empire; they make a wasteland and call it peace.'

Return to Rome: German Nazism

In Germany, the situation was very different in many ways. Its empire had been dismantled, its economy saddled with the debts of the First World War. It wasn't looking to speed up along the same path; it was trying to find a new way forward. Conversations in Germany around national identity were mostly dominated by ideas of the regional pre- and proto-history, the time before contact with Rome, and an idealized folk (or *Volk*) history. Rome was primarily associated with France, a nation Germany

---

19 A few years earlier, in 1930, the bimillenary of the Roman epic poet Virgil had also been celebrated. Virgil's epic poem, *The Aeneid*, had articulated a Roman identity that connected them with Troy and presented them as eternally opposed to Carthage, the empire based on the North African coast. Much use of this poem was made by Fascist Italy in its bid to conquer territories across North and East Africa.

20 The invasion was, in fact, unsuccessful; Ethiopia resisted and was never officially ruled by Italy or any European empire.

defined itself in opposition to, and Fascist Italy. The Holy Roman Empire, as a period of German-speaking leadership, was sometimes considered, but as an example of *German-ness,* not Roman-ness.

And yet, within a few years, Germany was also a violent dictatorship, determined to impose its ideas of racial supremacy on the world through a new empire, and articulating its identity and power with reference to Rome, in many of the same ways as in Italy.

In academia, in architecture, in the media, and in museums, the Nazi connection with Rome was proclaimed. One of the clearest examples of this was the new capital city that Hitler ordered for the German Empire he was conquering. Welthauptstadt Germania or World Capital Germania, was explicitly inspired by Rome. Together with his head architect, Albert Speer, Hitler planned a *via triumphalis,* a road of victory, that would be lined on both sides with military objects captured from conquered enemies, according to the ancient Roman practice, and ending in a new Arch of Triumph, like those that still decorated Rome. A new Great Hall, designed for mass meetings, was also planned based on the ancient Roman Pantheon. This city was never finished, although many of Speer's models and plans of his vision remain.[21]

Another telling example is that, in the final days of Germany's military defeat, it was common among the German media to recall how dark the military situation had seemed in the Second Punic War, when Rome had fought Carthage for Mediterranean supremacy and almost been completely destroyed.[22] Rome had turned the situation around and gone on to conquer a huge empire. Germany could still do the same, was the implication: could still emulate Rome, could still emerge stronger from this struggle and triumph.

21 After the war, Speer re-drew his plans but literally in ruins, like the sketches of ancient ruins that had been popular since the Grand Tour and frequently served as a metaphor for civilizational decline, a fear that haunted many of the Nazi elite.

22 Carthage, a Phoenician city, was often presented as a Semitic empire to support fascist anti-semitism, especially in Germany and Italy.

How did Rome become so important to the Nazi identity?

Just as in Fascist Italy, Nazism combined ideas about antiquity and modernity, anchoring the future of the nation in its history. The Nazis were obsessed with technological progress, with scientific racism, and with the idea that, if they could reform society quickly enough to conform to their idealized past, they could force the world to recognize their superiority.[23] That idealized past was Aryan, Nordic, Indo-European – different scholarly constructions that all meant, in the Nazi mindset, whiteness. In the Nazi hierarchical ranking of races, cultures, histories, and civilizations, Germany was superior.

Germany had not always meant whiteness: there had been people of African heritage living in German-speaking lands since the time of the Roman Empire. Africa and Europe have always been connected by the Mediterranean and there had consistently been regular contact between the two long before European empires had established African colonies. The establishment of those colonies, of course, brought more Africans to live in Europe, willingly and unwillingly, from the earliest colonial encounters.

In fact, German-speakers had identified with Africans as early as they identified as Christian: some of the most famous early Church Fathers had been from the African continent, a consequence of the Roman Empire. For example, Athanasius of Alexandria came from what is now Egypt; Augustine of Hippo came from what is now Algeria; and Tertullian of Carthage came from what is now Tunisia. In fact, the patron saint of the Holy Roman Empire, St Maurice, was, according to legend, an Egyptian soldier of the third century who had been sent to Gaul. In 961, Otto the Great had Maurice's remains interred in Magdeburg Cathedral to connect himself, his dynasty, and the Holy Roman Empire with the

---

23 The earlier German Empire, later renamed as the Second Reich, had committed the first genocide of the twentieth century between 1904 and 1908 against the Herero and Nama peoples in what is now Namibia. Many scholars have highlighted connections between the ideas of racial superiority that underpinned this genocide and Germany's other colonial atrocities and those that were later promoted in the Third Reich.

saint. Maurice later became linked with legends of the Holy Lance and was particularly prominent during the period of the religious Crusades. It has been estimated that more than 600 religious foundations across Europe were dedicated to him. From at least the thirteenth century, St Maurice was consistently depicted with black skin.[24]

This history was not part of the Nazi idealized past. Neither, at first, was Rome: the more popular appeals focused on prehistoric Germany, often articulated with reference to the stories written up by the Grimm Brothers, which were claimed to have captured an early, innate, non-elite German-ness that could be traced back to a pure form.

Where 'classical antiquity' was considered, ancient Greece was much more popular. Rome having been claimed by rival nations, it seems reasonable that Germany would look to the 'other' of the two ancient cultures that were held up across Europe as particularly special. There were other reasons, however; other interpretations of ancient Greece that better fit the Nazi way of seeing the world. One aspect of this was the art historical tradition begun in Germany by Johann Winckelmann's idealization of ancient Greek art, culture, and – not coincidentally – whiteness. Another was the understanding of ancient Sparta as a successfully totalitarian military state that maintained strict racial purity.

Rome was only one reference point among many for Nazi Germany, one way among many to show the world who it was. One key factor in its emergence was Hitler's personal interest. Another was, as we have seen elsewhere, the simple fact that Rome was considered so important by so many rival powers. For Nazi Germany to fully establish itself as superior, it seemingly faced a choice: show that it had a better claim to Roman-ness or show it was better than Rome. It found a third option: arguing that Rome was, in fact, German – or, more precisely, Nordic,

---

24 There were other Black saints acknowledged by European Christians at this time; while ideas about race certainly existed in this period, they were not fixed and, as we shall see in Chapter 9, changed over time in response to European colonialism.

the racial origin of German-ness and the supposedly superior branch of the 'Aryans'.[25]

This interpretation of Rome was not based on geography, religion, or institutions. It was based on race and the formulation was, in its own way, quite straightforward: the only explanation for superiority was racial and the superior race was Nordic. Rome's success, therefore, only made sense if some Romans – the best Romans – had actually been Nordic. It was well-known that peoples had migrated in the past.[26] At some crucial point, therefore, some Nordic peoples must have migrated to Rome (and, indeed, to the various ancient Greek city states).[27] More than this, when Rome had struggled, or even failed, the explanation lay in its failure to maintain racial purity. It had even been regenerated for a time by the arrival of new migrations of German-speaking military support, or the *foederati*, and then again in the German-led Holy Roman Empire.

This line of argument and its variations are often dismissed as illogical, even academically dishonest. Certainly, there is no evidence for it in the ancient texts that remain to us.[28] In fact, there is much evidence of the opposite: ancient Greeks and Romans regularly stated that paleness was a sign of femininity (in a pejorative sense) or 'barbarity'. Moreover, it does appear that many of the academics who supported it – actively or passively, openly or tacitly – did so for personal advancement. Some, however, seem to have fully believed their claims. It was the only explanation they could – or *would* – see.

---

25 Other groups considered to be part of the Nordic race in this period included 'Anglo-Saxons' and 'Franks', connecting England, the USA, and northern France with Germany.

26 In another example of how language can be used to frame ideas, German historians used the term Völkerwanderungen or "migrations of peoples" rather than "great invasions", which was popular in English and French histories of the time.

27 The German invasion of Greece in the Second World War was presented as a fourth wave of Nordic migration to 'redeem' Greece.

28 Scholars of race-science searched through the texts of Roman historians like Plutarch for descriptions of leading generals and emperors that mention blue eyes or blonde hair to connect them with their contemporary ideas of race.

Many German textbooks and teaching manuals taught this interpretation of history to young pupils, many German universities provided degrees that endorsed this interpretation of history to students and scholars, and many German propaganda films presented this interpretation of history to the general public.[29] Within the wider frameworks of race-science, civilizational hierarchies, and cultural heritage, this way of seeing Rome made sense to many people at the time. It was far from universal, however.

Resisting the renewed Roman Empires

In Germany and Italy, across Europe, and around the world, people everywhere rejected these individual ideas and these wider frameworks of thinking. Throughout the nineteenth and twentieth centuries, the ideas, language, and symbolism of first imperialism and then fascism were consistently contested and opposed.[30] Some of these opponents identified the Roman Empire as an original example of the problem they fought: one anti-fascist, the philosopher and French Resistance member Simone Weil, dismissed European efforts to portray themselves as inheritors of Rome, calling them 'bad imitations of undistinguished conquerors'. In particular, she claimed that 'Hitler alone has understood correctly how to copy the Romans' and compared him with Caesar in 'imposing submission by terror'. The comparison was meant as an insult; elsewhere, she argued that 'the brutality of the Romans horrified and paralyzed their contemporaries exactly as that of the Germans does today'.

For many who sought alternative ways to create community and identity, resisting imperialism and nationalism as the only alternative,

---

29 While many academics were complicit in the Nazi regime's behaviour, many others used their work and position to protest these narratives – at great personal risk.

30 For many intellectuals at the time, imperialism and fascism were inseparable from one another: the leaders of fascist empires were unelected and often inflicted their violence on European soil but no other distinction could be made.

inspiration could be found in rebels against Roman imperialism. Two examples stand out: the use of Spartacus in international socialism; and Hannibal as a reference point for pan-Africanism.

Spartacus was a former soldier who had been enslaved and forced to fight as a gladiator. In 73 BCE, he and a number of fellow enslaved gladiators escaped and, for the next three years, he helped lead one of the biggest revolts of enslaved people from around the empire against Rome.[31] The Roman records of this event are not clear about the motives of Spartacus and his fellow rebels, or the structure of the society they built during their long rebellion. However, the sources do clearly articulate the extraordinary military success of the men and women who freed themselves and fought against Rome. Among those who resisted imperialism, Spartacus was often a common reference point.[32]

Many international communists saw imperialism as inherently capitalist, connecting the exploitative and extractive practices of factory owners with the policies of imperial governments in the colonies. Rosa Luxemburg, a Jewish activist and intellectual who was born in Poland and later became a naturalized German citizen, argued that imperialism meant 'the destruction of all culture, and, as in ancient Rome, depopulation, desolation, degeneration, a vast cemetery'. In 1915, under the pseudonym Lucius Junius Brutus (named after the legendary founder of the Roman Republic, who overthrew the last tyrannical king of Rome), she argued that the cause of the First World War was the capitalist desire for imperial expansion in European nations. This imperialist expansion, she claimed, 'must sooner or later

---

31 Roman society relied heavily on enslaved labour; some scholars have estimated that 20-25 per cent, perhaps more, of the population of peninsular Italy was enslaved by the end of the Republican period. Rebellions were common, on a small and large scale.

32 Toussaint Louverture, one of the leaders of the successful Haitian Revolution against French imperial rule and enslavement, is often nicknamed 'the Black Spartacus', although it is not clear he personally took inspiration from Spartacus.

lead to a general reckoning, that the wind that was sown in Africa and Asia would return to Europe as a terrific storm'.

The Spartacus rebellion was frequently seen in these movements as an alternative to imperialist capitalism, an example of equality, internationalism, and self-government. The success of Spartacus and his allies against a seemingly overwhelming opposition, the society they might have built during the period of freedom, and their willingness to keep fighting to the end made it a popular precedent for many who opposed both imperialism and nationalism. Karl Marx, for instance, read the Roman historian Appian's account of Republican Rome's many civil wars and wrote to Friedrich Engels in 1861 to report that, 'Spartacus emerges as the most capital fellow in the whole history of antiquity. A great general [. . .], of noble character, a 'real representative' of the proletariat of ancient times'

One particularly famous example of this source of inspiration was the Spartakusbund, or Spartacus Group, a revolutionary movement co-founded by Luxemburg to oppose the German Empire's involvement in the First World War. Spartacus, said Luxemburg, 'stands for the fire and the spirit, the soul and the heart, the will and the deed of the proletarian revolution. Spartacus stands for all the misery, longing, and determination of the class-conscious proletariat. Spartacus stands for socialism and world revolution.' Towards the end of 1918 and start of 1919, the Spartakusbund joined the revolts by soldiers and workers across Germany to help bring about the end of the German Empire.[33] Its leaders were executed, a fate – like Spartacus – they must have known was likely.

Rome's great opponent, revived

In Fascist Italy, Rome's rivalry with Carthage had been interpreted and reinterpreted in numerous ways: to present Italian imperial ambitions

---

33 In response to this rebellion, the German government recruited the *Freikorps*, paramilitary forces of war veterans. Many of these soldiers would later join the Nazi movement.

as eternal, to justify invasions of North and East Africa, and to support their claims of racial hierarchies.[34] Both Virgil's epic poem the *Aeneid*, written in the first century BCE, and Petrarch's epic poem *Africa*, written on the same topic in the fourteenth century CE, were used to promote these ideas, in scholarship and in popular culture. In response, some of those who suffered from Italian imperialism in North Africa began to think of their own efforts at resistance in terms of Hannibal Barca (247–183 BCE), the Carthaginian general who was known for organizing the passage of an army – including nearly 40 war elephants – through the Pyrenees and then the Alps before leading several major military defeats of Rome and almost defeating it entirely.[35]

One of the most interesting ways we can see this is in the play *Annibal* by Käbbädä Mikael, the iconic Ethiopian intellectual. Ethiopia had successfully fought back against Italian invasion attempts, first in 1896 and then from 1935.[36] This success gave Ethiopia a powerful symbolism in the pan-Africanism movement, which emerged in the nineteenth century in opposition to colonialism, imperialism, and the connected ideas of civilizational hierarchies, race-science, and slavery. One strand of this self-determining approach focused on connecting indigenous peoples of Africa with diaspora peoples of African ancestry, such as in the Caribbean and United States of America, in a new communal identity that presented a different alternative to both imperialism and nationalism.

Ethiopia's relationship to Pan-Africanism was often complex and sometimes characterized by exceptionalism rather than solidarity among the elite. In the 1950s, however, Käbbädä wrote a version of the Hannibal story to address this and encourage a Pan-African unity. In

34 The wars between Rome and Carthage, known as the Punic Wars, had also been used by Nazi leaders and the media to promote its ideas of race-wars.

35 The Roman general who successfully led the response to Hannibal, Scipio Africanus, is referred to in the first verse of the Italian national anthem.

36 Despite Mussolini's claims, the Fascist occupation of Ethiopia was never formally recognized by anyone else and Ethiopians never stopped fighting a damaging guerilla war against the invaders.

this retelling, Rome explicitly stands for white Europeans and Carthage represents the continent and peoples of Africa. The Battle of Zama, the last stand between the two empires, one character proclaims, 'will decide the fate of the peoples of the world. If Rome resists successfully, she will be able to break the development of Africa and to block Africa's way to the future'. In the play, Hannibal is betrayed by senatorial elites who put themselves before unity, implied to be contemporary Ethiopian elites. An alternative future is possible, Käbbädä implies, if they commit to a wider unified community instead.

Today's world is still shaped by the legacy of empires, particularly European colonialism – and not just by lines on maps. Both Augustus and Tacitus explicitly defined the Roman Empire in terms of military conquest, resource extraction, and accumulated titles. Implicitly, they also both acknowledged the ability of the empire to define events for posterity, to have its version of events made official. The ideas, identities, and ideologies of the empires that claimed a right to rule based on Roman-ness can still be seen around the globe.

History is not just written by the victors, however, and, as Seneca said, 'unjust rule never lasts'. The interpretations of Rome by those who sought to end the unjust rule of empires help us see both ancient Rome and the modern world in full colour.

PART THREE
CULTURE

In the open forum, the centre of urban life, people mingle busily. The latest news is announced above the hum of the crowd as citizens, foreigners, and the enslaved all jostle at the many merchant stalls. In one corner, a law court has been assembled beneath the goddess of justice and an alleged crime is debated. In another corner, a popular poet performs their latest composition, surrounded by eager fans. Building work on the public baths, funded by a wealthy woman, spills dust and dirt into the street. A schoolteacher demands the attention of their pupils beneath the shade of the monumental columns, insisting they ignore the famous politicians weaving through the crowds to canvas for votes in the next election, ignore the strains of laughter from the ramshackle theatre, ignore the religious procession that can be seen in the distance.

The Roman forum was a busy, even chaotic place, offering a cross-section of a city's inhabitants and their lives. Crucially, the many ways in which these public spaces were used gives us a way to think about the customs, ideas, and important institutions of a wider group of people. They offer us a broader glimpse of Roman culture than we get from the formal letters and political histories written by elite men; after all, culture belongs to, and is shaped by, everyone in society.

A forum was not necessarily central to the lives of everyone inhabiting a city. Some would likely prefer more local gathering places, others would simply never have the money, need, or time to visit one. However, exploring these spaces and the ways they were used allows us to see beyond their aesthetic qualities and focus on social practices and norms, on popular art and literature, on everyday lives. It also allows us to connect everyday experiences to the political and literary preoccupations of the elites, which we tend to know more about. Just how much 'ordinary' inhabitants of a city were engaged with the elites of the empire is an ongoing question, one we are unlikely to fully answer. But we can make a good guess about some things based on what politicians did to make themselves popular.

Gladiator games were in demand, of course, but they were not the only sources of entertainment. A wide variety of major and minor public spectacles were staged by wealthy politicians to mark religious festivals that regularly punctuated the civic calendar and would often be more accessible for those only wanting to drop by for a short period. We know that theatre was sufficiently popular from early on in Roman history that temporary stages would be constructed and crowded around long before permanent spaces for performances were permitted (the Roman elite were initially quite snobby about theatre). Smaller-scale productions and poetry were often performed in the street, to engaged audiences. Letters from one politician to another, or to the Senate, far from being private, were often read out to public audiences to generate support or opposition from 'the people'. Political debates were often conducted in public, to audiences who demanded a good show and would make their reactions known.

Not everyone would have enjoyed these things or had the time to engage with them deeply but they were part of the fabric of urban life, the kind of thing you might walk past on your way to visit a particular merchant or temple.

Public baths were a major social activity, not just an opportunity to get clean. The buildings were often elaborately constructed and decorated and they were major examples of euergetism, an ancient form of philanthropy. Wealthy citizens would donate their money, in exchange for recognition, to facilities for communal use. Roman baths are frequently compared with modern-day spas as a way to convey the wide range of facilities available and the social function of these spaces but they had more than massage and hairdressing options – some even had libraries!

Gardens were also a major feature of Roman life: public gardens were another space often funded by wealthy donors for people to enjoy. As with public baths, such donations were very much done with an eye to the reputation of the donor: both Gaius Pompeius Magnus and Gaius Julius Caesar, political and military rivals, funded spectacular public gardens with the proceeds of their military campaigns before their rivalry spilled over into civil war.[1] At the highest levels of society, rich individuals paid for staggeringly lavish private gardens for personal relaxation and an ostentatious show of wealth, often also fuelled by personal rivalries. On a more everyday scale, it is very likely that small personal and communal gardens were used to grow food and support urban diets.

Not all of the finest examples of art and architecture were accessible to everyone; some of the most stunning examples that remain to us were private Roman villas and palaces whose architectural triumphs, gardens, luxury art, and water features would only be seen by an exclusive few. There is a reason, however, that monumental public buildings are one of the first things that come to mind when most people think about Rome and have been throughout history. Around the ancient Mediterranean, cities reached their highest populations and gained a correspondingly large number of monumental buildings in the first and second centuries CE, as the profits of imperial conquest were at their highest. Of course, the only way to maintain this wealth

---

1 In both cases, we can see an ancient example of reputation-laundering: both generals were accused of war crimes in their respective campaigns and of corruption in the administration of the booty and wealth they acquired (much of this wealth came from the sale of enslaved people, although the morality of this was not a concern raised by contemporaries).

and public building was to keep conquering new regions to exploit financially, an entirely unsustainable system. These huge public spaces meant that anyone who used them would also have the opportunity to engage with the art that decorated them, a visual representation of the might and wealth of Rome.

That visual language of power has made an impression across time and space and shaped the way many empires have referred to Rome in their own efforts to project authority and legitimacy. Monumental buildings, extraordinary art, and many other things we tend to vaguely categorize as expressions of 'culture' were part of the language of empire, as we shall see next.

8

Rivalling Rome:
the Empires of Early Islam

In recent years, fundamentalist groups like ISIS have connected 'Rome' with the USA, presenting themselves as returning to the earliest form of Islam, when the prophet Muhammad and his successors waged war against Rome in the eastern Mediterranean, and encouraging Muslims to consider themselves at war and the USA as the inheritor of that military opposition. But the various early Islamic empires engaged in multiple ways with Rome, not just militarily.

Pre-Islamic Arabia was deeply integrated into the Persian and Roman worlds, which is reflected in the ways the various early Islamic empires articulated and projected power. From the Atlantic to the frontier with China, old cities were expanded and new cities were built, centres of culture and intellectual activity to identify their rulers with long-standing traditions of imperial rule that included Rome. In Iberia, Syria, and Iraq, Muslim rulers engaged artistically, architecturally, diplomatically, and intellectually with the Christian Roman emperors in Constantinople and the Holy Roman emperors in Europe.

This interpretation of Rome, as an imperial example communicated by art, architecture, and scholarship, is strikingly similar to how many see Rome today.

Above the stone steps, through the arched gates, the Mediterranean sun reflects off an enormous golden dome. Elevated high into the sky, the glints from the dome are visible from afar, long before the beautifully colourful upper storey is visible or the pale marble lower walls. Outside, eight marble columns with intricately decorated capitals support an arched entrance. Inside, more columns create an arched colonnade to guide the visitor through the space. Dazzlingly detailed mosaics decorate the surfaces, covering the walls and the interior of the monumental dome. The jewels and golden glass of the mosaics refract the light that shines through the high windows, glittering and shimmering, overwhelming and inspiring the viewer.

THE DOME OF THE ROCK is the earliest example of Muslim architecture still standing, a stunningly beautiful monumental building.[1] It is also often described by scholars as the last great example of Roman architecture, with its elegant colonnades, extraordinary dome, and exquisite mosaics.[2]

How can this be?

The answer is quite simple. The world of Muhammad (*c.*570–632), the prophet of Islam, and the peoples he preached to, was a world that was not just connected with the Roman Empire but often a long-standing part of it. For centuries, many Arabian groups had traded with Romans, fought against and alongside Romans, led Romans, and *been* Romans.

The Romans divided the entire Arabian peninsula into three regions. Firstly, Arabia Petraea: their province, which neighboured Roman Syria to the north and Roman Egypt to the west. Secondly, Arabia Deserta:

---

1 The exterior has undergone significant changes since the original construction. The Umayyad marble and mosaic decoration of the upper part of the external walls was replaced by Suleyman the Magnificent with the now-famous Ottoman blue-and-white tiling style in the sixteenth century and the current gold-plating on the monumental dome was only introduced in the late 1950s.

2 Actually, it is often described as the last great example of *Byzantine* architecture but this is, as we have established, a way to describe something that is Roman.

also known as Arabia Magna, which described the interior desert areas that the Romans could not navigate themselves and where they therefore relied heavily on the trade and military support of nomadic peoples.[3] Thirdly, Arabia Felix: the southern part of the peninsula, known for its agricultural fertility. There was also Roman Syria, one of the most important provinces from an early period. Julia Domna, Roman empress from 193 to 211, was from a prominent Roman Syrian family, and Philip I, Roman emperor from 244 to 249, and referred to as 'Philip the Arab', was from the same region. It is actually suggested in some ancient sources that Philip I may have been the first Christian Roman emperor – that is, the first to personally practise the Christian faith (rather than encourage it publicly). Whether or not this is true, it reflects the association between Christianity and Arabian communities from the earliest period by Roman scholars.

Some cities in this wider region, like Antioch, were some of the most important in the Roman Empire while others, like Ayla, Bostra, Damascus, Gerasa, Palmyra, Petra, and Philadelphia, were all essential to trade and the Roman economy.[4] On the frontier with Persia, these places were also essential diplomatically and militarily.

From the third century onwards, the kingdom of the Jafnids, in the Levant and northern Arabia, and the kingdom of the Nasrids, in southern Mesopotamia and eastern Arabia, were Christian kingdoms whose military and trading strengths made them hugely important players in the ongoing Roman-Persian geopolitical relationship. In the southern part of the Arabian peninsula, the agricultural and trading strength of the Himyarite kingdom made it an important

---

3 This name for the region was often used by imperial administrators, scholars, and travellers in the nineteenth and twentieth centuries.

4 The Roman geographer Ptolemy listed around fifty important cities he was aware of in Arabia.

player in the Aksumite-Persian geopolitical relationship.[5] In the Hijaz, the western part of the peninsula where Muhammad lived, the many urban settlements and kingdoms were filled with Jewish and polytheist peoples who traded with this wider Aksumite-Roman-Persian world.

The Arabian peoples may have seemed on the periphery of the Roman Empire geographically but this way of reading a map misses both their significance and their deep engagement with the empires around them.[6]

Art and architecture from pre-Islamic Arabia across the peninsula reflects the interconnected world that Muhammad preached to. Both the visual styles and the scenes depicted would have been familiar to an Aksumite, Persian, or Roman traveller from the other side of any of these empires. From the Atlantic coast in the west across to central Asia, south to East Africa and the tip of the Arabian peninsula, there was a shared visual language of power that connected the region, influenced by its many participants. Local variations and practices existed, of course, and any long-distance traveller would have found much to confuse and interest them along their route, but there would also have been familiarities to be found from Italy to Yemen, the result of centuries of overlapping worlds.

By the seventh century, the various Arabian polities were fighting alongside one another, as part of the religious practice Muhammad had inspired. Rapidly, they conquered a large part of the empires who

---

5 The Aksumites were a Christian empire based in East Africa and often ruling territories in western and southern Arabia. This empire lasted for nearly 1,000 years and dominated trade in the important Red Sea region. It was likely the first place to adopt Christianity as a state religion, in the 320s. The Himyarite kingdom, located in modern-day Yemen, was ruled by both Christian and Jewish kings from at least as early as 375 CE and was home to sizable communities practising both religious traditions.

6 How much the different peoples living and working throughout the Arabian peninsula understood themselves to be connected before Muhammad's preaching is debated, just as it is not clear how much ancient Greek-speaking peoples saw themselves as one wider community. There were some cultural, linguistic, and societal overlaps and there were also some articulated differences – all of which could change over time and according to circumstance.

had previously dominated the region. Their long series of connections with Rome and Persia, inside and outside those empires, mean that it is easy to identify many earlier practices of both in the Muslim empires that followed.

An imperial example

In the ninth century, 228 years after the death of Muhammad, the court poet Ali ibn al-Jahm composed some verses to impress the Abbasid caliph al-Mutawakkil. This poem was performed in front of the caliph and his court in one of the magnificent palaces of the imperial capital Samarra and it offers us an extraordinary insight into how one of the most powerful Muslim rulers in history saw himself and his power.

> *I still hear that kings / build according to their acumen*
> > *And I know that the wisdom of men / is destroyed by their ruins*
> > *For Rome has that which their ancestors built / and the Persians inherited the monumental traces of their noblemen*
> > *[...]*
> > *You built, vindicating the Muslims / to their apostates and unbelievers,*
> > *Creations that Persia has not seen, / nor Rome, in the course of their lives!*
> > *[...]*
> > *If Solomon had been brought by his djinn, / some tales about it,*
> > *He would have known surely that the Hashemites / surpass him through their eminent majesty*
> > *The earth remains built and inhabited / through your life, the best of builders.*

Buildings were how great kings expressed their power: to their subjects, to their rivals, and to posterity. This was true for the great empires of the past and it was true for the Muslims. The physical record of Roman and

Persian power could still be seen but al-Mutawakkil, it is claimed here, had built on such a scale that even Solomon, the iconic builder king whose accomplishments were so extraordinary that it was believed he had commanded superhuman beings to produce them for him, would recognize the power and prestige of contemporary Muslim society.[7]

Al-Mutawakkil ruled from 847 to 861.[8] He was only one of many Muslim rulers who built to project their power and his capital, Samarra, was only one of many flourishing cities that showcased Muslim accomplishments in the first few centuries after Muhammad's death. In Córdoba, Damascus, Jerusalem, and Raqqa – all ancient and formerly Roman cities – incredible new buildings were constructed. In Baghdad, Basra, Cairo, Kufa, and Samarra, whole new cities were founded. All of these competed with Constantinople, still capital of the Roman Empire and one of the biggest cities in the world.

An elite traveller from Sasanian Ctesiphon to Roman Ravenna in the sixth century would likely have recognized visual similarities between the rock reliefs at Taq-e Bostan, built by successive Sasanian shahs, and the mosaic at San Vitale, ordered by Justinian and Theodora, and recognized them as statements of power. Four hundred years later, elite travellers from Constantinople, Samarkand, and Sanaa would all have recognized Abd al-Rahman III's Madinat al-Zahra outside Córdoba, Abd al-Malik's Dome of the Rock in Jerusalem, al-Mansur's Golden Palace in Baghdad as part of this same language of power, with many familiar visual references. Some things had changed but many things remained the same.

In fact, a great deal stayed the same in the territories that were conquered by Muhammad and the Muslim rulers that succeeded

---

7 Solomon is an incredibly important figure in Muslim tradition, as he was in the Roman and Persian worlds – for Christians, Jews, and Zoroastrians alike.

8 In the Hijri calendar, used by Muslims, which counts the years from the migration from Mecca to Medina by Muhammad and his followers, these dates correspond to 232–247 AH.

him. Archaeological evidence shows very few changes in the regions conquered by Arabian armies between 622 and 751.

On a modern map, these places stretched from the Atlantic coast in modern-day Morocco and Portugal and up to southern France, down into the Sahara desert and across to the entire Arabian peninsula, north up to Georgia and the Republic of Dagestan, and east to Kyrgyzstan, and down again to the Indian Ocean and Pakistan. This new empire covered much of the former Roman and Persian empires and their respective spheres of influence, bringing these formerly connected-but-separate worlds together.

In some places, the locals resisted fiercely and Muslim control was short-lived or tenuous. In others, exhausted by the military destruction inflicted by the wars of their previous imperial sovereigns, they were happy enough with new rulers. Moreover, although the invading armies were extremely militarily effective, their leaders were also adept diplomats who often negotiated with local leaders. They promised peace and prosperity under their rule and included existing local elites in the practicalities and profits of governing. In this, of course, they were no different from many of the empires we have already seen, who proclaimed the many benefits of their authority, particularly stability.

Conversion to Islam was not mandatory – far from it. Many existing religious groups were considered to share crucially significant traditions with the message proclaimed in the Quran. The most famous of these *dhimmi* or 'people of the book' were Jews and Christians but a number of other religious traditions were often included, such as the Sabians and the Zoroastrians in Mesopotamia and Persia, and Buddhists, Hindus, and Jains in south Asia. These groups did not have the same societal privileges as Muslims but they were given important legal protections in exchange for their taxes.[9]

---

9   Those legal protections were not always enforced and many of these peoples were still persecuted at different times and in different places.

Many people, of course, did choose to convert. Some found the egalitarian ideals attractive, others doubtless saw more pragmatic opportunities. However, it took around 500 years for these populations to become predominantly Muslim. Christian, Jewish, and Zoroastrian subjects lived in the newly built cities of the Muslim rulers, were frequently key players in the imperial administration, and were common guests in the fabulous new palaces of Muslim rulers.

'I still hear that kings build'

The first dynasty to rule the Muslim world was a family called the Umayyads.[10] They had been an important family in pre-Islamic Mecca but their power base was further north, in Syria.[11] Under their rule, the centre of gravity in the Muslim political world shifted to Damascus and Jerusalem, two of the oldest cities in the world. Both were major centres of worship, filled with Christian churches, Jewish synagogues, and Roman temples. In fact, when the first Umayyad caliph Muawiyah was criticized for 'having adopted the foreign ways of the Caesars [Romans] and the Khosrows [Persians]', he replied that Damascus was full of Romans and that none of them would believe in his power if he did not behave and look like them, as befitted an emperor.[12]

His successors would continue to behave like Romans to make their new subjects believe in their power.

---

10 In the period between Muhammad's death in 632 and the first Umayyad ruler in 661, there had been four caliphs (the Arabic word *khalifah* is usually translated to mean 'successor' or 'deputy' and denotes a political leader of the wider Muslim community). These four are often collectively referred to as the Rashidun (or 'rightly guided') caliphs and they were not hereditary but collectively agreed upon leaders – albeit not universally agreed upon.

11 The wider Arabian region was well-connected economically and socially and Damascus to Mecca was one such major connection.

12 This anecdote is recorded by the great historian al-Tabari and may not be true; it is possible it was a way to implicitly criticize the Umayyads and, perhaps discreetly, the Abbasid dynasty that had replaced them. It does, however, reflect the perception that Rome was both a reference point for authority (good or bad) and an audience for Muslim rulers in this period.

The first of the iconic Muslim builder-kings was Abd al-Malik, the fifth Umayyad caliph (r. 685–705). Among his many notable accomplishments was the construction of Qubbat al-Sakhra or the Dome of the Rock in Jerusalem. The tenth-century Palestinian geographer al-Muqaddasi, who came from a family of architects, recorded a conversation with his uncle where they discussed Umayyad building projects in Jerusalem and Damascus. He reports his uncle arguing that the Umayyad caliphs were worried that the many examples of impressive Christian architecture might make some Muslims waver in their faith. The uncle then added, 'For similar reasons Abd al-Malik built the Dome of the Rock. Like his son, he feared the grandeur of the dome of the Holy Sepulchre and the overall appearance of the church would dazzle Muslims.' Just as in the Roman world, politics and religion could not be separated and awe-inspiring buildings were proof of divine favour as well as practical power.

As al-Muqaddasi's uncle noted, Abd al-Malik's son and heir, caliph al-Walid (r. 705–715), was also a builder. He personally supervised the construction of the Great Mosque of Damascus, one of the largest and oldest mosques in the world. To do so, he had a formerly Roman temple to Jupiter, later converted into a Christian church, mostly torn down and the materials reused.[13] It has been estimated that as many as 12,000 labourers and artisans were needed to build the enormous complex. Al-Walid also funded a lavish expansion of the Prophet's Mosque in Medina, with yet more expert craftspeople and expensive materials used.

In Damascus and Jerusalem, these Umayyad builder-kings were conscious of their local and regional audiences and the imperial

---

13 This decision received much pushback from the local Christian communities and al-Walid is reported to have returned every other previously confiscated church in the city as a compromise. The area where John the Baptist's head was supposedly buried remained protected as, like many Christian traditions, it was also considered sacred by Muslims. In 2001, Pope John Paul II made the first papal visit to a mosque to visit these relics.

precedents for building to demonstrate power. They had other important audiences, however: the many (semi-)nomadic Bedouin tribes whose ongoing support was essential to the Umayyad government.[14] In the Umayyad-Bedouin relationship, we can see more references to Rome. Across modern-day Jordan, Iraq, Palestine, and Syria are numerous stone structures, often referred to as the Umayyad 'desert castles' (though many of them are neither in the desert, nor castles, and not all of them were built by the Umayyads). These buildings were probably the most consistent examples of Umayyad construction. They are often considered to have been on the periphery of the empire but that was no more the case under the Umayyads than it had been under the Romans – in fact, even less so, since the Bedouin were essential to Umayyad rule.

The so-called 'desert castles' were likely deliberately designed or repurposed as meeting places between the Umayyad and Bedouin elite.[15] Their construction was usually supervised by caliphal heirs in their capacity as regional governors in places close to important Bedouin territories and then used by them for diplomatic meetings with Bedouin leaders, the most important regional powers. Many of them reused Roman fortresses, such as Qasr Azraq, Qasr al-Hallabat, and Qasr Burqu. Others visibly reflect Roman (and Persian) architectural influences, cleverly combined with Arabian traditions in the construction, such as Qasr al-Hayr al-Sharqi and Qasr al-Mshatta.[16] Some of the most famous, Khirbat al-Mafjar, Qasr al-Hayr al-Gharbi,

---

14 The idea that nomadic peoples are permanently on the move and never use permanent architecture is incorrect; many Bedouin would have lived in settlements at various times of the year and there are many examples of permanent architecture built by nomadic peoples. It might be better to distinguish them by their pastoralism and the role of the changing seasons in their lives, without forgetting that trade was also significant.

15 They probably also had many other functions, not least the personal enjoyment of the governors who frequently stayed in them.

16 The most famous remains of Qasr al-Mshatta can be found in the Museum of Islamic Art in Berlin.

and Qusayr Amra contain luxurious bath-houses and are decorated inside with stunning Roman-style frescoes and mosaics. These were places built to impress important diplomatic allies, to relax, and to negotiate power; they are filled with Roman (as well as Arabian and Persian) aesthetic references because that was the visual language of power understood by both the Bedouin and Umayyad elites.

The Umayyads were overthrown and replaced from 749 by a new ruling dynasty, who exploited a widespread concern that they had relied *too* heavily on their Arabian allies to the detriment of their other subjects. Almost all the remaining members of the Umayyad family were assassinated, with the exception of Abd al-Rahman, who escaped and slowly made his way to Al-Andalus in Iberia,[17] where he acquired the support of the local elites and eventually established an independent polity, the Emirate of Córdoba.[18]

Mindful of the need to assert his legitimacy to his new subjects and project his power to the new Abbasid caliph, who still ruled the majority of Muslim territories, Abd al-Rahman quickly ordered the construction of a mosque. The later historical accounts describe the process in terms that are very similar to the narrative of his ancestor al-Walid's construction of the Great Mosque of Damascus – perhaps tweaking the story to clearly connect the new Umayyad state with the once-all-powerful caliphate, perhaps simply because the new emir had indeed used the same playbook. The Great Mosque of Córdoba was finished in 787 and, as at Damascus, the architecture made use of Roman remains.

Nearly 150 years later in Córdoba, Abd al-Rahman III promoted himself to caliph, the political leader of all Muslims, and set about

---

17 This corresponds to modern-day Gibraltar, Portugal, Spain, and southern France.

18 The Arabic word *emir* or *amir* is usually translated as 'commander' or sometimes 'prince'. In this early phase of local Umayyad-rule in Al-Andalus, the dynasty seems to have been cautious about asserting *too* much power in opposition to the Abbasids.

building a new capital city just outside Córdoba to support his claims. Madinat al-Zahra, 'the City of Radiance', was abandoned by 1015 and a great deal of the building materials were taken to be used elsewhere but the remains still offer a glimpse into the trends of the day. In addition to the caliphal palaces, there were numerous government complexes with extensive gardens to impress guests from Constantinople and Baghdad, public baths and fountains supplied by aqueducts, mosques and market places, military barracks and a coin mint – everything a major city in the Muslim world now needed.

Rivalling Rome: a new urban standard

By the time Madinat al-Zahra was built, the standard for a major Muslim ruler's capital city was high indeed. The Abbasids, the dynasty who had overthrown the Umayyads in 749, were prolific builders. The resources of their vast empire were put to work to build on a hitherto unseen scale to assert their legitimacy as the new rulers of the Muslim world.[19] The Abbasid caliphs founded a series of new cities between 754 and 836, enormous infrastructural projects completed at speed and luxuriously decorated. This was helped by the fact that, in Iraq, the local building material was the relatively cheap unfired mud brick. Additionally, as was often the case before and since, the bulk of the most expensive decorative items were portable and would be moved from one palace to another.

The most well-known of these Abbasid capital cities is Madinat al-Salam, the 'City of Peace' – otherwise known as Baghdad. Al-Mansur, the second Abbasid caliph, ordered a circular city to be built (and personally supervised its construction) between 762 and 766. The result almost immediately became shrouded in legends, probably helped by some astute self-promotion on the part of the caliph who seems to have known that, while buildings showed your power, they couldn't always

---

19 As in the Roman Empire, for example, the resources such large empires accrue through conquest and exploitation, including the profits of enslaved labour, made such projects possible.

be trusted to survive. This idea recurs in pre-Islamic Arabic poetry and contemporary Abbasid writings; specifically that, while kings build to memorialize their own power, kings also destroy the buildings of others to show their superiority (and, indeed, that time or natural disaster might destroy buildings). It was therefore essential also to record all your achievements in words.[20]

The Round City serves to demonstrate this idea very well. It was badly damaged in a civil war just 150 years later and irreparably damaged along with much of the city it had grown into by 1258. There are almost no material remains of the city al-Mansur hoped would be his legacy.

We do, however, have extensive written records that describe it, many based on contemporary reports. The city was perfectly circular, they claim, like none other in the known world.[21] It was concentrically organized, with the caliph's palace and the city's mosque in the exact middle. This symbolism showed the caliph and Islam not only as central to the city or even the empire but to everyone and everywhere: Baghdad rapidly became known as 'the crossroads of the universe'. It was also an execution of geometric principles popular across western Asia for a millennium or more, perhaps most associated with Euclid and Alexander the Great. Indeed, we know that al-Mansur had Euclid's *Elements* translated for him personally and many of the founding myths of Baghdad appear to associate him with Alexander the Great, famous across west Asia for founding cities as well as his military conquests. The geometric perfection of al-Mansur's Round City had multiple layers of symbolism in its projection of power.

20 This included written records for the literary elite, of course, but, perhaps more importantly, oral literature as well. Formally organized, orally transmitted histories were essential in this period, together with the millennia-long role of epic and vernacular poetry that functioned as literary archives of accomplishments, identities, and relationships.

21 The writers and scholars who claimed this must have known it was not accurate; there was at least one circular city nearby, the former Sasanian capital of Veh Ardashir. It is likely they were implying something more than just its circularity, perhaps just the degree of superiority.

In the heart of the city, al-Mansur's palace was topped with an enormous dome standing approximately forty metres high. The four monumental gates to the city were similarly crowned with domes, with slightly smaller examples. These domes did more than catch the eye of a far-off traveller; they connected the new city of Baghdad to other major cities across western Asia, showing off the building prowess of the new imperial dynasty.[22] The Abbasids, these domes showed, had arrived – and they were here to stay.

Al-Mansur didn't limit himself to Baghdad, however, and neither did his successors. His grandson, Harun al-Rashid, moved the imperial capital for the final thirteen years of his reign to Raqqa, an ancient city on the frontier with Rome.[23] No doubt keen to burnish his reputation as a military commander against the Abbasids' imperial Christian rivals, al-Rashid built a number of palaces with military-style exteriors. If that weren't clear enough, he constructed a huge monument around ten kilometres outside the city, reusing Roman stone, most likely to commemorate a military victory over the Romans.[24] Most interestingly of all, he had a floor made from blue and green glass tiles in one of his audience halls. This would have been beautiful and an extremely impressive display of craftsmanship – but it was more than that. In the Quran, Solomon has a glass floor in one of his palaces that looks so convincingly like water that Bilqis, the queen of Sheba, is amazed and immediately converts to Islam. On the border with Rome, as he waged war against the non-believers, al-Rashid was connecting himself

22 Similarly, the gate-doors used in the gateways were mostly re-used from other places to connect the Abbasid caliph with, respectively, Solomon and military conquest over Rome.

23 Harun al-Rashid is a recurring character in *One Thousand and One Nights*, the collection of folk tales and legends recorded in Arabic, where he is always connected with Baghdad, despite the fact he moved his capital elsewhere. This probably says something about the legendary nature of both the city and the ruler, brought together like magnets.

24 The reuse of Roman stone was a significant statement - it was not the usual practice for the Abbasids. It was likely intended to be understood in the same manner as the reused monuments of conquered peoples we saw in Chapter 7, an indication of ownership and superiority.

with the most legendary builder king of all, the king whose building accomplishments had converted a heathen queen.

A few years later, in 836, another new capital was built. Both Baghdad and Raqqa were flourishing cities, filled with artisans and scholars, monasteries and mosques, gardens and hammams. Each Abbasid caliph wanted to make his mark, however, and so a third city was founded, 120 kilometres north of Baghdad. This city was called Samarra, the great palace-city of the Abbasid caliphs. Once more, artisans and labourers were brought in from around the empire to create display after dazzling display of power. Canals and aqueducts were built to supply the many ostentatious, glittering fountains and beautiful, tiered gardens for leisurely strolls, numerous huge racecourses were erected for entertainment, markets and military barracks were established. More than anything, there were palaces. Caliph al-Mutawakkil, the recipient of the ninth-century praise poem that articulated the Abbasid understanding of building as power, reportedly ordered the construction of eight palaces.

A Roman audience

The Abbasids had a clear audience for their building efforts: Rum, or Rome, their imperial rival.

Rome and Persia, Caesar and Khosrow: again and again, the Arabic sources of the time note these two great imperial examples (with both approval and condemnation). The Persians, however, had by now been conquered; the last Sasanian ruler, Yazdegerd III, had been killed trying to escape in 651. Rome, on the other hand, remained.[25] The majority of the territories that had once comprised the Roman Empire had been conquered but a Caesar still ruled in Constantinople. Every year, with

---

25 Local elites who still identified as Persian in some way remained an important audience for the Abbasid caliphs too and Persian traditions never went out of fashion; in fact, they became increasingly significant as those elites reasserted their power from the late ninth century.

varying ratios of effectiveness to symbolism, the Umayyad and then Abbasid caliphates campaigned militarily against Rome. The idea of capturing Constantinople – of ruling from Constantinople – as a proof of the triumph of Islam was a powerful one.

It was not, however, an all-consuming idea. Commercial and diplomatic relationships were maintained, seemingly consistently. Whether from Damascus, Baghdad, or Córdoba, Muslim rulers regularly exchanged communications and gifts with Rome.[26] Indeed, Arabic sources tell us that the Roman emperor sent craftsmen and materials to support the Umayyad building works in Damascus, Jerusalem, and Medina. We also have reports of embassies to Baghdad and their reactions to Abbasid displays of power. How accurately these sources describe events has been questioned, as with any historical account. They clearly show, however, that Rome was *understood* as a diplomatic relationship – and an audience by successive Muslim rulers for their projection of power.[27]

At times they were a literal audience. We have at least two reports of official embassies from Constantinople to Baghdad, one during the reign of al-Mansur (r. 754–75) and another in 917. Arabic accounts clearly convey the significance of the visits for both parties. Likewise, we know of a number of diplomatic embassies from Constantinople to Córdoba and vice-versa.

What would a visitor from Rome have seen in these cities? After all, for all that monumental buildings can impress and inspire, a city is more than its buildings. No amount of palace building can compensate

---

26 Charlemagne himself had a military alliance with local Umayyad rulers in Al-Andalus against Christian territories considered to be mutual rivals; he later conducted a diplomatic exchange with the caliph in Baghdad, as part of which the Abbasid ruler Harun al-Rashid sent him an elephant, probably less a recognition of the Frankish ruler's power than a display of the caliph's wealth.

27 They were not the only audience, of course, nor necessarily the most important – these were huge empires with many competing audiences. Rome was, however, their imperial rival and therefore an important audience.

for that indefinable buzz of a thriving city, the lived experience of citizens and visitors.

Just as there were certain features of art and architectural styles that could be found from the Atlantic coast to central Asia, from northern Italy to southern Arabia, so were there similar aspects of urban life. Similarities do not add up to the *same*, of course; there were always regional variations and also major differences. A well-travelled visitor to the many cities across Afro-Eurasia would experience striking contrasts; they did, in fact, according to accounts of geographers like al-Muqaddisi. There would be little charm in travel if everyone and everywhere was the same.

Consistently, however, we know that travellers to these major cities of the early Muslim empires would also encounter some key characteristics that repeated from city to city. Monumental architecture, striking from a distance, and flourishing trade hubs were only the start.

Just as the forum can be seen as the centre of Roman urban life, so we can capture a glimpse of urban life in a place like eighth-century Baghdad or tenth-century Córdoba by considering the mosques. These were far more than spaces for religious worship, they were huge complexes that served as centres of the community. Increasingly, the major urban mosques were built with extensive stone courtyards, completed with shaded arcades on each side – gorgeously decorated, of course, in colours a Roman guest would probably find familiar (mustard yellow, olive-green, blue-green, deep-blue, and red). In these courtyards, local markets thrived and families strolled. People socialized on the way to or from prayer, consulted legal experts to help with their problems, and gave charity to those who needed it (or requested it for their own needs).

On the way to or from the mosque complex, a visitor might experience a performance of street poetry from a local celebrity or perhaps even a poetry-battle, where a promising upstart tested their skills against an established expert, cheered (or booed) on by delighted crowds.

Any traveller to a city would almost certainly walk past a hammam or three, perhaps experiencing one for themselves.[28] These were public baths that had tweaked and perfected ancient Greek and Roman public baths for local practice while retaining the same essential features: vital social institutions where people moved between rooms with water of varying temperatures to relax and rest as well as clean themselves before perhaps getting a haircut or one of many other spa treatments. Just as in the Roman Empire, many of these spaces were enormously expensive public works of architecture, beautifully decorated in vibrant colours, to remind the users of the power of their rulers and the benefits of empire.

These visitors would probably also pass by or through many extraordinary gardens, elaborately planned and which were frequently enormous outdoor spaces that required huge amounts of resources to create and maintain. These spaces were designed to restore body and soul, but they were also an expression of control over the natural world, of power and wealth. Both Roman and early Muslim public gardens actually developed from the longstanding Persian tradition of 'paradises', beautiful garden spaces – a reminder of how interconnected ancient west Asia and the Mediterranean were.[29]

One other Persian tradition that was developed very early on by Muslim rulers in their cities that might have surprised an ancient Roman guest was the bimaristan, literally 'the place of the sick' (what we might call a hospital).[30] These spaces were founded by caliphs, rulers, and wealthy elites from a very early period and were for everyone (irrespective of gender, religion, wealth, or severity of problems). Outdoor spaces,

---

28 One writer from the tenth–eleventh century, Hilal al-Sabi, estimated that Baghdad at its height had 60,000 bathhouses – almost certainly an exaggeration but a reflection of how important they were to public life.

29 Throughout the Quran, *Jannah* or heaven, is described as a garden or more specifically a 'paradise' in the Persian tradition.

30 These would only have been a surprise to an ancient Roman visitor – Romanland had public hospitals of its own in Constantinople from perhaps the late fourth century.

especially gardens, were considered essential in a bimaristan to help patients of all ailments heal, as was a variety of entertainment, places of worship, and good food. Again, though, these spaces had a broader remit than a modern association; many included libraries and lecture halls, places for people to learn, to practise surgical techniques, and to teach.

Scholarship, at every level, was one of the most important elements of life in these cities. No visitor to Muslim Baghdad, Cairo, or Córdoba would walk away without encountering a flourishing academic scene – it was inescapable.

Rivalling Rome: new centres of scholarship

A love of learning was common across the many different regions ruled by Muslim leaders: the famous exhortation of the prophet Muhammad, to 'seek knowledge even as far as China' reflected the world Muhammad had lived in, one that valued scholarship for its own sake, as well as its practical application. For instance, there was a long tradition in the Arabian peninsula of expertise in sciences like astronomy (and navigation), agriculture, and water engineering. This was not always recognized by scholars, as we saw in the previous chapters. For example, for a long time, it was incorrectly assumed that the water infrastructure at Nabatean Petra indicated it had been occupied by Rome from a much earlier period, as many scholars struggled to believe the Arabian Nabateans had such a sophisticated level of expertise.

Additionally, the merchants that connected Mecca and Medina across land and sea carried more than goods to trade; they also brought reports of new science and technology, new wisdom and philosophy. Sometimes they escorted scholars and their works from India, central Asia, and Persia to the Mediterranean or the other way, from Alexandria, Nubia, and Pergamon to the Indian Ocean. As the Umayyad and then Abbasid Caliphates brought these regions under one central rule, it was easier to collect the scholarly traditions together and formalize these connections.

From at least as early as al-Mansur, founder of Baghdad, and perhaps earlier, the caliphs and the elites of their courts sponsored education and research on an extraordinary scale.[31] The investment was enormous and the salaries reportedly available to reliable research assistants, never mind leading scholars, were enough to make a career in scholarship extremely tempting. Women as well as men worked in research, Christians, Jews, and Zoroastrians, as well as Muslims, enslaved people as well as free subjects – academia cut across all levels of society.[32]

This widespread interest in education and research, especially in the early period, was explicitly understood as part of the rivalry with Rome. The fact that Abbasid scholarship engaged extensively with the works of, for instance, Aristotle and Galen, is often highlighted and it is clear that Abbasid society felt an ownership over the academic traditions they found in the Roman Empire. However, that was true of *all* academic traditions. Greek or Latin scholarship was not more prized in Baghdad than Persian or Sanskrit research, for instance. As before, a crucial distinction is that Rome remained as the major imperial rival for the Abbasids.[33] Excelling them in this field, as in all others, was another way to assert superiority.

31 This is often referred to as the 'Translation Movement', which implies the main activity was translating prior research. Translation was a substantial part of the work: making the scholarship of one place understandable to much wider audiences, an important research skill and contribution. However, it was only one aspect of the work being done across nearly every discipline and this name means the huge leaps in mathematics, medicine, and philosophy (among many others) tend to be overlooked.

32 By far the most famous scholars of the time were free men and mostly Muslim. However, we know of many important Christian and Jewish scholars and some women. We also know that the most famous scholars were supported by many assistants, as is always the case, and these were frequently women and the enslaved .

33 We can see this in the way that, as the central control of the Abbasid caliphs faded, the various regional powers began to compete with each other for the best scholarly reputation. Just as with monumental buildings, this was about power: the best city walls, the best gardens, the best poets, the best scholars – all millennia-old ways for a city to assert itself across Afro-Eurasia that continued.

Part of this assertion of superiority was not just to surpass their rival in scholarly accomplishments but to add a moral claim to the best scholarship available in the Roman world, arguing that it was produced by pre-Roman Greek speakers. One example of this argument can be found in the letters of al-Jahiz (776-868/9), a famous polymath who spent time at the caliphal courts in both Baghdad and Samarra. He argued that the ancient Greek 'religion was different from the religion of the Romans, and their culture was different from the culture of the Romans. They were scientists, while [the Romans] are craftspeople who appropriated the books of the Greeks on account of geographical proximity.'

A century later, the geographer and historian al-Masudi (896-956) made similar claims, more explicitly blaming the Roman conversion to Christianity for the decline in scholarship. Their religious superstitions, he contended, meant they now persecuted scholars rather than supported them. The Abbasid caliphs hosted theological debates between Christian leaders and Muslim experts and proclaimed their sponsorship of free speech, contrasting themselves with Constantinople. In fact, it is quite likely that, by the reign of caliph al-Mamun (r. 813–833), Roman neglect of scholarly traditions was being used as another justification for renewed military campaigns against them.

Intriguingly, there are hints from contemporary Roman sources that Baghdad was understood, at least in the ninth century, as a great centre of scholarship – one worth travelling to. John the Grammarian, Leo the Mathematician, and St Photios, some of the intellectual giants of ninth-century Romanland, all reportedly spent time in the Abbasid courts, according to Roman sources. As always, it is hard to tell how far the stories of their travels are true but it is clear that there was an understanding in ninth-century Rome that the very best scholars spent time in Abbasid academies (just as today many people might interpret a stint at the universities of Cambridge, Harvard, or the Sorbonne as an indication of the same international scholarly acclaim).[34]

Science, technology, engineering, and mathematics

The benefits of all this focus on scientific research, of course, were considerably more than the ability to claim superiority over an imperial and religious rival. In fact, although the caliphs in this period wielded considerable power, their interest and support alone would not have been enough to ensure such widespread societal investment of energy, finances, identity, and time in scholarship. Abbasid Baghdad rapidly became famous as the gold standard of Muslim academia but it was not able to make itself such overnight. Rather, it was the product of longstanding investment in scientific research and its practical usages.

From the time of Abd al-Malik, the first Muslim 'builder-king' in the late seventh century, the expanding bureaucratic elites of the empire had been developing and applying scholarship, in part to ensure their own relevance to government and society. An empire can be conquered with the profits of military campaigns but those proceeds rapidly run out. Stable government of an empire usually requires taxes and taxes require surplus. Existing scientific knowledge was put to work to increase the assessment, exploitation, and taxation of agriculture and trade, making them more efficient. The skills acquired in this process provided the foundation for later research.

By the time of the Abbasids, this application of research was well-established and new avenues were pursued: exploring the nature of the world and the relationship to the divine, the obligations of people to

---

34 One of the most commonly mentioned Abbasid institutes of learning is called Bayt al-Hikma or 'the House of Wisdom'. There was almost certainly an important archive known as this in Baghdad, perhaps in the Sasanian-Persian tradition, but the idea that it was a library or even a proto-university is more likely another example of seeing the past through the lens of what is familiar to us – just as the Library of Alexandria is often used as a stand-in for the wider intellectual climate of the ancient Mediterranean, so Bayt al-Hikma is used as shorthand for the Abbasid scholarly environment.

one another, and the best ways to govern and navigate society.[35] New technologies were being invented, including ones that could astonish and delight as well as serve more practical functions. In the tradition of Solomon, the builder-king whose marvels were legendary, the Abbasid caliphs and their courts applied scientific research to produce increasingly spectacular wonders. Harun al-Rashid's floor that appeared like water in his palace at Raqqa was only the start; at Samarra, the caliphs' craftspeople produced porcelain that shimmered and walls that appeared like silk textiles, moving gently in the breeze. An audience with the imperial court must have been a dizzying, enchanting experience.

The rivalry with Rome fuelled this further. Contact and competition between Rome, Baghdad, and the increasingly confident emirate based in Córdoba produced astonishing self-propelled mechanical devices called automata. These feats of technology and craft imitated roaring lions, moving beasts, and singing birds on trees and decorated the courts and gardens of all three cities to impress and overwhelm visitors. The automata displayed at these imperial courts were created by brilliant craftspeople drawing on African, Chinese, Greek, Persian, and Sanskrit precedents, a reminder of how many different traditions of scholarly expertise were being combined in these cities.[36]

Baghdad is the city most associated with this culture of research and it was clearly very important to the city's identity. When the caliph al-Mamun was trying to heal the wounds of the civil war he had successfully waged against his brother and earn the faith of Baghdadi residents, he did so by increasing support for research in the city to

---

35 These topics would probably now fall under the categories of philosophy, theology, and law, with some overlap.

36 This courtly tradition of mechanical devices to project power would continue for centuries; in 1599, Elizabeth I of England gifted a type of automaton to Mehmed III in the hopes of improving diplomatic relations with the Ottoman Empire, as we saw in Chapter 5. Well into the eighteenth century, some of the most powerful rulers of the world, including Catherine the Great of Russia, Frederick the Great of Prussia, and Tipu Sultan of Mysore, were all delighted by automata.

appeal to its bureaucrats, merchants, and soldiers. However, as the Abbasid caliphate started to fracture and powerful local governors began to acknowledge their authority in name only, cities across the Muslim world competed to be centres of learning. Bukhara, Fez, and Nishapur, to name only a few, rapidly developed reputations for academic excellence and scholarly institutions.[37]

This understanding of monumental building, craftsmanship, and scholarship as expressions of power, or the gold standard of imperial rule, continued for centuries in Muslim-ruled empires. They emerged as a result of centuries of close contact between Arabia, Persia, and Rome before being expanded and finessed in Umayyad and then Abbasid imperial centres. From there, they proliferated across Afro-Eurasia – we can see more examples in Palermo, Samarkand, and Timbuktu. Over time, these traditions developed different nuances, different local variations, and different interpretations of core ideals. And yet, similarities still remained.

The early Ottoman rulers could easily present themselves as 'Renaissance rulers' to European audiences because many of the traditions that the Italian Renaissance claimed to be reviving were as much a part of Ottoman culture as they were Italian – or Abbasid, German, Romanland, or Russian. All these languages of power had developed along slightly different paths from the same starting point and so they were still recognizable to one another, even where they were believed to be distinctly different.

What the word 'Rome' meant, however, continued to shift over time. For much of the Ottoman period, outside of Constantinople, it was informally used in ways that reflected its earlier associations of both craftsmanship and governance.[38] 'Rumi' or 'Romans' could be

---

37 In present-day Uzbekistan, Morocco, and Iran, respectively.

38 This is in addition to various meanings we have already seen 'Rum' have *in* Ottoman Constantinople.

used to describe a group of highly skilled travelling artisans in many of the Ottoman provinces, for example, a reminder of the city's earlier reputation. Elsewhere, historical accounts of Arabia and Egypt written in Arabic regularly referred to the imperial officials sent to govern a region as the *Rum*.

In the eighteenth and nineteenth centuries, many Muslim intellectuals confronted the power of the European empires in the region. For some, as we have seen so often elsewhere, the answer to the problems of the present lay in their past. Reformist movements like the Wahhabis, and later the Salafis, looked to the earliest period of their faith and, particularly, the Quran and hadith (the actions and advice traditionally associated with Muhammad). The idea of Rome as a Christian imperial rival was revived, narrowed down to an enmity, and shorn of its nuances.

It is this interpretation of Rome that groups like ISIS use in their propaganda, casting their fight as eternal and existential, divinely sanctioned.[39] Much as we saw in Chapter 4 with conservative Russian ideas about Byzantium, this view of Rome relies on terms set by their so-called enemies: in this case, that the historic empire based in Constantinople has, in some meaningful way, been inherited by the United States of America.

---

39 One of ISIS's online propaganda magazines was actually called *Rumiyah* for two years. It was published in English, German, and French as well as Arabic, Bosnian, Indonesian, Turkish, Uyghur, and Urdu.

9

The New Republic: USA Edition

Ever since the Declaration of Independence, the United States of America has presented itself as an heir to Rome. Thomas Jefferson's understanding of Roman liberty, tyranny, and republicanism was central to his proposed new form of government. He also reflected the civilization he drew inspiration from in the architecture of the White House and Washington DC, a city with so many classical-style colonnaded and domed buildings that the Irish poet Thomas Moore called it the 'Modern Rome'. In fact, Capitol Hill, the seat of the US government, takes its name from Capitoline Hill, the centre of Republican Rome. Elite American universities are filled with busts of iconic Roman men, their libraries boast some of the biggest collections of Roman manuscripts, their departments have world-renowned expertise in Roman scholarship.

When Donald Trump's supporters attacked the Capitol Hill in January 2021 to protest at what they claimed was a rigged election, many of them consciously referred to Julius Caesar's illegal military attack on his own capital city of Rome more than two millennia previously, to protest at what he believed to have been a rigged election. Trump's supporters carried banners saying #CrossTheRubicon and their forums are filled with Latin references. They did so not only because of the enduring legacy of ideas about Rome in neo-Nazi movements around that world but because of the uses of Rome in the earliest years of the USA.

*In front of two large Corinthian columns, on a stage famous
for oratory, the speaker addresses a rapt audience. The acoustics,
perfectly designed, help his carefully chosen words carry to the very
back of the hall. He reminds the crowd of their shared values, of
their hard-won rights, of their laws and obligations. His powerful
rhetoric is peppered throughout with clever references to remind
the assembled people of his education and to reassure them he is
one of them. He speaks of liberty and tyranny, of behaviour that
befits a great people and acts that condemn barbarians. In a rousing
conclusion, he speaks of his hope for the future and the crowd's
renewed commitment to freedom.*

THIS MAN WAS FREDERICK DOUGLASS, the Black self-emancipated
former slave, and his speech directly addressed the hypocrisy of celebrating
liberty and the overthrow of tyranny in the United States of America when
around 3.2 million men, women, and children were enslaved.

The particular discrepancy between the ideal of liberty and the
reality of enslavement that Douglass challenged in his speech had its
roots in Roman ideas. Many of the so-called Founding Fathers of the
USA explicitly used Republican Rome as an ideal precedent when
they wrote the constitution for their new nation. The country they
established had, and still has, many parallels with ancient Rome – just
perhaps not the ones we think.

Echoes and reflections of all the previous interpretations of ancient
Rome that we have looked at so far can be found in this last entry, the
United States of America: a nation formed quite explicitly around the
idea of the right to inherit Rome.

In fact, the white, 'classical-style' colonnaded and domed buildings
of Washington DC and the interpretation of Rome that they represent
might be the clearest example of the modern inability to see Rome in
full colour, no matter how many times a day we think about it.

The Founding Fathers, the men who fought the British Empire for their independence, framed their struggle in terms of Roman-ness. They wrote letters to one another filled with references to Roman political theory and used the names of ancient Roman heroes as pseudonyms. They wore togas in public, used Latin slogans taken from Cicero, and identified themselves with Roman statesmen. They proclaimed to crowds of listeners that they would build a new empire, one that was a worthy descendant to Rome.

After their successful rebellion, these men debated the ideal Roman virtues and wrote a constitution designed to imitate the Roman Republic. They set about conquering the new Roman Empire that they considered themselves worthy of,[1] constructed imitations of Roman buildings across their cities, and navigated their political struggles by drawing yet more inspiration from Rome.

This eighteenth-century vision of Rome drew on the interpretations popular in Europe over the previous centuries: one that was Republican without sacrificing imperial ambitions, one that sat at the top of a civilizational hierarchy, one that could be passed on genealogically.

Above all, this Rome – its buildings and its people – was white.

A Roman solution

The first four presidents of the United States of America were classicists. George Washington taught himself, while John Adams, Thomas Jefferson, and James Madison were all university educated. Their particular idea of Rome was formed, inevitably, by that education and thus reflected their intellectual conversations and scholarly traditions of Europe, brought by European invaders to the American continents.

1 The Founding Fathers were opposed to the British Empire but not the concept of empire itself. In fact, the idea that they would conquer their own empire was very much a part of the revolutionary rhetoric. In just one example, George Washington himself said to his soldiers that they were men who had 'shared in the toils and dangers of effecting this glorious revolution, of rescuing Millions from the hand of oppression, and of laying the foundation of a great Empire'.

It was also, however, an idea of Rome formed in opposition to Europe, one that allowed the Founding Fathers of the United States to address the specific problems they encountered in building a new nation for themselves.

This new nation was very much for *them* – and them alone.

The European empires who had spent the last 300 years conquering, colonizing, and committing genocides against the indigenous nations and peoples of the American continents were not welcome – they were unworthy heirs to Rome. Moreover, neither the people of the indigenous North American nations, nor the Black people – enslaved or free – who had been trafficked there were considered to be participants in this new nation; they, of course, could not be heirs to Rome.[2]

The United States of America was going to be different, just as the Roman Republic had been. Liberty would be proclaimed for elite men while others were enslaved, just as in the Roman Republic. The profits of empire would not go to an unelected monarch who could exploit all colonial subjects with impunity but instead would be shared among elite men, just as in the Roman Republic. The contradictions pointed out by people like Frederick Douglass were a feature of this system, not a bug – just as in the Roman Republic.

It is important to acknowledge that these *were* all features of the Roman Republic.

Roman stories of its earliest period highlight violence, conquests, and rape. At every stage in its long history, Rome relied on enslaved labour. The Republican voting system didn't just refuse the vote to

---

2 There are many different ways to describe the indigenous peoples of the Americas. The early use of 'tribe' was intended to devalue and erase the legitimacy of indigenous culture and rule, another example of a civilized/barbarian approach to the world that was rooted in ideas about ancient Rome and a desire to create a civilizational hierarchy in the present. Yet again, these descriptions and what we know of the reality on the ground don't match up. In fact, the Founding Fathers were partly inspired by the federated, representative union of the Haudenosaunee or Iroquois Confederacy as a way to balance local and national government. They were rather less keen to promote this example for their thinking, however.

many, it literally treated the votes of rich men as more important[3]. The lost ideal of liberty that the elite men of the early imperial Roman period like Seneca and Tacitus mourned was only for some; equality was never a Roman goal.

Yes, the people who built the USA in their image of Rome selected those elements that spoke most clearly to their fear and needs, just as everyone else we have encountered in these chapters did. But Rome has been a reference point for so many empires since because it was powerful – and that power was achieved at the expense of huge numbers of people.

In consciously creating what they thought of as a 'new' nation, a more perfect civilization than their peers or predecessors, the Founding Fathers painted a picture of ancient Rome for a modern audience that sharpens our perspective. These ideas weren't unique, they are just easier to see in this context.

When William Thornton designed the United States Capitol building to reference Roman monumental architecture and project the identity and power of the USA, he was using the same neoclassical style, for the same reason, as that seen across Enlightenment Europe: in the Brandenburg Gate of Prussian Berlin, the Panthéon of Louis XV's Paris, and the Pavlovsk Palace of Catherine the Great's Saint Petersburg.

When James Madison wrote that Athenian-style democracy would always lead to mob rule because, when people gathered together to vote, 'passion never fails to wrest the sceptre from reason', and that a Roman-style republican system that balanced a monarchy, an aristocracy, and a democracy was ideal, he was drawing on the ideas of leading Enlightenment thinkers like Montesquieu.[4]

---

3 It was a complicated system that, as previously discussed, was intentionally undemocratic: wealthier, more aristocratic men, if they were citizens, literally got to vote first and with a weighted vote that usually effectively determined the outcome. Women of any status, the substantial enslaved population, and the vast majority of those who lived outside the city of Rome were not allowed to vote.

4 Madison wrote this under the pseudonym 'Publius', a common name in ancient Rome.

When Thomas Jefferson wrote in 1781 that he believed Black people were 'in reason much inferior' to white people, that they have 'a very strong and disagreeable odour', and that 'Their griefs are transient', he was making the same arguments as the famous philosopher Immanuel Kant.[5] In 1764, Kant wrote, 'The Negroes of Africa have by nature no feeling that rises above the trifling' and 'This fellow was quite black from head to foot, a clear proof that what he said was stupid', while, in 1775, he claimed that 'Negroes stink'.

When Joseph Warren, dressed in a Roman toga, addressed a Boston crowd in 1775 and argued that, although Britain had conquered lands that even the Romans hadn't, their love of tyranny made them unworthy heirs to the legacy of Rome, he was speaking a language the British understood – just using it against them (technically, of course, at this stage Warren and those he was addressing were all still British citizens, however much they were pushing for a new identity and citizenship). One of the key arguments of Edward Gibbon's famous *The History of the Decline and Fall of the Roman Empire*, the first part of which was published the year after Warren's speech, was that the decline in civic virtues led directly to the decline of Roman power. It was a popular argument amongst the Enlightenment thinkers of Europe; Gibbon's history followed the same lines of argument as Montesquieu and Voltaire.[6]

---

5 This was in Jefferson's publication *Notes on the State of Virginia*. Elsewhere, Jefferson noted that enslaved people in the Roman Empire had been artists and intellectuals, which he claimed was evidence that the inferiorities he identified in Black people were not a consequence of slavery but being Black. Jefferson had, of course, famously stated that 'all men are created equal' as part of the 1776 Declaration of Independence.

6 Intriguingly, Gibbon's six-volume history covered the years 98–1590, beginning in the imperial Roman period and ending well after Constantinople had been conquered by the Ottomans. His history of Rome, in his own words, focused on, 'the artful policy of the Caesars, who long maintained the name and image of a free republic; the disorders of military despotism; the rise, establishment, and sects of Christianity; the foundation of Constantinople; the division of the monarchy; the invasion and settlements of the barbarians of Germany and Scythia; the institutions of the civil law; the character and religion of Mohammed; the temporal sovereignty of the popes; the restoration and decay of the Western empire of Charlemagne; the crusades of the Latins in the East; the conquests of the Saracens [Muslims] and Turks [Ottomans];] the ruin of the Greek [Romanland] empire; the state and revolutions of Rome in the middle age.'

Moreover, the ideas and values proclaimed by the Enlightenment – like fraternity, individual liberty, progress, rational thought, and religious tolerance – were inspired by ideas about the ancient world, particularly 'classical' Athens and Rome. Again and again, philosophers such as Denis Diderot, David Hume, Montesquieu, Jean-Jacques Rousseau, and Voltaire referred to Roman examples and Roman thinkers. In fact, Kant suggested that the Enlightenment could be summed up with a quotation taken from the Roman poet Horace (65–8 BCE): '*sapere aude*', or 'dare to know'. That he was using Horace to encapsulate the wider philosophical movement was essential to the point: Rome underpinned everything.

A view from the Roman Republic

How much would an ancient Roman have recognized these ideas and their implementation in the newly formed United States of America?

We cannot really say, of course. Firstly, as we have seen, we are always looking at the past with the eyes of the present – the most impartial efforts to sift through the evidence will still be *looking* for something and that influences what is found.

Secondly, although we have a lot of evidence for ancient Rome compared with many other past societies, the entire total still only offers a relatively tiny insight. In terms of a jigsaw puzzle, we are missing most of the pieces and the guiding image.

Thirdly, which ancient Roman's perspective would we want? A member of the imperial family or an enslaved person, a carpenter or a sex-worker, a general or a poet, a resident of Rome or someone who had never visited? Just as in any society, no single person can represent every perspective of the collective group.

This is especially true of an entity as long-lived as Rome. Someone who lived in the fifth century BCE, when Rome was a city state struggling for supremacy against the cities and towns around it, would have a significantly different experience of being Roman than someone 400 years later, as the Republic tore itself apart fighting over the profits of the empire. By 212 CE, when Roman citizenship was granted to all free men in that empire, Roman society was very different, and not just because of the law change. The same is true for 532 CE, when the Nika riots in New Rome destroyed much of the city, or in the twelfth century, during the life of Anna Komnene, whom we met in Chapter 2. Across more than 2,000 years, Rome changed in hugely significant ways while still identifying as *Roman*.

We can stretch the jigsaw metaphor a little further: the pieces we have are jumbled together from many different puzzles, in different styles and formats.

That's not to despair. We can look at the evidence we do have, specifically for elite men in late Republican Rome, the period of government that the Founding Fathers of the USA took as their model, and make some useful comparisons.

For a start, as we have already seen, we know that Republican Roman monumental buildings and statues were extremely colourful. We also know that the temples would have been overwhelming sensory experiences: filled not just with colour but smells and sounds. So we can guess that anyone who had experienced a monumental Roman temple, which were often used as government buildings in the Republican period, would find the pale white columns and domes of neoclassical architecture like the United States Capitol very different.

There are some institutions of the early United States that might have struck these elite Republican men as familiar, however. They would probably have recognized the separation of powers that balanced an elected leader of the armed forces (the consuls in Rome, the president in the USA) with a legislative body of men from the highest societal class (the Senate, in both cases), and legal judges from that same body of men.

Another element of government in the early USA that would also probably have been recognized by an elite ancient Roman was the requirement in most states that voting was limited to free men who owned land – and the connection such laws had with imperial expansion.[7] Recent scholarship has highlighted the ways in which nineteenth-century legal theory around property ownership, which claimed to derive its principles from ancient Roman practice, was different in a number of crucial ways from what we know of how Romans regulated and understood ownership and, in fact, much more rooted in Enlightenment ideals of what *should* be the case. However, it is certainly true that property ownership was integral to ideals of Roman Republican citizenship and political participation.

More than that, imperial expansion, confiscation of land and the cheap reallocation of that land to citizens willing to move, ensure control of the new territories, and spread Roman customs and traditions was an essential feature of Roman Republican history. It therefore also seems very likely that most elite Romans would have recognized the steady expansion of the territory controlled by the state, as both individuals and elected leaders of the USA sought more land, more resources, and more power. Gaius Julius Caesar, for instance, wrote a calm, detailed account of precisely this type of behaviour in *Commentarii de Bello Gallico*, his account of his nine-year military campaigns across central and northern Europe.[8]

On the other hand, the idea that religion was a matter only for individuals and something that could be kept separate from

---

7 This was predominantly the case in the original thirteen colonies, inherited from the British regulations. New states often experimented with ways to limit or expand suffrage, often as a way to attract new citizens. These also included gender, military service, race, religion, tax payment, and wealth. The last state to remove a property qualification for voting was North Carolina in 1856.

8 This is an excellent example of the diversity of opinion present even in a narrow group of people at a specific time – some of Caesar's political peers considered this an illegal war, a brutal suppression and mass murder of native peoples in the name of Rome that discredited them and were sufficient for legal proceedings against him. Part of the elite opposition to this was no doubt the huge wealth that Caesar acquired and the building projects he spent it on, which they worried might make him too popular with non-elites, in the armies and in Rome.

government would have been deeply confusing to any elite Roman of any time, whatever his individual beliefs and religious practices. Proper acknowledgement of the gods, in the domestic and public spheres, was essential to Roman life.

Certainly, any elite ancient Roman would have recognized the enslavement of people as part of the economy of the USA and the brutal reality of an enslaved person's life, although some aspects, particularly the racialization of slavery would have been puzzling to them: as we will see, ideas about both race and slavery were different in important ways in the ancient world.

An elite man of the Roman Republic would surely also have recognized the way the American network of roads spread out across the landscape, connecting the newly conquered places with the existing centres of power. The Romans prided themselves on the efficiency and quality of their road infrastructure and the role it played in maintaining their empire.[9]

We know that Romans in the Republic worried about the 'decline' of their society and its civic values. Elite Roman men wrote about this frequently and they passed laws about it throughout – not just towards the 'fall' of the Republic – that regulated the behaviour of themselves, of elite women, of so-called foreigners, of other minority groups. They passed laws restricting what you could eat and wear, how you could worship, or who you could worship. We don't know how effective these laws were in terms of changing behaviour; the fact that many such laws were repeatedly passed suggests that perhaps they weren't a successful deterrent for long. However, we do know that people were punished and sometimes killed for behaving in a way that was seen as threatening the collective.[10]

9 Indeed, this aspect of Roman roads was often commented on in the British Empire and by men of both Hitler and Mussolini's governments, for example.

10 Many examples of Romans being officially executed for their behaviour would now strike us as religious: Vestal Virgins, a group of elite priestesses with a sacred, symbolic connection to wider Roman society, or worshippers of Dionysus, or early Christians. This is because religion was inseparable from everyday life to Romans and proper practice of religion was always about the health of the wider state, not that of the individual.

We also know that Romans considered the right way to behave to be in the same manner as their ancestors, holding onto what was perceived to be traditional. The *idea* of civilizational decline and its relationship with the right to rule would probably have struck elite Roman men of the Republic as familiar, if not the details.

Having said all that, it is clear from their art, laws, and literature that elite Roman men had very different ideas about the specifics of correct behaviour as well as things like beauty, class, gender, race, religion, sexuality, and many other ways to think about individual and collective identities.

One way to see this is their repeatedly expressed belief that men with pale skin who wore trousers were barbarians, people with customs that were fundamentally different from Rome's. So we can guess that many elite Roman men would have found the idea that they were white to be confusing, likely even offensive.[11]

This gap, between the ways in which ancient Romans understood and expressed their identity in a society and the ways that we think about identity now, is difficult to bridge. After all, buildings, governing institutions, and literary references might look familiar to a Roman but they don't add up to *being* Roman. It is precisely this tricky gap, however, that we need to think about if we want to see both ancient Rome and the modern world in full colour.

Inheriting Rome in the United States of America

The ideas of Rome that circulated and were put to use in the eighteenth-century USA hold the key to this gap. How does the USA, from its position on a totally separate continent, claim to have inherited Rome in some way?

---

11 It seems likely that this would have been different for elite Roman women, for whom pale skin was an indication of wealth and virtue. This meant, among other things, that they did not have to go outside to work and were appropriately covered when they did leave their homes.

The answer is the idea of 'Western civilization' and the central position of ancient Rome within that.

In the 1770s, the men rebelling against the British Empire to form their own state had a conundrum. They needed to create a collective identity strong enough to bring people together to potentially fight multiple empires, because, although the American War of Independence brought those men to fight the British Empire, there were other empires – French, Russian, and Spanish – that all ruled vast swathes of territory in the American continent as well and were therefore a potential threat. This identity, therefore, had to be prestigious. It had to be powerful. It had to be something that spoke to people of all backgrounds to unite them with pride.

Their only real option, they felt, lay with the ancient world and, specifically, ancient Rome.

Of course, everything that made ancient Rome an obvious choice also presented a problem: how could they simultaneously define themselves in opposition to European empires and still lay claim to the ancient societies that, by this stage, were considered to be the ancestors of Europe? If Britain, France, and Spain all claimed to be Roman in some way (as well as the connection to Rome of the German-speaking regions many had immigrated from), how could the men trying to create a new Republic in opposition to them?

The answer lay in one of the Enlightenment talking points we have already encountered, the idea of decline. It wasn't enough to have inherited Rome, men like Joseph Warren argued. You had to keep demonstrating the right to that inheritance through your civic virtue. Britain, along with the rest of Europe, had become decadent, just like the Romans did after the fall of the Republic. The men who would soon define themselves as Americans had demonstrated their bravery in leaving decadent Europe and conquering new territories; they would soon demonstrate their commitment to liberty by fighting tyranny. They would earn the right to call themselves Roman, a right that Europe had lost.

This was, in a way, a Roman idea.

The ancient Romans had lots of ideas and ways to think about people collectively: by birth (according to their mythological descent); by culture (according to their customs, languages and political structures); and by environment (their shared geography).

One example of this thinking was environmental determinism, the idea that one's environment created characteristics in people. For example, people from cold and wet climates, like northern Europe, were believed by Romans to be sluggish and slow learners. However, they were also considered to be courageous because the wet climate made it easy for them to produce more blood, thus allowing them to be reckless in fights. Pale skin and red hair were the classic aesthetic attributes of such people and Germans the most common example. The reverse was believed to be the case for people from hot, dry climates: they were highly intelligent, but not very brave – because the heat of the sun dried up their blood and thus they had to take care to preserve it. The most common example given in Roman texts was the Ethiopians (the word comes from the Greek for 'burnt-face' or 'sunburned' and was originally used to refer to a far wider region than the modern nation state).[12]

It was not just the environment that Romans believed formed character, however: tyrannical political systems could create people with servile characteristics; mythological founders could pass down bravery through generations. Some people were considered different in ways that were respected and even worthy of emulation,

12 Environmental determination was hugely important in scientific racism. As a theory, particularly the version espoused by Aristotle, it has been engaged with for millennia. During the Enlightenment, it was 'proved' by scientists, in connection with other evidence from the natural world, and endorsed by thinkers like Montesquieu before being picked up and adapted by the Nazis and eugenicists of the early-to-mid twentieth century.

while others were dismissed as different in ways that could never be overcome.

Crucially, none of these things necessarily prevented a person from becoming Roman. Indeed, as we have already seen, Romans thought of themselves as immigrants from Asia, refugees who fled Troy to build a new life in Italy. It didn't stop there: the foundation myth of Romulus explains that, in desperate need of men for his new city, he opened his city to criminals who were willing to become Roman. Finding themselves lacking women and being rejected as suitors by the neighbouring cities, they used a religious festival as cover to abduct and rape the women there. These myths might not reflect what actually happened but they do reflect what Romans believed: that anyone could *become* Roman.

There are many ways to see this. Roman citizenship is one – an individual man could be granted citizenship and all the privileges that came with it for noteworthy services to the state; entire regions could be granted citizenship for their men after certain periods of time as allies or subjects (women were always granted specific, different rights, not full citizenship). Citizens were documented and their rights were enshrined in legislation that was repeatedly debated, updated, and sometimes even fought over. These debates and laws give us an insight into ideas about becoming Roman.

Perhaps the easiest way to get a sense of Roman ideas about identity, however, is in the practice of adoption. This was common among elite families and for clearly articulated purposes: Cicero tells us that sons were legally adopted to carry on the family name, to inherit the family wealth, and to be responsible for the household's religious obligations.[13] An adopted son was expected to take on all the legal responsibility of the male head of the family and the customs that came with his new

13 A household was not just the immediate family but often included many generations and branches of the family as well as all of its enslaved workers. They were considered an important, inter-connected unit.

family, resigning those of his previous family – however different.[14] Ancestry and even upbringing were less important in determining identity than customs, the way that one behaved.

For a Roman, citizenship was the most important identity marker and, just like family, citizenship was defined by customs. Correct behaviour could earn citizenship if you weren't fortunate enough to acquire it by birth; failure to behave appropriately could, in rare cases, cost you citizenship (however it had been acquired).[15]

The idea put forward in the eighteenth century, that the European empires had lost their right to be considered Roman by their civic decline and the newly founded USA had earned a claim to Roman-ness by their virtuous behaviour, is one that had its origins in Republican Rome.[16] Behaviour mattered more than ancestry or geography.

And yet, as Frederick Douglass noted, this only applied to white people.

In the early United States of America, white people could earn or lose the inheritance of Rome through their behaviour. For Black or indigenous peoples, ancestry meant it could never be earned.

This idea would have been alien to the ancient Romans. Skin colour did not signal inferiority or superiority; it did not even signify a universal ideal of beauty. It was the scientific racism of the Enlightenment that insisted skin colour indicated irreconcilable mental, psychological, and physical differences that could be ranked hierarchically and used as justification for exploitation and enslavement. For all their idealization

---

14 Frequently these were adult adoptions and, while they were sometimes from the wider family (as in the case of Gaius Julius Caesar, who adopted his great-nephew as his heir), they might also be adoptions from the family of a friend or political ally. Since re-marriage was common in Roman society, children from a wife's former marriage were also frequently adopted.

15 The laws around citizenship and crimes against the state changed over time, according to the concerns and needs of the ruling elite. However, citizenship was always intimately connected with both military service and tax so desertion and lying under oath to the censors about your property were consistently among the most serious offences in Roman law.

16 By the imperial period, this accusation could be – and often was – levelled against Roman citizens for failing to resist one-man rule.

of ancient Rome, most Enlightenment thinkers, including the Founding Fathers, were extremely selective about which Roman ideas they were willing to endorse for themselves.

Inheriting Rome, after all, was about inheriting power.

Inventing Western civilization

The Founding Fathers selected the various existing strands of thought that most suited their purposes and wove them together to create a powerful new unifying identity: 'Western civilization'.

It is here that the popular modern vision of Rome emerged: one of white men and white buildings, one that is connected with democracy and liberty, capitalism and Europe, Christianity and culture. It is a house of mirrors image of Rome, reflected and distorted by different angles and interpretations: still just about recognizable but certainly not the same as the original, no longer the Rome of the ancient Mediterranean but instead the Rome of the West.

This new concept connected the USA with the northern European ancestors of its leading men while marking them as something slightly different, the men who travelled west to seek liberty. In the Rome of 'Western civilization', as men like Joseph Warren defined it, ancient Greekness and Christianity were combined again with Roman-ness – those elements that, together, had disqualified Romanland from being considered properly Roman were now reunited as a prestigious and indivisible tripartite inheritance, worthy of the superpower status they aspired to.

Still, though, this didn't have to mean white. Ancient Greek-speaking societies had been as diverse as ancient Rome, Christianity was a religion that emerged and developed in southwest Asia and North Africa. The literary and material evidence for ideas about group identity in the ancient world were available to scholars in this time but, just like Johann Winckelmann, who we encountered in the opening chapter, most scholars simply refused to see it. They believed in scientific racism, they believed white people were superior, and they scrubbed the paint off the ancient statues they found until they were as white as can be.

Black people repeatedly confounded these ideas and were repeatedly ignored.

In Haiti, from 1791 to 1804, different peoples of colour joined together in a revolution against both enslavement and French colonial rule. They declared themselves to be free people with the right to self-government on the same basis as the American and French revolutions, invoking, among others, the legendary Spartacus. They were dismissed, ignored, fought against, and, eventually, saddled with debt to pay for the freedom they had fought for.

Phillis Wheatley (c.1753–1784), an extraordinarily talented poet, produced works that drew on Latin literature and Biblical traditions and earned her fame around the English-speaking world. She wrote in support of the American Revolution and was invited to visit George Washington in 1776. As an enslaved Black woman, however, there was such disbelief in her ability to have produced the work she did that her first book of poetry was investigated by a legal trial. When the book was published, it was accompanied by a text insulting her background as 'an uncultivated Barbarian from Africa and [. . .] under the Disadvantage of serving as a slave' but verifying her as the author.

There are countless more examples but no amount of proof could overcome this new interpretation; the Rome of 'Western civilization' was a Rome of white buildings, run by white men.

USA citizenship is no longer limited to white men.[17] Most scholars who teach about the ancient world work hard to reveal the complexity, nuance, and difference of the societies they study. Phillis Wheatley

17 Although significant numbers of people, mostly peoples of colour, are still denied citizenship and therefore many basic rights by a very restrictive immigration policy.

is acknowledged as the author of her poetry. Frederick Douglass' descendants have the vote.

And yet, the White House still 'looks' more Roman to most people than the Dome of the Rock. One is a plain white building in a continent that ancient Romans weren't aware existed, the other is decorated with Roman mosaics in a city they knew very well.

How much does this matter?

After all, this book isn't really concerned with what it meant to *be* Roman, although sometimes it helps to look at what the Romans themselves did and said. Nor is this an attempt to assign grades to different interpretations of Roman-ness; as we have already seen, early US political thinkers were not alone in their ideas or in applying those ideas to form a national identity. Some of their interpretations would have seemed deeply strange to an inhabitant of ancient Rome. Many of them, however, would have been very recognizable.

Two things make the interpretation of Rome in the early USA essential to understand: firstly, the specific context of their identity formation and the influential ideas of the European empires, and, secondly, the amount of cultural, financial, intellectual, military, and political power the USA has exercised globally since.

It's not just that we need to take seriously the ideas of a nation with this much influence. The USA is almost synonymous with the concept of 'Western civilization', a fuzzy category that has expanded since its origin to bring together certain parts of the world and differentiate them from the rest and has perhaps had the most to do with the gap between our *idea* of ancient Rome and ancient Rome itself. Western civilization comes up in school textbooks, university courses, popular histories, and political speeches. It's an origin story, an explanation for who we are and how we got here. It's just that this version of the origin story really begins in eighteenth-century Europe and the USA, not first-century Rome (nor fifth-century BCE Athens).

The Protestant Reformation that began in the late fourteenth and early fifteenth centuries in the Holy Roman Empire had been led by people who were frequently unwilling to relinquish their Roman identity while still trying to separate themselves from the Roman Catholic Church. They focused on Roman law, literature, and philosophy over religion and dismissed the colour, pageantry, and pomp of Catholic practices and spaces as pagan. In fact, they literally whitewashed their churches, removing all traces of colour – finding, as we would expect, justifications in ancient texts for the use of white. These new, pale religious spaces were proclaimed as beautiful, serene, and virtuous whereas colour was gaudy, foreign, and ugly.

Throughout the Renaissance and then the Enlightenment, intellectuals defined a new sense of time and history, that of the glorious ancient past, the backwards 'middle ages', and the modern day. The ruins of this glorious ancient past were the most popular tourist attractions of the day and they just happened to be pale cream and white (their original colours long faded by sun exposure or soil erosion, of course), in contrast with the bright colours so popular in the widely-derided medieval spaces. This thinking also infused the racial science of the day: whiteness, it was well-established, was *aesthetically* superior and that contributed to its racial superiority. It was this mindset that made it so easy for Winckelmann to believe that ancient Greek and Roman statues had to be white, and made it so easy for him to be widely believed, against the evidence.

By the time the Founding Fathers were creating their new nation state, these ideas had taken hold, consciously and unconsciously. Bright colours were chaotic, foreign, and pagan, unworthy of intellectual, rational, elite white men. They articulated their identity and power with buildings and statues – in serene white. It was ancient Rome through an Enlightenment, Protestant lens: whitewashed of colour.

As the USA has become increasingly powerful globally, images of these white, neoclassical buildings and statues are beamed around the world, combined with the rhetoric of 'Western civilization'. Over time, the sheer cultural dominance of the USA has made this eighteenth-century interpretation of Rome one that is very difficult to see past.

'The Roman tradition of statues'

We can see the impact of eighteenth-century ideas of Rome in the USA in the world today by returning to statues. Not the statue of Artemis that Johann Winckelmann so firmly believed was white in the 1760s but those that were removed by protestors and local governments during the summer of 2020: in the UK and USA, in Canada and the Caribbean, in Bangladesh and India, in South Africa and New Zealand. Across the former territories of the British Empire, statues commemorating men of the eighteenth, nineteenth, and twentieth centuries were debated, defaced, and destroyed.[18]

Many of these statues were created in a style based on ancient Roman (and Greek) precedents. The clothes and hairstyles of these statues may have been updated for more contemporary references but the locations, the plinths, the poses, and frequently even the accessories, were very much designed to reflect Roman statues, just like the columns and domes of the buildings in which they were so often housed. Our imaginary visitor from ancient Rome would likely have found much to recognize in these statues, despite their lack of colour and togas.

The debate over the removal of statues, however, would probably have confused a Roman.

18 This was far from the first such movement: 1660s England, 1800s French Martinique, 1960s India, 1990s former Soviet states, and 2003 Baghdad are only a few such celebrated examples of statue removal. The 2020 movement was itself rooted in the Rhodes Must Fall campaigns of 2015, begun in Cape Town, South Africa.

In ancient Rome, statues of public figures were regularly adapted, destroyed, or replaced.[19] Heads of statues were often sculpted separately to be removable so they could represent the person with detailed accuracy, while still leaving open the possibility of an exchange at a later date. It was such a common practice to change the person represented by the statue that it seems some might even have come with removable hairstyles and accessories – clip-on beards and fringes – to reflect changing trends. Sometimes, it seems it was just the inscription describing who the statue was supposed to represent and why. At other times, the statue would be entirely removed and recycled. Marble statues could be smashed into pieces and thrown into a kiln to make limestone for new buildings rather than waste them.[20] The appropriate option to take changed according to circumstances but there was no sense that these statues were untouchable.

Modern statue practice in 'the West' might be inspired by ancient Rome but it turns out we just don't see the world in the same way. A hero in an ancient context was a person with a super-human level of ability to influence events, for good *and* bad, to a degree that connected them with the divine in some way. The same was true of the gods: divinity was about power, not morality. Honouring people with a statue, in the same way gods and goddesses were honoured, was an acknowledgement of their ability to influence events. It was a way to earn their favour so they would use their power to help rather than harm you, not a stamp of approval for their specific actions (if you read any epic poem or tragic play from the ancient world, it is clear that being a 'hero' does not make you a 'good' person in a way that we would understand today). Once their ability to directly influence your life had passed, so did the need for the statue.

19 This is not the case for statues depicting divinities, for which there were very different practices.

20 Interestingly, in the early days of the American Revolution, a statue of King George III was not only removed but melted down for bullets to be used by the Revolutionary army.

It's not that an ancient Roman would have considered Edward Colston or Christopher Columbus unworthy of a statue: after all, ancient Romans traded in enslaved people and committed genocides. It is simply that they would not have recognized the need to keep statues of them unless they were still serving a particular purpose, like earning the favour of a powerful descendant or powerful admirer.

Statues, in ancient Rome, were a language of power. More than that, they were *understood* as expressing power.

This is the major distinction, the gap in understanding between ancient Rome and the present day that helps us see the world more clearly. Every reference to Rome, every interpretation of Rome, that we have seen in this book has been about power. On some level, we do know this: otherwise we would not care so deeply about statues of men who lived and died decades or even centuries ago. But, scrubbed of the metaphorical or literal paint, we struggle to recognize this language of power clearly. Instead, we file it under 'heritage', echoing the ideas of the men and women in the eighteenth and nineteenth centuries who were using Rome to define themselves in connection with some people – and in opposition to others.

This vision of Rome has been so influential that it is now hard to see past it, even when we know how it came about. It is not just comforting and familiar, it cements a connection with people we don't know but instinctively feel are similar to us in some way, whether that is across an ocean in the modern day or 2,000 years ago. It allows us to explain differences that seem too deep for us to bridge the gap. It tells us who we are – and who we are not.

So where does that leave us? Back at the start, of course.

10

Conclusion: All Roads Lead to Rome

In the heart of Rome, at the centre of a large square of glistening grey cobblestones, worn smooth by millions of visitors, an obelisk towers proudly upwards. At its base, water emerges from the mouths of stone lions to pool in the bases of four fountains. All around the square stand pale white buildings with domed roofs. The ancient Via Flaminia, the road north, runs through a monumental, triple-arched gateway, inscribed with Latin that honours its founder. A stone's throw away runs the river Tiber, the city's lifeblood. The scent of poplar trees wafts gently on the breeze, as the Mediterranean sun beats down.

This is the Piazza del Popolo, one of the many busy tourist hotspots in the modern Italian city of Rome. It is popular in photos and paintings, both as a backdrop and as a subject in its own right, a perfect snapshot of the Eternal City.

It is probably not a surprise to learn that all is not quite as it seems in this iconic Roman scene.

The piazza itself was redeveloped in the early ninetenth century, in the neoclassical style that stripped the colour from ancient Rome. The two domed churches are from the late seventeenth century, and the monumental gate dates from a slightly earlier rebuilding phase in the mid-sixteenth century. That Latin inscription refers to Pope Pius IV

217

(1499–1565), of the Medici family. The lion-fountains were constructed as part of the late sixteenth-century rebuild ordered by Pope Sixtus V (1521–90) and the obelisk's position in *this* particular square dates to the same period. In just this one part of Rome, we can peel back layers and layers that seem ancient but, in reality, only go back a few centuries.

The obelisk, though, goes back a few millennia – it is older than the city of Rome itself by around 500 years.

If you visit Rome today, the chances are high that you will encounter at least one obelisk. There are currently thirteen ancient examples in the city, as well as five modern versions (There are only thirty ancient obelisks that we know of still standing in the world, including Egypt). The history of these monuments, all made in ancient Egypt, tells us something important about how ancient Romans saw themselves.

The obelisk in the Piazza del Popolo dates back to the period of ancient Egypt known as the New Kingdom (1550–1070 BCE). Its construction was ordered during the reign of pharaoh Seti I (r.1290–1279 BCE) and its first home was Heliopolis, the city of the sun.[1] It arrived in Rome on the order of Augustus, the first man to rule Rome alone, in 10 BCE – more than 1,200 years later. Decades previously, Augustus and his allies had warned their fellow Romans about the dangers of Egypt, as personified by Cleopatra.[2] The luxuries, religious traditions, and enormous wealth of Egypt would tempt good old-fashioned Romans away from their values, just as Cleopatra had tempted Marcus Antonius away from his Roman wife (and Augustus's sister). Egypt was presented as foreign, a handy way to make the fight between two rivals look less like another civil war (or worse, a family squabble inflicted on everyone else) and more like a battle for Rome's soul.

---

1 This is the Roman name for the city, based on the Greek name. Locally, we think it was known as 'the Pillars' or 'the House of Ra'.

2 In this, they were following in the footsteps of earlier elite Roman politicians who preached against the dangers of contact with powerful and wealthy cultures like the Carthaginians, Egyptians, Greeks, and Persians.

Twenty years after Augustus' victory over his political rival (or Rome's deadly foe, as you prefer), he went to an enormous effort to have two Egyptian obelisks transported across the Mediterranean. When they finally arrived in Rome, the best engineers were put to work erecting them in their new home.[3] In 10 BCE, that home was the Campus Martius, one of the many public spaces of Rome that Augustus was dramatically rebuilding to make the city fit to be the capital of an empire (in his own record of his accomplishments, Augustus said that he 'found Rome a city of brick and left her one of marble'). On the pedestal, a new inscription was carved to tell the viewers that, having conquered Egypt for the people of Rome, Augustus dedicated this obelisk to Rome. A monument to one of Egypt's dangerously foreign gods now lived in the heart of Rome.

The obelisk was rediscovered in 1587, when another ruler of Rome sought to demonstrate his power with a rebuilding of the city. This time it was Pope Sixtus V who was digging up some parts of the past and destroying others to tell a story about the present.[4] Again, it was erected by the best engineers in Rome, this time in the Piazza del Popolo, where public executions were held. The inscription was updated and the obelisk topped with a cross, a reminder of the authority it now represented.

What does this ancient Egyptian monument, covered in hieroglyphs, standing in the centre of modern Rome tell us about the ancient Roman view of the world? Why did Augustus go to such extraordinary lengths to ship these gigantic representations of Egyptian religion to Rome, having spent decades warning about the dangers of Egypt and its gods?

---

3 This was no small effort: the Flaminio Obelisk that stands in the Piazza del Popolo is more than 23 metres high and weighs more than 200 tonnes. Pliny the Elder (23–79 CE) gives some detail on how they were transported; it was clearly considered an astonishing feat at the time.

4 Sixtus was more than happy to use ancient monuments for his building projects in a way that often elicits gasps of horror from tourists now, despite being common practice for much of the city's history. Three other obelisks as well as a number of other monumental columns and statues were reused and other ancient buildings were destroyed for raw materials.

The answer, of course, is power. The obelisks didn't just represent his military victory and his political authority over Egypt, they also represented Rome's technological ability to transport anything it wanted from anywhere and the finances to pay for it. With Augustus in charge, Rome could have whatever it desired. Specifically, it could have the power of fabulously, famously wealthy places like Egypt.

This book has traced more than 1,500 years of people and places looking to Rome as an example of how to express power, sometimes in surprising ways. The obelisk tells us something about where the ancient Romans looked, about who their examples of power were. The answer is not just Egypt but Carthage, Persia, and Troy: great empires of Africa and Asia.

We have already seen how the *Aeneid*, Virgil's epic account of ancient Rome's origins, traces Roman history back to the fall of Troy. We have seen how, as the Romans recovered from a series of civil wars and confronted their transition from republican rule to a dynastic system, they formed a new collective identity by reaching for the prestige of the past.

Virgil's poem does more than position the Romans as Trojan refugees, however. One third of this Roman epic is spent with Aeneas and his fellow Trojan refugees on the North African coast, in the newly founded city that will one day become known as Carthage. Rome's own origin story takes us on a journey from one legendary city to another, highlighting the importance of both Troy and Carthage, before its hero reaches the Italian coast. This plot device allows the poet to subtly play around with a number of important narratives, including setting up the rivalry between Carthage and Rome that would dominate Rome's early history. It also reinforces just how important Carthage was to ancient Rome.

It is easy now to see Carthage through the lens of its wars with Rome, an empire doomed to be absorbed by its rival (partly because most of the local records of Carthage were destroyed by the Romans, along with the rest of the city, at the conclusion of the third and final Punic War in 146 BCE, so it is difficult to see Carthage on its own terms). We zoom in on the years between 264 and 146 BCE, when the two powers fought three devastating conflicts collectively known as the Punic Wars, framed as one of the first major tests along Rome's road to power. We might pause to gasp at the audacity of Hannibal's famous march across the Alps and perhaps the more military-minded among us pore over the details of the campaigns by Quintus Fabius Maximus Verrucosus and Publius Cornelius Scipio Africanus that ultimately defeated him. Some of us might glance at a map and observe that the Carthaginian imperial provinces form the basis of Rome's empire.

Despite these reminders, despite the starring role of Carthage as a flourishing, model city in the *Aeneid*, it is often forgotten just how important Carthage was in the ancient Mediterranean. Far back in the mists of Roman history, in 509 BCE, Carthage was well-established as the local superpower. And Carthage certainly was a superpower compared with Rome: its territories were spread around the Mediterranean, its navy dominated the seas and trade, and its wealth allowed it to pay the best rates for mercenary armies. The first trade agreement with Carthage was recorded by the Romans on bronze tablets, a sign of its significance to them – it needed to be indestructible. The two remained allies for hundreds of years; not surprising, since the only way to grow as a new city state in this region was to keep the Carthaginians on-side. Carthage's system of government was even praised by ancient Greek-thinkers like Aristotle for the way it balanced aristocracy, democracy, and monarchy – the only non-Greek-speaking government to be given such recognition.

When Rome was finally confident enough to go to war against their ally in 264 BCE, over control of Greek-speaking Sicily, they had to capture a Carthaginian naval vessel and reverse engineer it to build their own navy, which didn't exist until then. Rome wanted to learn from the best.

By the early years of the second century BCE, Rome had finally succeeded in destroying the regional superpower to the south of them but their attention had already been dragged east: to Persia, where the real regional superpowers lay.[5] First to the Seleukids, the dynasty that succeeded to Alexander the Great's territories from the eastern Mediterranean into central Asia from 312 to 63 BCE; then the Arsakids, known to Rome as the Parthians, who slowly conquered the territories east of Anatolia, ruling from 247 BCE to 224 CE; and finally the Sasanians, the dominant cultural, economic, and military power of western Asia from 224 to 651 CE.

We can see how important Persian empires were to the Romans by once again looking at the Augustan period, the time when Romans grappled with their identity, guided by their new ruler. One of the great military defeats of Rome, as they understood it themselves, had been the destruction by the Parthians of seven legions under the command of Marcus Licinius Crassus at Carrhae in 53 BCE.[6] Such was the scale of the defeat that Crassus was killed and the eagle standards of the legions, deeply significant symbols of Rome, were captured. Augustus negotiated a peace settlement in 20 BCE that, amongst other things, secured the return of the eagles to Rome.

This was a huge propaganda opportunity for Augustus and he made the most of it, representing the Parthians as not only having returned Rome's military symbols but as having formally submitted to Rome's

---

5 It is very simplistic to group these three empires as 'Persian'; the Seleukids, for instance, spoke Greek – a reminder of how deeply interconnected the ancient Eurasian world was and how differently they conceived of and marked their collective identities. For our purposes, however, all three of these empires ruled much of the former Achaemenid Persian imperial territories, engaged deeply with Persian traditions of power, and were conceived of by their Roman peers as in some way Persian.

6 The Parthian forces were quite small, they suffered minimal losses, and seemed generally unconcerned by the event – increasing the damage to Rome's sense of its reputation.

authority. Three separate entries of the *Res Gestae,* Augustus' official record of his acts, deal with examples of his authority on behalf of Rome over the Parthians.[7] On coins issued by the Senate, on new buildings around the city of Rome, including a triumphal arch, and in his official iconography, Augustus depicted the Parthians retreating in battle, returning the standards and kneeling to Rome.[8] These quickly became part of imperial Rome's visual culture and later emperors would also use these images to project their own power, partly to connect themselves with Augustus and partly because, of all the foreign powers Rome encountered, Parthia was *the* foreign power to beat.

In fact, Rome's foreign policy was dominated by its rivalry with Persian powers until the end of the Sasanian Empire in 651 CE. The Roman historian Cassius Dio (*c.*165–*c.*235 CE) observed the wars between the two seemed never-ending and certainly successive emperors seemed to have jumped at the chance to present themselves as victors over the Persians. Military matters in the east almost always took precedence over those in the west, a matter of economics and access to trade as well as prestige. When it came to the international power relations of western Asia, Persia had the most important seat at the table.[9]

This focus on Persia continued to be translated into Rome's visual culture. At an imperial level, it was developed by regular diplomatic exchanges between the two powers. This was also fuelled by the interest of Roman elites in getting their hands on the latest fashionable Persian goods, from stunning silk textiles to elaborately carved metalwork.

By the fifth century, these two empires had created a visual language

---

7 There are thirty-five sections of the *Res Gestae* in total.

8 It is important to note that this is the *Roman* version of events; the agreement made with Augustus does not seem to have been so significant to the Parthians, who quite quickly ignored the other terms they supposedly agreed to.

9 If we zoom out further, however, the empires of east Asia would emerge as the dominant powers – certainly from an economic point of view.

of power to communicate with one another, elements of which had spread across their respective empires and areas of influence. The Oratorio di Santa Maria, built in the eighth century by the Germanic-speaking Lombards in present-day north-east Italy, has many details we can also find in late Sasanian examples – in presenting themselves as Roman, they drew, knowingly or not, on Persian visual traditions. This is just one of many, many examples in elite art and architecture across Afro-Eurasia; we encountered more in Chapter 8.

Even today, we can see the results of Rome's references to Persia in their projection of power: the official mascots of the Paris 2024 Olympic and Paralympic Games, named 'The Phryges', are based on the Phrygian cap. The history of this one symbol and its journey from Persepolis to Paris could fill a book on its own, detailing the connections, confusions, and cultural exchanges of Eurasia for the past 2,500 years. The short version is that, in Revolutionary France, it was associated with formerly enslaved Romans and liberty and allowed the revolutionaries to connect themselves with Rome while opposing the aristocracy and monarchy.[10] In ancient Rome, the Phrygian Cap was used to visually identify someone as Persian – *their* major reference point for power.

We have one final stopping point, a place where all these threads come together in very recent history.

That place is Tadmor, an oasis town in Syria that dates back at least as far as the second millennium BCE. Its fertile soil, water supply, and advantageous position made it a common stopping place for Eurasian trade networks. For a time, it accumulated wealth and adeptly exploited its position on the frontier between two empires to increase its regional importance. Stunning private and public art and architecture that combined local and regional traditions to create a unique style articulated the community's place in the world to their many visitors.

---

10 They appear to have confused it with a similar piece of Roman headgear that was given to formerly enslaved people when they were manumitted.

For a few years, it became the capital of a new empire led by a warrior queen. After, its power decreased and the stream of visitors declined. Its people remained, however – generation after generation, century after century. They lived in and around the monumental architecture, cared for the land, and produced crafts to trade. In the 1980s, a French military barracks nearby was used as a prison, famous for human rights abuses and a massacre. In 2015, it became famous all around the world.

Tadmor is more commonly known by its Roman name: Palmyra.

As Palmyra, it is a city famous for destruction and ruins: first, by the Romans in 273, when the Emperor Aurelian brutally repressed Queen Zenobia's rebellion by destroying much of the city, and again in 2015, when it was occupied by ISIS and those same ruins became the focus of international attention.

Despite the devastation wreaked by the Romans on Palmyra and the restriction for a time of its trading rights, and thus its ability to get back on its feet, the city survived. It became a centre of Christianity, important enough to have a bishop under the rule of Romanland, alongside a significant Jewish population. The Temple of Baal, built in the first century and dedicated to a local god, became a church, then a mosque, and then a communal shelter for family homes – transformed over time in response to local needs.

Palmyra's ruins attracted visitors just as its markets once did, under Umayyad and Abbasid rule, through to Ottoman government, and into the modern day. Descriptions, paintings, and sketches of those ruins (rarely featuring the inhabitants of the town) were part of the European revival of interest in the ancient world from the seventeenth century, brought back by tourists who tended not to mention their local hosts and tour guides. The neoclassical style of architecture we have seen deployed again and again in this book to project power was very much inspired by sketches of Palmyra; it is actually quite likely that the Great Seal of the United States is partly inspired by the town. Kaiser Wilhelm II, the last German emperor, visited in 1898 and encouraged archaeological research there. In the 1930s, a French archaeological team evicted the inhabitants living in the old town and 'restored' the site, discarding centuries of historical remains to get to the Roman version.

These regional and international histories collided in 2015 when ISIS, having occupied Tadmor for the local symbolism of destroying its notorious prison, realized they were also in control of a site with global symbolism. The international media furore over their occupation suggested that, to many, Palmyra's Roman-era ruins mattered more than Tadmor's people and so ISIS filmed themselves destroying many of those ruins.[11] They also publicly murdered Khaled al-Asaad, the Syrian scholar and curator of the archaeological site and distributed images of their acts on social media to maximize their impact.

The impact was enormous. More than fifty projects sprang up, dedicated to 'preserving' and 'protecting' Palmyra's Roman heritage using cutting-edge technologies. A partial recreation of Emperor Septimius Severus' third-century Arch of Triumph was produced and transported from city to city in Europe and the USA, photographed and reported on everywhere it went. Palmyra's ruins had the attention of international audiences once more.

In 2016, Russian forces assisted Syrian President Bashar al-Assad in driving ISIS from Tadmor-Palmyra. In celebration, a classical Russian orchestra held a concert in front of international reporters, local soldiers, Russian officials, and UNESCO representatives. It was shown live on Russian state television, part of a broadcast that included a speech by President Vladimir Putin about the preservation of global heritage and an introduction by the conductor, Valery Gergiev, who

---

11 They also filmed themselves destroying some funerary sculptures; the vast majority of their engagement with the archaeological remains of the site, however, was to loot and sell what they could on the black market.

described the performance as a protest 'against barbarians who have destroyed monuments of world culture'.

The venue for this concert was the same ancient theatre that ISIS had used for many of their public executions the year before: a Roman stage for the projection of power.

Where does this final stopping point leave us?

To put it another way: do we learn history to avoid repeating past mistakes or to help see ourselves a little more clearly?

Rome is about power, a way to define and present one group of people as superior to everyone else, as this recent use of Palmyra's ruins shows. In languages like Arabic, English, French, German, Greek, Italian, Portuguese, Russian, Spanish, and Turkish, in languages we no longer speak but still read in medieval manuscripts, and in a visual language that we can all see, Rome has been used and interpreted as power again and again.

This interpretation of Rome as power is what links sixth-century Constantinople, thirteenth-century Frankfurt, and twenty-first-century Moscow; it's a thread that runs through the Ottoman, British, German, and Italian imperial projects; it's why we can connect eighth-century Baghdad with eighteenth-century Virginia. It's also why we see so many of these places as inextricably opposed in the present day: this idea of power is one that dominates, that is superior to others. It can't be shared.

But that interpretation of Rome is not an inevitable legacy of a long-gone empire. It is a consequence of the way that people have chosen to see Rome and what they have focused on as meaningful to them. The people and places explored throughout this book are also a reminder of the many different ways we can see Rome – and of the many different ways that Romans saw themselves. Instead of using Rome to articulate oppositions, we could consider how this long and varied history of engaging with Rome reveals our many connections.

Seeing this history clearly doesn't change the world we live in but perhaps understanding the choices people made before us helps us with the decisions we will go on to make ourselves. Perhaps it gives us new ways to see the world, new roads to take.

Want to Know More?

'Citation is how we acknowledge our debt to those who came before; those who helped us find our way when the way was obscured because we deviated from the paths we were told to follow.'

Sara Ahmed, *Living a Feminist Life*,
Duke University Press, 2017.

There are so many scholars whose brilliant work I have relied upon to form my thoughts in the process of researching and writing this book. Here, I have highlighted the people whose research I particularly relied upon and suggested some of their public scholarship that you might enjoy, if you want to learn more. I have included podcasts and writing intended for a popular audience, as well as books that you might be able to find in your local bookstore or library. These suggestions are organized by chapter to help the reader, although, of course, the influence of these scholars is not limited to just one section or chapter.

This is intended as a way for me to properly acknowledge those who helped me find my way and as a place for interested readers to start exploring. If you are looking for a more exhaustive list of references, a full bibliography follows.

Chapter 1: Introduction

In this first chapter, I want to recommend the public scholarship of Dr Sarah E. Bond and, particularly, her piece entitled *Why We Need to Start Seeing the Classical World in Color* on the website Hyperallergic. You can find a lot more of her work and links to other public scholarship on the ancient world at https://sarahemilybond.com/.

I also want to acknowledge Dr Aimee Hinds Scott's blogpost, *Pygmalion, Polychromy, and Inclusiveness in Classics,* which helped me think much more clearly about the layers of history in interpretations of Rome.

If you want to become more familiar with the ancient world for yourself, you can find an excellent collection of links to freely accessible material and textual resources at the Working Classicists website https://www. workingclassicists.com.

Chapter 2: The New Rome

I could not have written this chapter without the work of Dr Anthony Kaldellis, Dr Marion Kruse, and Dr Leonora Neville. If you want to know more about this topic, their work is a good place to start. Helpfully, Dr Kaldellis has a podcast series called Byzantium & Friends, on which these other two excellent scholars have guested.

Of the many fascinating topics covered on this podcast, I would especially recommend:

- *Byzantium & Friends, Episode 15. When does Roman history end and Byzantine begin? with Marion Kruse*
- *Byzantium & Friends, Episode 43. Is it time to abandon the rubric "Byzantium"?, with Leonora Neville*

If you want to read more in-depth scholarship on the specific issues explored in this chapter, I would recommend:

- *Anthony Kaldellis, Romanland: Ethnicity and Empire in Byzantium*
- *Marion Kruse, The Politics of Roman Memory: From the Fall of the Western Empire to the Age of Justinian*

Chapter 3: The Holy Roman Empire

In this chapter, I would like to acknowledge the work of Dr Judith Herrin and Dr Eleanor Janega. In different ways, their work helped me to rethink my own ideas on this topic. Dr Herrin has featured on the Byzantium & Friends podcast:

- *Byzantium & Friends, Episode 41. Ravenna, Capital of Empire Between East and West, with Judith Herrin*

Dr Janega co-hosts the BBC's *Gone Medieval* podcast as well as the *We're Not So Different* podcast, both of which are filled with fascinating episodes on this period of history. You can find more of her public scholarship on her website, https://going-medieval.com/

She has also written two books on the topic:

- *Eleanor Janega, The Middle Ages: A Graphic History*
- *Eleanor Janega, The Once and Future Sex*

Dr Herrin has written many books on Romanland (or Byzantium). To learn more about its role in medieval Europe, I recommend:

- *Judith Herrin, Byzantium: The Surprising Life of a Medieval Empire*
- *Judith Herrin, Ravenna: Capital of Empire, Crucible of Europe*

Chapter 4: The Third Rome

In particular, I found the research of Dr Maria Alessia Rossi, Dr Eugene Smelyansky, Dr Alexandra Vukovich, and Dr Monica White extremely helpful and interesting while researching this chapter.

Some podcasts featuring these scholars can be found here:

- *Byzantium & Friends, Episode 115. Imaginary Byzantiums in modern Russia, with Eugene Smelyansky*

- *Well That Aged Well, Episode 186. Kievan/Rus, with Alexandra Vukovich*

- *Byzantium & Friends, Episode 114. Byzantium and the early Rus', with Monica White*

You can find an interview with Dr Rossi and one of her colleagues, Dr Alice Isabella Sullivan, discussing their research on links between Romanland/Byzantium and Eastern Europe in *Medieval World* magazine, November 2020 issue: https://www.karwansaraypublishers. com/blogs/medieval-world-blog/byzantium-eastern-europe. You can also explore the art, culture, and history of this region for yourself on their digital platform, North of Byzantium: https://www. northofbyzantium.org/.

Dr Vukovich has worked with TORCH (the Oxford Research Centre in the Humanities) on a number of podcasts, YouTube videos, and blogposts to introduce people to her research and the wider world of medieval northern Eurasia; for example: https://www.torch.ox.ac.uk/ article/orientalism-in-2020.

Chapter 5: Conquering Rome: the Ottoman Empire

I want to begin this section by acknowledging the team behind the Ottoman History Podcast: Dr Sam Dolbee, Dr Can Gümüş, Dr Chris Gratien, Dr Önder Eren Akgül, Dr Zeinab Azarbadegan, Dr Marianne Dhenin, Dr Susanna Ferguson, Dr Matthew Ghazarian, Dr Shireen Hamza, Dr Maryam Patton, and Dr Brittany White. This digital platform is an extraordinary resource that has been a gateway for me into so much of the amazing research on the Ottomans.

Additionally, I want to highlight the research of Dr Molly Greene, Dr Gülru Necipoğlu, and Dr Diana Mishkova, which underpinned my thinking in this chapter in important ways.

- *Ottoman History Podcast Episode 217. Greeks in the Ottoman Empire, with Molly Greene*

- *Byzantium & Friends 102. Byzantium and Balkan national identities, with Diana Mishkova*

Dr Necipoğlu is a hugely influential scholar of art and architecture who has published on a wide range of topics, including artistic exchange between different cultures and empires. Two of her books are now available for free online:

- *Architecture, Ceremonial, and Power: The Topkapi Palace in the Fifteenth and Sixteenth Centuries, 1992; available on the MIT Press website.*

- *The Topkapi Scroll: Geometry and Ornament in Islamic Architecture, 1996; available on the Getty Publications website.*

Chapter 6: Pax Romana, Pax Britannica

Again, I want to begin by acknowledging an entire podcast series and the team behind it: *Khameleon Classics* by Shivaike Shah, Malin Hay, Stephanie Chungu, Sara Tabar, Cara Vaitilingam, and Francesca Amewudah-Rivers. This series explores some of the most meaningful ideas and interpretations of the ancient world and their consequences for the world we live in, in conversation with expert scholars. Each episode is fascinating. I have highlighted two here:

- *Khameleon Classics, Episode 12: Classics and the British Empire in India, with Phiroze Vasunia*

- *Khameleon Classics, Episode 18: Classics and Colonial Presences in Egypt, with Heba Abd el Gawad and Usama Ali Gad*

Additionally, I would not have found my way in this chapter without the scholarship of Dr Arabella Currie, Margaret Freeman, and Dr Phiroze Vasunia.

Dr Currie specializes in the ways people interpret the past to think about the present. Two examples of her work that I enjoyed are *William Golding's use of the Trojan War*, which you can find here: https://william-golding.co.uk/goldings-trojan-war and *Ireland and the classics*, available here: http://www.apgrd.ox.ac.uk/learning/short-guides/ireland-and-the-classics.

Margaret Freeman hosts the podcast *Nomads, Past and Present*, where she explores the architecture, material culture, and histories of nomadic peoples and their interactions with empires. I also recommend *Something in the Sand: The Haunted Landscapes of Bedouin Nomadic Pastoralists*, here: https://niche-canada.org/2023/10/17/something-in-the-sand-the-haunted-landscapes-of-bedouin-nomadic-pastoralists/ and *Between a Rock and a High Place: Picturing Bedouin Geographies in ibn Sbayyil's "Arabian Romantic"*, available here: https://www.libraryofarabicliterature.org/2023/bedouin-geographies/.

Finally, Dr Vasunia's book is indispensable for anyone wanting to know more about this topic:

- *The Classics and Colonial India*

Chapter 7: Roman fasces, European fascism

I am very much indebted to the research of Dr Samuel Agbamu, Dr Zena Kamash, Dr Olivette Otele, and Dr Helen Roche; this chapter is considerably better for my engagement with their work.

These podcast episodes will introduce you to the work of Dr Kamash, Dr Otele, and Dr Roche:

- *Khameleon Classics, Episode 20: Tadmor-Palmyra: Reconstruction and Digitisation, with Zena Kamash*
- *History Extra podcast, African Europeans with Olivette Otele*
- *Khameleon Classics, Episode 8: Classics in Nazi Germany, with Helen Roche*

Dr Agbamu has written some excellent introductory pieces on this topic, including *Rethinking Rome: Cityscapes of Empire, Ancient and Modern*, which you can find here: https://bsr.ac.uk/ rethinking-rome-cityscapes-of-empire-ancient-and-modern/ and *Whose Aeneid? Imperialism, Fascism, and the Politics of Reception*, available here: https://classicalstudies.org/scs-blog/samagbamu/ blog-whose-aeneid-imperialism-fascism-and-politics-reception

You can find some of Dr Kamash's public research on the ancient world, such as *Three ancient cities to rival London, Paris and New York*, here: https://theconversation.com/three-ancient-cities-to-rival-london-paris-and-new-york-48107 and *From washing machines to computers: how the ancients invented the modern world*, here: https:// theconversation.com/from-washing-machines-to-computers-how-the-ancients-invented-the-modern-world-53147.

Dr Roche has a personal website where you can find many more resources: www.helenroche.com.

Finally, I recommend Dr Otele's excellent book:

- *African Europeans*

Chapter 8: Rivalling Rome: the empires of early Islam

This chapter came from my PhD research. I would therefore like to take the opportunity to introduce you to some of my favourite public scholarship on the early Islamic world, which has influenced how I communicate my own work. These are Dr Glaire D Anderson, Dr Amira Bennison, Dr Ali A Olomi, and Dr Rachel Schine.

Dr Anderson and Dr Olomi both worked on the videogame *Assassin's Creed Mirage*, which is set during ninth-century Baghdad and is extremely well-researched and beautifully produced.

Dr Anderson has a personal website filled with resources, including a number of interviews and talks she has given about her work on various video games: https://glairedanderson.com/

Dr Bennison is a frequent expert guest on podcast episodes, such as:

- *In Our Time: The Almoravid Empire*

- *The Essay – The Islamic Golden Age, Episode 17: Cities of Learning*

- *You're Dead to Me: Al-Andalus*

I also highly recommend her book:

- *The Great Caliphs: The Golden Age of the 'Abbasid Empire*

Dr Olomi co-hosted two series of the official Ubisoft podcast *Echoes of History*, with Deana Hassanein, to accompany *Assassin's Creed Mirage*:

- *Baghdad Soundwalks*

- *Figures of Baghdad*

Additionally, Dr Olomi is the host of the *Head On History* podcast, which covers a range of topics and is a great introduction to Islamic history. He is a prolific public scholar and you can find more resources on his personal website: http://aliolomi.com/.

Finally, I love Dr Schine's blog *Lyric Poets*, where she writes about classical and contemporary lyricism in Arabic and English. You can find the archive at: https://www.tumblr.com/lyricpoets and another example of her writing, *Boss Moves Are Bloody Moves,* here: https://www.libraryofarabicliterature.org/2018/antarah-and-cardi-b/

Chapter 9: The New Republic: USA edition

There has been a huge amount of research on this topic, for both academic and public audiences. I am especially grateful to Dr Rebecca Futo Kennedy, Dr Jackie Murray, Dr Denise Eileen McCoskey, and Dr Dan-el Padilla Peralta for lighting up this area for me. I could not have written this chapter without their excellent scholarship.

You can find some introductory podcast episodes to the work of Dr Kennedy, Dr Murray, and Dr McCoskey here:

- *Khameleon Classics, Episode 2: Race in Antiquity, with Denise McCoskey*

- *Khameleon Classics, Episode 16: Classics and Eugenics in the USA, with Rebecca Futo Kennedy*

- *Khameleon Classics, Episode 27: Classics and the Reconstruction, with Jackie Murray*

Another fantastic resource for you to explore the ancient world and its reception today is Eidolon, which can be found at:

- *https://eidolon.pub/*

This site includes pieces by Drs Kennedy, McCoskey, and Padilla Peralta, as well as many others. I particularly recommend:

- *White People Explain Classics to Us by Young In Chae*

- *We Condone It by Our Silence by Rebecca Futo Kennedy*

- *Why I Teach About Race and Ethnicity in the Classical World by Rebecca Futo Kennedy*

- *Bad to the Bone by Denise Eileen McCoskey*

- *What Would James Baldwin Do? by Denise Eileen McCoskey*

- *Barbarians Inside the Gate* by Dan-el Padilla Peralta
- *From Damocles to Socrates* by Dan-el Padilla Peralta

Chapter 10: Conclusion: All Roads Lead to Rome

If the people as well as the ruins of Palmyra have caught your attention, I encourage you to visit *Palmyrene Voices*, a group that works to support the local people of Tadmor-Palmyra in returning to their homes, rebuilding their city, and honouring the full range of their heritage.

If you want to know more about the ways people have used the past to build the present, I very much recommend reading *Uncivilised* by Subhadra Das and *The West: A New History of an Old Idea* by Naoíse Mac Sweeney. For a longer and more detailed history of these contacts and connections, tracing our world back 4,000 years, *How the World Made the West* by Josephine Quinn is also excellent.

A full bibliography for each chapter can be found next.

Full Bibliography

Collected primary sources/translations used in manuscript

1.

Winckelmann, Johann Joachim. *Geschichte der Kunst des Alterthums*, 1764

https://digi.ub.uni-heidelberg.de/diglit/winckelmann1764

Part One

Plutarch, *Life of Julius Caesar*, 61

2.

Niketas Choniates. *Nicetae Choniatae Historia*, ed. Jan Louis van Dieten, Berlin, 1975: 585

3.

Conring, Hermann. De origine iuris Germanici, 1643

https://pure.mpg.de/pubman/faces/ViewItemOverviewPage. jsp?itemId=item_2430805

Godfrey of Viterbo. *Gesta Friderici I et Heinrici VI*, ed. Georg Waitz, Hanover, 1872

4.

Ivan IV's justification for wars, in van den Bercken, Wil. *Holy Russia and Christian Europe. East and West in the Religious Ideology of Russia*, SCM Press, 1999: p. 152

Michelangelo Gianetti: 'All the glory of all the heroes presented by Rome / All the glory of those men embodied in you.' in Proskurina, Vera. *Creating the Empress: Politics and Poetry in the Age of Catherine II*, Academic Studies Press, 2011: p. 37

Nikolai Patrushev on security and Sophia Palaiologina: 'A Byzantine Sermon,' The Economist, February 14, 2008: https://www.economist.com/europe/2008/02/14/a-byzantine-sermon

Aleksandr Dugin: https://vk.com/@rossia3-a-g-dugin-absolut-vizantizma

Part One

Cicero, *In Verrem*: 2.4.14

Seneca the Younger, *Medea*: 196.

Tacitus, *Agricola*: 30

Augustus, *Res Gestae*: 2

5.

Bayezid II: The Jewish Encyclopedia: a descriptive record of the history, religion, literature, and customs of the Jewish people from the earliest times to the present day, Vol. 2 Isidore Singer, Cyrus Adler, Funk and Wagnalls, 1912 p. 460

Ottoman titles in Kołodziejczyk, Dariusz. 'Khan, Caliph, Tsar and Imperator: Multiple Identities.' in *Universal Empire: A Comparative Approach to Imperial Culture and Representation in Eurasian History.*, Dariusz Kolodziejczyk and Peter Fibiger Bang (Eds.), Cambridge University Press, 2012, pp. 175–193

6.

Leathes' claims in Symonds, Richard. *Oxford and Empire. The last lost cause?*, Oxford University Press, 1991

Lucas, Charles Prestwood. *Greater Rome and Greater Britain*, Clarendon Press, 1912

Cecil Rhodes in Baker, Herbert, and W. T. Stead, *Cecil Rhodes: The Man and His Dream*, Books of Rhodesia, 1977, p. 161

Lord Palmerston, speech, House of Commons, 25 June 1850: https://www.oxfordreference.com/display/10.1093/acref/9780191826719.001.0001/q-oro-ed4-00008130

Macaulay's 'Minute' on Indian education: the India Office Records in the British Library: F/4/1846, No. 77633, 127–46:

https://dn790002.ca.archive.org/0/items/Minutes_201311/MinutesNew.pdf

Trevelyan, Charles Edward. *On The Education Of The People Of India*, 1838, 196–7

https://archive.org/details/oneducationofpeoooochar/page/n1/mode/2up

Baring, Evelyn. *Modern Egypt*, MacMillan, 1908, p. 69

Rutilius Claudius Namatianus quote in Baring (91):

https://thelatinlibrary.com/rutilius.html

Glubb, John. 'A Monthly Report on the Administration of the Transjordan Desert for the Month of December 1936,' CO 831/41/11, The National Archives, Kew, United Kingdom

Zissu, Theodore AL 'Notes on the Negeb: Palestine's Empty Half,' n.d., GB165-0312 Zissu, Middle East Centre Archive, St. Antony's College, Oxford, United Kingdom

Treaty of Versailles, Article 22

Lord Curzon's letter to George Hamilton, dated 23 April 1900,

https://www.qdl.qa/en/archive/81055/vdc_100160355870.0x00008b

Nehru, Jawaharlal. *Glimpses of World History*, Penguin Books, 1934: p. 117

Lugard, Frederick. *The Dual Mandate in British Tropical Africa*, Blackwood & Sons, 1922, p. 618–19

Horton, James Africanus Beale. *West African Countries and Peoples*, W. J. Johnson, 1868

7.

Mussolini, Benito, Speech: 9 May 1936 https://flt.hf.uio.no/texts/work/171

Weil, Simone. *'Reflections on Barbarism,'* 1939, and 'Some Reflections on the Origins of Hitlerism,' in *Nouveaux Cahiers*, 1940.

Luxemburg, Rosa. The Junius Pamphlet, 1915: https://www.marxists.org/archive/luxemburg/1915/junius/ch01.htm

Letter from Marx to Engels about Spartacus in 1861:

https://www.marxists.org/archive/marx/works/1861/letters/61_02_27-abs.htm

Luxemburg, Rosa. *What Does the Spartacus League Want?*, 1918

https://www.marxists.org/archive/luxemburg/1918/12/14.htm

8.

Ali Ibn al-Jahm. *Diwan*, Edited by Khalil Marum, Al-Majma 'al-'Ilmi al-'Arabi, 1949: p. 29

al-Tabari, cited in Grabar, Oleg. *The Formation of Islamic Art*, Yale University Press, 1973: p. 40

al-Muqaddasi 159 and 168, translated in Lassner, Jacob. *Medieval Jerusalem: Forging an Islamic City in Spaces Sacred to Christians and Jews*, The University of Michigan Press, 2017: p. 177, 178

al-Jahiz, translated in Fowden, Garth. *Before and After Muhammad: The First Millennium Refocused*, Princeton University Press, 2014: p. 151

9.

Jefferson, Thomas. *Notes on the State of Virginia*, 1781

Kant, Immanuel. *Observations on the Feeling of the Beautiful and Sublime*, 1764, and *On the Different Races of Man*, 1775

Madison, James. *Federalist No. 55*, 1788

Preface to Wheatley, Phillis. *Poems on Various Subjects, Religious and Moral,* A. Bell, 1773

10.

Gergiev, Valery. Mariinsky Orchestra

https://abcnews.go.com/International/russian-orchestra-striking-chord-ancient-palmyra-amphitheater/story?id=38898866

Ancient Roman history
(Chapters 1 and 10 and introductions to Parts One,
Two and Three)

Agut-Labordère, Damien, and M.J. Versluys. *Canonisation as Innovation: Anchoring Cultural Formation in the First Millennium BCE.* Leiden, Brill, 2022

Aldrete, Gregory S. *Daily Life in the Roman City: Rome, Pompeii, and Ostia.* Norman, University Of Oklahoma Press, 2008

Ando, Clifford. *The Matter of the Gods: Religion and the Roman Empire.* Berkeley, University of California Press, 2009

Angelova, Diliana. *Sacred Founders: Women, Men, and Gods in the Discourse of Imperial Founding, Rome through Early Byzantium.* Oakland, California, University of California Press, 2015

Arena, Valentina, and J.R.W. Prag. *A Companion to Roman Political Culture.* Hoboken, NJ, John Wiley & Sons, 2022

Baird, Jennifer and Zena Kamash, 'Remembering Roman Syria: Valuing Tadmor-Palmyra from "Discovery" to Destruction', *Bulletin of the Institute of Classical Studies* 62.1 (2019), 1-29

Baird, Jennifer, and Claire Taylor. *Ancient Graffiti in Context.* Routledge, 2010

Beard, Mary, et al. *Religions of Rome. 1: A History.* Cambridge University Press, 1998

—. *Religions of Rome. Volume 2: a Sourcebook.* Cambridge, Cambridge University Press, 1998

Bernard S., Mignone L.M., Padilla Peralta D., eds. *Making the Middle Republic: New Approaches to Rome and Italy,* c.400–200 BCE. Cambridge University Press; 2023

Birk, Stine, and Birte Poulsen. *Patrons and Viewers in Late Antiquity.* Aarhus, Aarhus University Press, 2012

Bond, Sarah. Trade and Taboo: Disreputable Professions in the Roman Mediterranean. University of Michigan Press, 2016

Borg, Barbara. *A Companion to Roman Art.* Chichester, Wiley, Blackwell, 2020

Brown, Peter. *The World of Late Antiquity: From Marcus Aurelius to Muhammad.* London, Thames And Hudson, 1971.

Burrell, Barbara. *A Companion to the Archaeology of the Roman Empire.* Wiley-Blackwell, 15 Apr. 2022.

Canepa, Matthew P. *The Two Eyes of The Earth: Art And Ritual Of Kingship Between Rome And Sasanian Iran.* University Of California Press, 2009

Cohen, Beth. *Not the Classical Ideal: Athens and the Construction of the Other in Greek Art.* Leiden, Brill, 2000

Dillon, Matthew, and Lynda Garland. *The Ancient Romans.* Routledge, 21 Apr. 2021

Flower, Harriet I. *The Cambridge Companion to the Roman Republic.* Cambridge, Cambridge University Press, 2014

Flower, Harriet I. *Roman Republics.* Princeton University Press, 2011

Futo Kennedy, Rebecca, et al. *Race and Ethnicity in the Classical World: An Anthology of Primary Sources in Translation.* Indianapolis, Hackett Pub. Company, Inc., 2013

Futo Kennedy, Rebecca and Molly Jones-Lewis (eds). *Identity and the Environment in the Classical and Medieval Worlds*. Routledge, 2016

Gruen, Erich S. *Rethinking the Other in Antiquity*. Princeton, N.J., Princeton University Press, 2011

Hall, Edith. *Inventing the Barbarian*. Cambridge University Press, 1989.

Harper, Kyle. *The Fate of Rome: Climate, Disease, and the End of an Empire*. Princeton University Press, 2017

Haselswerdt, Ella, et al. *The Routledge Handbook of Classics and Queer Theory*. Routledge, 2023

Hilsdale, Cecily. 'Imperial Monumentalism, Ceremony, and Forms of Pageantry: The Inter-Imperial Obelisk in Istanbul,' in *The Oxford World History of Empire*, v. 1: The Imperial Experience (Oxford University Press, 2021) pp 223–265.

Kaldellis, Anthony. *Romanland: Ethnicity and Empire in Byzantium*. Harvard University Press, 2019

Kaldellis, Anthony. *The New Roman Empire*. Oxford University Press, 2024

Laurence, Ray. *Rome, Ostia, and Pompeii: Movement and Space*. Oxford, Oxford University Press, 2011

Lincoln, Bruce. *Gods and Demons, Priests and Scholars*. University of Chicago Press, 2015.

Loar, Matthew P., MacDonald, Carolyn and Dan-el Padilla Peralta. *Rome, Empire of Plunder. The Dynamics of Cultural Appropriation*, Cambridge University Press, 2017

Morley, Neville. *The Roman Empire: Roots of Imperialism*. Pluto Press, London, 2010.

Padilla Peralta, Dan-El. *Divine Institutions: Religions and Community in the Middle Roman Republic*. Princeton, New Jersey, Princeton University Press, 2020.

Peña, J. Theodore. *Roman Pottery in the Archaeological Record.* Cambridge University Press, 2007.

Popkin, Maggie L. 'Decorum and the Meanings of Materials in Triumphal Architecture of Republican Rome.' *Journal of the Society of Architectural Historians*, vol. 74, no. 3, 1 Sept. 2015, pp. 289–311

Potter, D.S. *A Companion to the Roman Empire.* Wiley-Blackwell, 2010

Rüpke, Jörg. *On Roman Religion.* Cornell University Press, 2016

Scheid, John. *The Gods, the State, and the Individual.* University of Pennsylvania Press, 2015

Snowden, Frank Jr. *Blacks in Antiquity: Ethiopians in the Greco-Roman Experience.* Cambridge, MA: Harvard University Press, 1970

—. Before Color Prejudice: *The Ancient Views of Blacks.* Cambridge, MA.: Harvard University Press, 1983

—. 1997. 'Misconceptions about African Blacks in the Ancient Mediterranean World: Specialists and Afrocentrists.' Arion 4: 28-50

Ulrich, Roger B., and Caroline K. Quenemoen. *A Companion to Roman Architecture.* John Wiley & Sons, 2013

Umachandran, Mathura, and Marchella Ward. *Critical Ancient World Studies.* Taylor & Francis, 2023

Vasunia, Phiroze. *The Gift of the Nile.* University of California Press, 2001

Vout, Caroline. *Classical Art: A Life History from Antiquity to the Present.* Princeton, New Jersey, Princeton University Press, 2018

Wiedemann, Thomas. *Greek and Roman Slavery.* Routledge, 2003

Woolf, Greg. *Rome: An Empire's Story.* Oxford; New York, Oxford University Press, 2014

Chapter 2: The New Rome

Anderson, Benjamin and Mirela Ivanova (Eds) *Is Byzantine Studies a Colonialist Discipline?* Penn State Press, 2023

Betancourt, Roland. *Byzantine Intersectionality: Sexuality, Gender, and Race in the Middle Ages.* Princeton, Princeton University Press, 2020

Brubaker, Leslie. *Inventing Byzantine Iconoclasm.* London, Bristol Classical Press, 2012

—. 'Memories of Helena: Patterns in Imperial Female Matronage in the Fourth and Fifth Centuries.' *Women, Men and Eunuchs: Gender in Byzantium*, edited by Liz James, 1997, pp. 52–75

Cameron, Averil. *Byzantine Matters.* Princeton, Princeton University Press, 2019

Chatterjee, Paroma. *Between the Pagan Past and Christian Present in Byzantine Visual Culture.* Cambridge University Press, 2021

Churchill, Neil. *Power and Representation in Byzantium.* Taylor & Francis, 2024

Demacopoulos, George E. *Colonizing Christianity: Greek and Latin Religious Identity in the Era of the Fourth Crusade.* Fordham University Press, 2019

Herrin, Judith. *Byzantium: The Surprising Life of a Medieval Empire.* Princeton, Princeton University Press, 2009

James, Liz. 'Making a Name: Reputation and Imperial Founding and Refounding in Constantinople.' *Wiener Jahrbuch* Für *Kunstgeschichte*, vol. 60, no. 1, 1 Jan. 2012, https://doi.org/10.7767/wjk-2012-0108. Accessed 23 June 2019

—. *Mosaics in the Medieval World: From Late Antiquity to the Fifteenth Century.* Cambridge; New York, Cambridge University Press, 2017

Kaldellis, Anthony. *Byzantium Unbound.* Leeds Arc Humanities Press, 2019

—. *Romanland: Ethnicity and Empire in Byzantium*. Harvard University Press, 2019

—. *The New Roman Empire*. Oxford University Press, 2024

Kruse, Marion. *The Politics of Roman Memory: From the Fall of the Western Empire to the Age of Justinian*. Philadelphia, University Of Pennsylvania Press, 2019

Leonora Alice Neville. *Anna Komnene: The Life and Work of a Medieval Historian*. New York, NY, Oxford University Press, 2019

—. *Byzantine Gender*. Arc Humanities Press, 2019

—. *Guide to Byzantine Historical Writing*. Cambridge University Press, 2018

Luca Zavagno. *The Byzantine City from Heraclius to the Fourth Crusade, 610–1204*. Springer Nature, 2021

Mango, Cyril A. *The Art of the Byzantine Empire, 312-1453: Sources and Documents*. Toronto, University Of Toronto Press, 2013

Radle, Gabriel. 'The Veiling of Women in Byzantium: Liturgy, Hair, and Identity in a Medieval Rite of Passage.' *Speculum*, vol. 94, no. 4, Oct. 2019, pp 1070–1115

Schwartz, Ellen C. (ed.). *The Oxford Handbook of Byzantine Art and Architecture*. Oxford University Press, 2021

Tannous, Jack. *The Making of the Medieval Middle East: Religion, Society, and Simple Believers*. Princeton, New Jersey, Princeton University Press, 2018

Usherwood, Rebecca. *Political Memory and the Constantinian Dynasty*. Springer Nature, 2022

Chapter 3: The Holy Roman Empire

Arnold, Jonathan J. *Theoderic and the Roman Imperial Restoration*. Cambridge, Cambridge University Press, 2014

Aschenbrenner, Nathanael, and Jake Ransohoff. *The Invention of*

Byzantium in Early Modern Europe. Dumbarton Oaks Research Library And Collection, 2021

Bavuso, Irene. 'Balance of Power across the Channel: Reassessing Frankish Hegemony in Southern England (6th-7th C)' *Early Medieval Europe*, 2021, pp 283–304

Boeck, Elena. 'Fantasy, Supremacy, Domes, and Dames: Charlemagne Goes to Constantinople.' *Byzantium in Dialogue with the Mediterranean: History and Heritage*, edited by Daniëlle Slootjes and Mariette Verhoeven, Brill, 2019.

Davis, Jennifer R. *Charlemagne's Practice of Empire*. Cambridge University Press, 2015

Fasolt, Constantin. *Past Sense: Studies in Medieval and Early Modern European History*. Brill, 2014

Foerster, Thomas. *Godfrey of Viterbo and His Readers*. Routledge, 2016

Herrin, Judith. *Ravenna: Capital of Empire, Crucible of Europe*. Princeton University Press, 2022

— *Unrivalled Influence: Women and Empire in Byzantium*. Princeton University Press, 2013

— *Women in Purple: Rulers of Medieval Byzantium*. Princeton University Press, 2004

Hilsdale, Cecily J. *Byzantine Art and Diplomacy in an Age of Decline*. New York, Cambridge University Press, 2014

James, Liz. *Empresses and Power in Early Byzantium*. Burns & Oates, 2001

— *Mosaics, Empresses and Other Things in Byzantium*. Taylor & Francis, 2024

Pegg, Mark Gregory. *Beatrice's Last Smile*. Oxford University Press, 2023

Scales, Len *The Shaping of German Identity: Authority and Crisis, 1245–1414*. Cambridge University Press, 2015

Watts, Edward J. *The Eternal Decline and Fall of Rome*. Oxford University Press, 2023

Wickham, Chris. *Framing the Early Middle Ages.* Oxford University Press, 2006

— *The Inheritance of Rome*. Penguin, London, 2009.

Wijnendaele, Jeroen W.P. *The Last of the Romans*. Bloomsbury Publishing, 2014

— *Late Roman Italy*. EUP, 2023

Wilson, Peter H. *The Holy Roman Empire: A Thousand Years of Europe's History*. London, Penguin Books, 2017

Chapter 4: The Third Rome

Bonacchi, Chiara. *Heritage and Nationalism*. UCL Press, 2022

Bushkovitch, Paul. *A Concise History of Russia*. Cambridge University Press, 2011

Dutsch, Dorota et al. (Eds.). *A Handbook to Classical Reception in Eastern and Central Europe*. John Wiley & Sons, Ltd, 2017

Ibn Fadlan. *Ibn Fadlan and the Land of Darkness*. Penguin, London, 2012.

Matheou, Nicholas S. M. *'Methodological Imperialism.' Is Byzantine Studies a Colonialist Discipline?* edited by Benjamin Anderson and Mirela Ivanova, Penn State University Press, 2023

Mayhew, Nick. 'Moscow: The Third Rome.' *Oxford Research Encyclopedia of Literature*, OUP, 2021

McReynolds, Louise. 'Excavating Byzantium: Russia's Archaeologists and Translatio Imperii.' in *Kritika: Explorations in Russian and Eurasian History*, 21: 4, 2020, pp 763–789

Raffensperger, Christian. *The Kingdom of Rus'*, Arc Humanities Press, 2017

Rossi, Maria Alessia, and Alice Isabella Sullivan. *Byzantium in Eastern European Visual Culture in the Late Middle Ages*. Brill, 2020

—. *The Routledge Handbook of Byzantine Visual Culture in the Danube Regions, 130 –1600*. Taylor & Francis, 22 Feb. 2024.

Smelyansky, Eugene. *Medievalisms and Russia: The Contest for Imaginary Pasts*. Arc Humanities Press, 2024

Shepard, Jonathan. 'Byzantinorussica.' in *Revue Des Études Byzantines*, 33:1, 1975, pp. 211–225

—. 'Closer Encounters with the Byzantine World: The Rus at the Straits of Kerch.' *Pre-Modern Russia and Its World: Essays in Honor of Thomas S. Noonan*, Reyerson, Kathryn L, et al. (Eds.), Harrassowitz Verlag, 2006, pp 15–77

—*The Expansion of Orthodox Europe: Byzantium, the Balkans and Russia*. Routledge, 2007

Sullivan, Alice Isabella and Kyle G. Sweeney. *Lateness and Modernity in Medieval Architecture*. Brill, 2023

Teibenbacher, Elena. 'Catherine the Great: How the Question of Legitimacy Influenced Her Politics.' in *Dynastic Change*, Rodrigues, Ana Maria S.A. et al. (Eds.), Routledge, 2019, pp 255–274

Torres Prieto, Susana and Andrei Franklin. *Medieval Rus' and Early Modern Russia*. Taylor & Francis, 2023

van den Bercken, Wil. *Holy Russia and Christian Europe. East and West in the Religious Ideology of Russia*, SCM Press, 1999

Vukovich, Alexandra. 'Enthronement in Early Rus: Between Byzantium and Scandinavia.' *Viking and Medieval Scandinavia* 14, 2018, pp. 211–239

— 'Enthronement Rituals of the Princes of Rus' (Twelfth-Thirteenth Centuries)' in *FORUM University of Edinburgh Postgraduate Journal of Culture & the Arts* 17, 2013

— 'How Byzantine Was the Moscow Inauguration of 1498?' *Byzantium in Eastern European Culture in the Late Middle Ages, East Central and Eastern Europe in the Middle Ages, 450-1450*, edited by Maria Alessia Rossi and Alice Sullivan, Brill, 2020, pp 35–71

—. 'The Yardsticks by Which We Measure Rus.' *Russian History*, 46:2-3, 2019, pp 213–224

Chapter 5: Conquering Rome: the Ottoman Empire

Eldem, Edhem. 'Rescuing Ottoman History from the Turks.' *Turkish Historical Review*, 13 (2022), pp 8–27

Ferguson, Heather L. *The Proper Order of Things: Language, Power, and Law in Ottoman Administrative Discourses.* Stanford University Press, 2020

Gathorne-Hardy, Jonathan. *Sultan's Organ.* Propolis, 2017

Greene, Molly. *A Shared World: Christians and Muslims in the Early Modern Mediterranean.* Princeton University Press, 2000

—. *The Edinburgh History of the Greeks, 1453 to 1774: The Ottoman Empire.* Edinburgh, Edinburgh University Press, 2015

İnalcık, Halil. *Studies in Ottoman Social and Economic History.* Aldershot, Ashgate/Variorum, 1985

— *The Middle East and the Balkans under the Ottoman Empire: Essays on Economy and Society.* Bloomington (Ind.), Indiana University, 1993

—*The Ottoman Empire and Europe: The Ottoman Empire and Its Place in European History.* İstanbul Kronik 2017

İnalcık, Halil, and Suraiya Faroqhi. *An Economic and Social History of the Ottoman Empire 1: 1300-1600.* Cambridge, Cambridge University Press, 1999

Kafadar, Cemal. 'A Rome of One's Own: Reflections on Cultural Geography and Identity in the Lands of Rum.' *Muqarnas 24: History and Ideology: Architectural Heritage of the 'Lands of Rum,'* 2007, pp 7–25

Kane, Eileen. *Russian Hajj: Empire and the Pilgrimage to Mecca.* Cornell University Press, 2017

Key Fowden, Elizabeth. 'The Parthenon Mosque, King Solomon, and the Greek Sages.' *Ottoman Athens: Archaeology, Topography, History,* edited by Maria Georgopoulou and Konstantinos Thanasakis, Gennadius Library and the Aikaterini Laskaridis Foundation, 2019, pp 67–95

Kołodziejczyk, Dariusz. 'Khan, Caliph, Tsar and Imperator: Multiple Identities.' *Universal Empire: A Comparative Approach to Imperial Culture and Representation in Eurasian History.* Dariusz Kołodziejczyk and Peter Fibiger Bang (Eds.), Cambridge University Press, 2012, pp 175–193

Mackintosh-Smith, Tim. *Travels of Ibn Battutah.* Collectors Library, 2016

Mishkova, Diana. *Rival Byzantiums.* Cambridge University Press. 2022

Morton, Nicholas. *The Mongol Storm: Making and Breaking Empires in the Medieval Near East.* Basic Books, New York, 2022

Necipoğlu, Gülru. 'Süleyman the Magnificent and the Representation of Power in the Context of Ottoman-Hapsburg-Papal Rivalry.' *The Art Bulletin* 71: 3, 1989, pp. 401–427

— *Architecture, Ceremonial, and Power.* MIT Press, 1991

— *The Age of Sinan: Architectural Culture in the Ottoman Empire.* Reaktion Books, London, 2011

— 'The Aesthetics of Empire: Arts, Politics, and Commerce in the Construction of Sultan Süleyman's Magnificence.' *The Battle for Central Europe: The Siege of Szigetvár and the Death of Süleyman the Magnificent and Nicholas Zrínyi (1566),* Pál Fodor (Ed.), Brill, 2019, pp 115–58

Peirce, Leslie. *A Spectrum of Unfreedom: Captives and Slaves in the Ottoman Empire.* Central European University Press, 2021

—. *Empress of the East: How a European Slave Girl Became Queen of the Ottoman Empire*. Basic Books, New York, 2017

Sitaridou, Ioanna. 'Romeyka.' *Endangered Languages in Turkey*, edited by Metin Bagriacik et al., The Laz Institute, Istanbul, 2024, pp 6–8

Universal Empire: A Comparative Approach to Imperial Culture and Representation in Eurasian History. Peter Fibiger Bang and Dariusz Kołodziejczyk (Eds.), Cambridge University Press, 2012

Yaycioglu, Ali. *Partners of the Empire: The Crisis of the Ottoman Order in the Age of Revolutions*. Stanford University Press, 2020

Zarakol, Ayse. *Before the West: The Rise and Fall of Eastern World Orders*. Cambridge University Press, 2022

Zeynep Çelik. *About Antiquities: Politics of Archaeology in the Ottoman Empire*. University Of Texas Press, 2016.

Chapter 6: Pax Romana, Pax Britannica

Abd el-Gawad, H., & Stevenson, A. "Egypt's dispersed heritage: Multi-directional storytelling through comic art' in *Journal of Social Archaeology*, 21: 1, 2021, pp 121–145.

Bhambra, Gurminder K., *et al.* (Eds.). *African Athena: New Agendas*, Oxford University Press, 2011

Bradley, Mark (Ed.), *Classics and Imperialism in the British Empire*, Oxford University Press, 2010

Cormack, Raphael. *Midnight in Cairo: The Divas of Egypt's Roaring '20s*. W. W. Norton & Company, 2021

Currie, Arabella. 'Moderns of the Past, Moderns of the Future: George Sigerson's Celtic-Romans in Ireland, 1897–1922', in Francesca Kaminski-Jones and Rhys Kaminski-Jones (Eds.), *Celts, Romans, Britons: Classical and Celtic Influence in the Construction of British Identities*, Oxford University Press, 2020

—. 'Abjection and the Irish-Greek Fir Bolg in Aran Island Writing', in Isabelle Torrance and Donncha O'Rourke (Eds.), *Classics and Irish Politics, 1916-2016*, Oxford University Press, 2020

Freeman, Margaret. 'Rendre leur âme aux fantômes: nomadisme et hantologie de l'architecture chez les Bédouins,' in *Perspective: actualité en histoire de l'art* (2), 2021, p. 221-238

— 'The Sheikh's Castle: Architecture as Control in Jordan's Southern Desert.' *Journal of Architectural Education* 77 (2) 2023, 472–79.

Gilmore, John. 'The British Empire and the Neo-Latin Tradition: The Case of Francis Williams', in Barbara Goff (Ed.), *Classics and Colonialism*. Duckworth, 2005, pp 92–106

Goff, Barbara (Ed.), *Classics and Colonialism*. Duckworth, London, 2005

Goff, Barbara. *'Your Secret Language': Classics in the British Colonies of West Africa*. Bloomsbury Academic, London, 2013

Hagerman, Christopher. *Britain's Imperial Muse: The Classics, Imperialism, and the Indian Empire, 1784-1914*. Oxford University Press, 2013

Hall, Edith and Phiroze Vasunia (Eds.). 'India, Greece, and Rome, 1757 to 2007', in *Bulletin of the Institute of Classical Studies Supplements* 108, 2010

Hardwick, Lorna and Carol Gillespie (Eds.). *Classics in Post-Colonial Worlds*. Oxford University Press, 2007

Kumar, Krishan. 'Greece and Rome in the British Empire: Contrasting Role Models.' *Journal of British Studies*, 51: 1, 2012, pp. 76–101

Morgenstein Fuerst, Ilyse. 'Locating Religion in South Asia: Islamicate Definitions and Categories,' *Comparative Islamic Studies* 10: 2, 2017, pp. 217–241

Reid, Donald M. 'Cromer and the Classics: Imperialism, Nationalism and the Greco-Roman Past in Modern Egypt.' *Middle Eastern Studies*, 32: 1, 1996, pp. 1–29

Said, Edward W. *Orientalism*. Routledge & Kegan Paul Ltd, 1978

— *Culture and Imperialism*. Chatto & Windus, 1993

Vasunia, Phiroze. *The Classics and Colonial India*. Oxford University Press, 2013

—'Barbarism and Civilization: Political Writing, History, and Empire', in Norman Vance & Jennifer Wallace (eds.), *The Oxford History of Classical Reception in English Literature*, Volume 4: 1790-1880.Oxford University Press, 2015), pp 131–158

—'Memories of Empire: Literature and Art, Nostalgia and Trauma', in Peter Fibiger Bang, C.A. Bayly & Walter Scheidel (eds.), *The Oxford World History of Empire*, vol. 1: The Imperial Experience. New York: Oxford University Press, 2020, pp 497–522.

Chapter 7: Roman fasces, European fascism

Agbamu, Samuel. 'The Return of Rome. *The Epic World*, 2 Jan. 2024, pp. 484–497, https://doi.org/10.4324/9780429286698-39. Accessed 20 Aug. 2024

— *Restorations of Empire in Africa*. Oxford University Press, 2024

— 'The Reception of Petrarch's Africa in Fascist Italy.' *International Journal of the Classical Tradition*, vol. 29, no. 1, 5 Feb. 2021, pp 83–102

Andersen, Maria et al. *Classical Heritage and European Identities*, Routledge, 2019

Anderson, Benedict. *Imagined Communities: Reflections on the Origin and Spread of Nationalism*. Verso, 1983

Aimé Césaire. *Discourse on Colonialism*. 1950. NYU Press

Cullen, Helen E. *A Selection of Short Essays on Simone Weil's Life and Writings*. FriesenPress, 2023.

Fanon, Franz. *Les Damnés de la Terre*. François Maspero, 1961

Hejlskov Larsen, Ane, et al. (Eds.) *Museologi Mellem Fagene*, Aarhus Universitetsforlag, 2021

Hell, Julia. *The Conquest of Ruins: The Third Reich and the Fall of Rome*. University Of Chicago Press, 2019

Kamash, Zena. 'Postcard to Palmyra: Bringing the Public into Debates over Post-Conflict Reconstruction in the Middle East.' *World Archaeology*, vol. 49, no. 5, 20 Oct. 2017, pp 608–622

— 'Remembering the Romans in the Middle East and North Africa: Memories and Reflections from a Museum-Based Public Engagement Project' in *Epoiesen: A Journal for Creative Engagement in History and Archaeology*, 2017

Mac Sweeney, Naoíse, et al. 'Claiming the Classical: The Greco-Roman World in Contemporary Political Discourse.' *Council of Classical Departments Bulletin*, vol. 48, 2019

Marzagora, Sara. 'Ethiopian Intellectual History and the Global: Käbbädä Mikael's Geographies of Belonging.' *Journal of World Literature* 4: 1, 2019, pp 107–128

Nelis, Jan. "Back to the Future: Italian Fascist Representations of the Roman Past." *Fascism*, 3: 1, 2014, pp. 1–19.

Noronha, Ricardo. 'The Myth of Spartacus and the Tradition of the Oppressed.' *Theory & Event* 22: 4, 2019, pp 1082–1104

Otele, Olivette. *L'histoire de l'Esclavage Transatlantique Britannique*. Michel Houdiard Editeur, 2008

— *African Europeans*. Basic Books, 2021

Roche, Helen. 'Mussolini's Third Rome, Hitler's Third Reich and the Allure of Antiquity: Classicizing Chronopolitics as a Remedy for Unstable National Identity?' *Fascism: Journal of Comparative Fascist Studies* 8: 2, 2019, pp 127–52

— *The Third Reich's Elite Schools*. Oxford University Press, 2021

Roche, Helen, and Kyriakos Demetriou (Eds.) *Brill's Companion to the Classics, Fascist Italy and Nazi Germany*, Leiden, Brill, 2018

Rose, Jacqueline. 'Woman on the Verge of Revolution: Rosa Luxemburg.' in *Women in Dark Times*, by Jacqueline Rose, Bloomsbury, 2014

Rossol, Nadine. *Performing the Nation in Interwar Germany: Sport, Spectacle and Political Symbolism, 1926–36*. Palgrave Macmillan, 2010

Stewart, Susan. *The Ruins Lesson: Meaning and Material in Western Culture*. University Of Chicago Press, 2020

Stobiecka, Monika. 'Archaeological Heritage in the Age of Digital Colonialism. *Archaeological Dialogues* 27: 2, 2020, pp. 113–125

Umachandran, Mathura, and Marchella Ward. *Critical Ancient World Studies*. Taylor & Francis, 2023

Chapter 8. Rivalling Rome: the empires of early Islam

Al-Azmeh, Aziz. *The Emergence of Islam in Late Antiquity: Allah and His People*. Cambridge University Press, 2014

Alami, Mohammed H. *Art and Architecture in the Islamic Tradition: Aesthetics, Politics and Desire in Early Islam*. I.B. Tauris Publishers, 2011

Anderson, Glaire D., and Jennifer Pruitt. 'The Three Caliphates, a Comparative Approach.' *A Companion to Islamic Art and Architecture*, edited by Finbarr Barry Flood and Gülru Necipoğlu, John Wiley & Sons, 2017, pp 223–249

Borrut, Antoine. *Entre mémoire et pouvoir: L'espace syrien sous les derniers Omeyyades et les premiers Abbassides (v.72–193/692–809)*, Brill, 2011

Bauer, Thomas. *Die Kultur der Ambiguität: Eine andere Geschichte des Islams*, Verlag der Weltreligionen, 2011

— *Warum es kein islamisches Mittelalter gab. Das Erbe der Antike und der Orient*. Beck, 2018

Canepa, Matthew P. *The Two Eyes of The Earth: Art And Ritual*

Of Kingship Between Rome And Sasanian Iran. University Of California Press, 2009

El-Cheikh, Nadia. *Byzantium Viewed by the Arabs.* Harvard University Press, 2004

El-Hibri, Tayeb. *The Abbasid Caliphate: A History.* Cambridge University Press, 2021

Flood, Finbarr B. and Gülru Necipoğlu, *A Companion to Islamic Art and Architecture*, John Wiley & Sons, 2017

Garth Jones, Rhiannon. 'Building a Language of Power: Early Abbāsids use of al-Rūm and Near Eastern building traditions to project imperial authority and power.' *Politics of pasts and futures in (post) imperial contexts*, edited by Sebastian Fahner et al., De Gruyter, 2024

— *References to Rome in the early Abbasids' visual language of power, 762-861*, Unpublished Dissertation, Aarhus University, 2024

Iafrate, Allegra. *The Wandering Throne of Solomon: Objects and Tales of Kingship in the Medieval Mediterranean.* Brill, 2015

Levy-Rubin, Milka. 'Why was the Dome of the Rock built? A new perspective on a long-discussed question.' *Bulletin of the School of Oriental and Africa*n Studies, 80:3, 2017, pp 441–64

Masood, Ehsan. *Science and Islam: A History.* Icon Books Ltd, 2017

Meinecke, Katharina. 'Circulating images: Late Antiquity's cross-cultural visual koiné.' in *A Globalised Visual Culture? Towards a Geography of Late Antique Art*, Guidetti, Fabio and Katharina Meinecke (Eds.), Oxbow Books, 2020, pp 321–40

Northedge, Alastair. *Samarra I: The Historical Topography of Samarra.* Oxbow Books, 2008

Saba, Matthew D. *Impermanent Monuments, Lasting Legacies: The Dār al-Khilāfa of Samarra and Palace Building in Early Abbasid Iraq.* Reichert Verlag, 2022

Saliba, George. *Islamic Science and the Making of the European Renaissance.* MIT Press, 2007

Webb, Peter. *Imagining the Arabs: Arab Identity and the Rise of Islam.* Edinburgh University Press, 2016

Chapter 9: The New Republic: USA edition

Appiah, Kwame Anthony. *The Lies that Bind: Rethinking Identity.* Liveright, 2019

Bindman, D., H. Gates Jr, and K. Dalton, (Eds) 2010. *The Image of the Black in Western Art: From the Pharaohs to the Fall of the Roman Empire. Vol. 1.* Harvard University Press

Bond, Sarah E. 'The Story of the Black King among the Magi.' *Hyperallergic*, 6 Jan. 2020, hyperallergic.com/535881/the-story-of-the-black-king-among-the-magi/.

Du Bois, W.E.B. *Black Reconstruction in America.* Oxford University Press, 2007

Futo Kennedy, Rebecca. 'Teaching Race in Greco-Roman Antiquity: Some Considerations and Resources.' The Classical Outlook 97.1: 2-8, 2022

George, Victoria. *Whitewash and the New Aesthetic of the Protestant Reformation*, Pindar Press, 2012

Hanses, Mathias. 'Cicero Crosses the Colour Line: "Pro Archia Poeta" and W.E.B. DuBois's "The Souls of Black Folk".' *International Journal of the Classical Tradition*, vol. 26, no. 1, 2019

Isaac, Benjamin. *The Invention of Racism in Classical Antiquity.* Princeton University Press, 2013

McCoskey, Denise. 1999. 'Answering the Multicultural Imperative: A Course on Race and Ethnicity in Antiquity.' *Classical World* 92: pp 553-561

— 'By Any Other Name? Ethnicity and the Study of Ancient Identity' in *Classical Bulletin* 79.1 (2003), pp 93–109.

— 'On Black Athena, Hippocratic Medicine, and Roman Imperial Edicts: Egyptians and the Problem of Race in Antiquity,' in *Race and Ethnicity: Across Time, Space and Discipline*, Rodney D. Coates (Ed.), Brill, 2004, pp 297-330

— *A Cultural History of Race in Antiquity*. Bloomsbury Publishing, 2023

Nasrallah, Laura, and Elisabeth Schüssler Fiorenza, (Eds). *Prejudice and Christian beginnings: investigating race, gender, and ethnicity in early Christian studies*. Fortress Press, 2010

Painter, Nell Irvin. *The History of White People*. W. W. Norton & Company, 2011

Ricks, Thomas E. *First Principles: What America's Founders Learned from the Greeks and Romans and How That Shaped Our Country*, HarperCollins, 2020

Scott, Aimee Hinds, and Paprocki, Maciej. 'Casting Black Athenas: Black Representation of Ancient Greek Goddesses' in *Modern Audiovisual Media and Beyond. Journal of Popular Film and Television 51: 1.* 2023, pp 29–38

Shields, John C. 'Phillis Wheatley's Use of Classicism' in *American Literature 52: 1*, 1980, pp 97–111

Sullivan, Marek. *Secular Assemblages: Affect, Orientalism and Power in the French Enlightenment*. Bloomsbury Publishing, 2020

Trouillot, Michel-Rolph. *Silencing the Past: Power and the Production of History*. Boston, Massachusetts, Beacon Press, 1995

Yoffee, Norman. *Negotiating the Past in the Past: Identity, Memory, and Landscape in Archaeological Research*. University of Arizona Press, 2007

Timeline

Accurate dates for ancient historical events are tricky and often quite contested – different perspectives on these events would frequently label them differently. The ones below are commonly accepted dates, phrased and ordered to help anchor you in the events discussed in this book.

BCE

753	Foundation of Rome
550	Achaemenid rule begins in Persia
509	Roman Republic begins
390	Rome is sacked by the Gauls
336	Alexander the Great begins his campaigns across Eurasia
323	Alexander the Great dies
321	Seleukid rule begins across central and west Asia
305	Ptolemaic rule begins in North Africa
264–241	First Punic War between Rome and Carthage
247	Parthians emerge as rulers in central Asia
218–201	Second Punic War between Rome and Carthage
150	Aksumite rule begins in East Africa and southern Arabia
149–146	Third Punic War between Rome and Carthage
110	Himyarite rule begins in southern Arabia
91–88	Rome's Italian allies request citizenship, leading to the Italian War

73–71	Spartacus' revolt
63	Seleukid rule ends in west Asia
58–50	Caesar's campaigns in Gaul, Britain
53	Battle of Carrhae, Rome defeated by Parthians
49	Caesar crosses the Rubicon; Civil War begins
44	Assassination of Caesar
31	Antony and Cleopatra defeated at Actium; Ptolemaic rule ends in North Africa
27	Octavianus granted the name Augustus; Roman Empire begins
CE	
43	Romans invade Britain again
65	Seneca the Younger, critic of Roman imperial rule, dies
120	Tacitus, critic of Roman imperial rule, dies
224	Sasanian rule begins across central and west Asia
270–73	Palmyrene rule across formerly Roman provinces of Syria Palaestina, Arabia Petraea, and Egypt, as well as much of Asia Minor
284–305	Rule of Diocletian; tetrarchy instituted to restore order after fifty years of military and political upheaval
312	Constantine seizes power, ends tetrarchy
330	Christianity becomes official religion of Aksumite rulers Foundation of Constantinople/Nova Roma
380	Judaism becomes official religion of Himyarite rulers
410	Sack of Rome by Alaric
476	Romulus Augustulus deposed after eight months; Odoacer rules in Italy
493	Odoacer murdered; Theodoric rules in Italy
496	Pope Gelasius I fails to end Lupercalia celebrations in Rome
525	Aksumite rule expands to Himyarite territories in southern Arabia

527–565	Rule of Justinian and Theodora; many of the former western territories are recaptured, a new legal code is instituted, major building programme begins
537	Hagia Sophia completed in Constantinople
572	Roman-Persian wars renewed
622	Migration of Muhammad's followers from Mecca to Medina; beginning of Hijri calendar
632	Death of Muhammad, Rashidun rule begins, expanding across Afro-Eurasia
651	Sasanian rule ends
661	Umayyad rule begins, expanding across Afro-Eurasia
692	Dome of the Rock completed in Jerusalem
711	Great Mosque completed in Damascus
717	Romanland rule across most of Italian peninsula ends
730	Leo III bans image worship in Romanland
749	Abbasid Rebellion succeeds, Abbasid rule begins across Afro-Eurasia
756	Umayyad Emirate of Córdoba established
762	Madinat al-Salam/Baghdad founded, becomes Abbasid capital
762–775	Diplomatic embassy from Romanland to Baghdad
775	Eirene becomes co-ruler of Romanland
785	Works begins on the Great Mosque of Córdoba
787	Eirene works to unite the churches of Rome and Romanland at the Second Council of Nicaea
788	Idrisid dynasty declares independence in Maghreb
797	Eirene deposes Constantine VI and rules Romanland alone
800	Aghlabid dynasty takes governorship in Ifriqiya
	Pope Leo crowns Charles in Rome
802	Eirene deposed
836	Samarra founded, becomes Abbasid capital

907	Earliest known treaty between Romanland and Rus
917	Diplomatic embassy from Romanland to Baghdad
939	Madinat al-Zahra founded
940	End of Aksumite rule in east Africa
961	Emperor Otto the Great inters St Maurice's remains in Magdeburg Cathedral as patron saint of his new dynasty
988	Vladimir the Great converts to Christianity
989	Vladimir the Great marries Anna Porphyrogenita
1054	'Great Schism' between the churches of Rome and Romanland
1071	Battle of Manzikert; Seljuks defeat Romanland in Asia Minor
	Normans defeat Romanland in the last of their Italian peninsula territories
1077	Sultanate of Rum established, based in Nicaea
1096–1099	First Crusade
1121–1269	Almohad rule in north Africa and southern Iberia
1146–48	Second Crusade
1155-90	Reign of Frederick I, during which period the name 'Holy Roman Empire' begins to be used officially
1183–90	Godfrey of Viterbo publishes (and revises) his history of the Holy Roman Empire
1189–92	Third Crusade
1203–4	Fourth Crusade sacks Constantinople and deposes the rulers of Romanland
1261	Rulers of Romanland return from exile to Constantinople
1288	Ottomans emerge as regional power
1321	Dante finishes his *Divina Commedia*
1330s	Italian scholar Petrarch argues for a distinction between the 'light age' of ancient Rome and the 'dark age' of the intervening period and proposes an Italian Renaissance

1346–1353	Black Death
1419–1434	Hussite Wars (or Crusades against Bohemian Reformists)
1431–1449	Council of Florence attempts to reunite the churches of Rome (Catholic) and Romanland (Orthodox)
1439	Bessarion leaves Romanland for Rome, converts to Catholicism
1453	Mehmed II conquers Constantinople
1472	Sophia Palaiologina marries Ivan III, Grand Prince of Muscovy
1492	Isabella and Ferdinand defeat the last Muslim ruler in Iberia
	The Alhambra Decree formally expels all practising Jews from Spain
	Zosimus of Moscow promotes idea of Moscow as the Third Rome
	Christopher Columbus lands in Guanahani in the Caribbean
1512	Selim I deposes Bayezid II and begins rule of Ottoman territories
1517	Martin Luther publishes his Ninety-five Theses, Protestant Reformation begins
1520	Suleyman I (aka the Magnificent) becomes Ottoman sultan
1526	The Portuguese complete the first transatlantic slave voyage to Brazil
1532	Suleyman I's triumphal parades in Europe
1533	Treaty of Constantinople, Hungary acknowledges Ottoman seniority
1576	Britannia imagery revived in England
1579–1595	Safiye Sultan of the Ottomans and Elizabeth I, Queen of England, correspond

1599	Elizabeth, I sends a clockwork organ as a gift to Sultan Mehmed III
1600	English East India Company founded
1607	English attempts to colonize North America begin in Jamestown, Virginia
1618–1648	Thirty Years War in Europe and some European colonies
1630s	Hermann Conring proves Roman law is not used in the Holy Roman Empire
1672	Charles II puts Britannia on the coinage of England
1682	Peter the Great co-rules Russia; from 1696, he rules alone
1745	Catherine the Great marries Peter, heir to the Russian throne
1762	Peter and Catherine begin to rule Russia; in the same year, Catherine deposes him and rules alone
1765–1783	American Revolution against British rule
1773	Phillis Wheatley publishes *Poems on Various Subjects*
1774	Treaty of Küçük Kaynarca ends the 1768-74 war between the Ottomans and Russia, granting many concessions to Russia
1781	Catherine the Great forms alliance with the Holy Roman Empire to partition the Ottoman territories, if conquered
1788	New constitution of the United States of America ratified
1789–1799	French Revolution against monarchy
1789	George Washington elected first President of the United States of America
1791–1804	Haitian Revolution of self-liberated slaves against French rule, the first successful slave uprising in history
1798-1801	Napoleon invades Egypt during the French Revolutionary Wars
1804–1835	Serbian Revolution against Ottoman rule
1804–1865	Russian imperial expansion across central Asia, Siberia, and the Pacific

1806	Napoleon officially dissolves Holy Roman Empire; Habsburg rule continues in the Austro-Hungarian Empire
1807	Britain declares the international slave trade is illegal
1821–32	Greek Revolution
1833	British Slavery Abolition Act 1833 makes slavery illegal in most of the empire; compensates slave-owners
1834–38	Thomas Babington Macaulay writes his *Lays of Ancient Rome* while a member of the Governor-General of India's Supreme Council
1839–42	Britain wages First Opium War against China
1845–1852	Irish Great Hunger
1850	Lord Palmerston, British Prime Minister, tells Parliament that British foreign policy should be like that of the Roman Empire
1852	Frederick Douglass gives his famous *What to the Slave Is the Fourth of July?* Speech at Corinthian Hall in Rochester, New York
1857–58	First War of Indian Independence
1858	Imperial Civil Service formally established in India and East India Company rule ended
1861	Kingdom of Italy formed
1861–1865	Civil War of the United States of America
1871	German Empire formed
1878	Montenegro, Romania, and Serbia achieve formal independence from Ottoman rule; Bulgaria gains formal autonomy while remaining under Ottoman control
1878–1886	German excavations at Pergamon; the relief panels from the Pergamon Altar transferred to Berlin
1882	Anglo-Egyptian War; Britain occupies Egypt
1896	Italy tries to invade Ethiopia
1904–1908	Herero and Nama genocide under German rule

1908	Austria-Hungary annexes Bosnia and Herzegovina from Ottoman rule
1914–1918	First World War
1915–17	Armenian genocide under Ottoman rule
1918	Austro-Hungarian rule formally dissolved
1919	Spartakusbund rebellion in Germany; Rosa Luxemburg executed
	League of Nations distributes former German and Ottoman territories to be ruled as Mandates by Australia, Belgium, Britain, France, Japan, New Zealand, and South Africa
1919–1922	Greco-Turkish War
1922	Fascist Party marches on Rome, demands Benito Mussolini be appointed as prime minister
1923	Treaty of Lausanne declares amnesty for crimes committed between 1914 and 1922; creates borders of Greece, Bulgaria, and Türkiye; and mandates involuntary population transfers on the basis of religion, including around 1.5 million Anatolian Christians and 500,000 Greek Muslims.
1929	Mussolini declares the Vatican City a sovereign microstate
1933	Nazis seize power in Germany
1936	Italy tries to invade Ethiopia
1937	Fascist Italy celebrates 2,000th anniversary of Augustus' birth
1939–1945	Second World War
1947	Partition of India and Pakistan
1997	Sovereignty over Hong Kong formally transferred from the United Kingdom of Great Britain and Northern Ireland to the People's Republic of China
2020	Resurrection of Christ Cathedral in Moscow officially opened and dedicated to the Russian Armed Forces

Acknowledgements

I couldn't tell you how many books I've read without pausing to read the acknowledgements until recently. I realize now how many people contribute to what I'm reading and I slow down to enjoy these words, to appreciate the way each author acknowledges their debts and expresses their gratitude. The idea of writing my own overwhelms me – so many people helped, in so many ways, and 'I couldn't have done this without you' doesn't seem to cover it. Every 'quick question' answered, every consult over phrasing and framing, every chat to untangle an idea, every informal peer-review, every pep-talk: the generosity of colleagues, friends, and total strangers has been incredible. It kept me going in the difficult moments and made me almost giddy in the good ones. I hope I managed to privately let you all know what your kindness meant to me. This is my effort to do so publicly.

First thanks go to my team (what a mind-blowing thing to write), who have done so much amazing work to produce these pages. Katie Fulford, my agent, Richard Green, my editor, and everyone at Aurum Press: Michael Brunström, Paileen Currie, Róisín Duffy, Stephanie Lee, Philip Parker, and all the other dedicated people behind the scenes.

So many people answered a cold email or message on social media with detailed help and offers of more. I never stopped being astonished at the kindness of strangers while writing this. Liz James, Eleanor Janega, Anthony Kaldellis, Ilyse Morgenstein Fuerst, Eugene Smelyansky, Rolf Strootman, David Veevers, Alexandra Vukovich,

Marchella Ward, Jeroen W.P. Wijnendaele – thank you for your answers to my random questions, your reading recommendations, and your words of encouragement. Thanks also to Alex Body, Raphael Cormack, Adrian Kelly, Laura McAtackney, and Orçun Urgun for your answers to my panicked questions. That I thought you would help doesn't make me any less grateful that you did.

So many brilliant people generously read chapter or section drafts and sent detailed feedback that helped me to think differently, more clearly, more confidently. Ledetta Asfa-Wossen, Irene Bavuso, Sarah Croix, Arabella Currie, Ioana A. Dumitru, Jonn Elledge, Rowan S. English, Maggie Freeman, Guido Furlan, Becky Haasbroek, Stephanie Melvin, David van Oeveren, Eoin Redahan, Khodadad Rezakhani, Rachel Schine, Alexandra Sills, Julia Steding, Maria S. Thomas, Tonicha Upham: I owe you the finest gelato and then some. This book is so much better for your input – I hope you can see that. I can't stress enough that any remaining factual mistakes or fanciful interpretations are mine alone.

Then to my friends: Marine Debray, Arabella Currie, Jonn Elledge, Maggie Freeman, and Jessica Hayden believed in me from the start, when I needed it most; my MW magazine teams taught me to write all those years ago and help to this day; Maria Thomas worked with me while I wrote so much of this book that she probably doesn't need to read it, then hosted me while I recovered; Alba Antía Rodríguez Nóvoa, Amel Bouder, and Patricia Vieira had an uncanny ability to text me with inspiration and love at the perfect times; my WLWB gang (especially Phil Lewis, Josh Gardner, Jonny McGinty, and Gavin Thomas) had a confidence in me that was sometimes expressed in unorthodox fashion but always unwavering; Rowan English, Derek Parrot, and Izzy Wisher kept me going with silliness, seriousness, and everything in between; and my Burnley people have always shown me the way, holding me up with love and laughter and teasing loyalty. You mean the world to me.

ACKNOWLEDGEMENTS

To my family: every one of you, across every branch of the tree. What a team I was lucky enough to grow up with. Those who are no longer with me: my godmother, Judith; my uncles, Dave and Llew; and my grandparents, Anne, William, Eric, and Joan – their voices, belief, and love remain in my memory. To my godfather, Francis Flynn, for getting to the end of the first two draft chapters and helping me believe in his own inimitable way that I had written something worthwhile. To my brothers, Tomas and Liam, for the consults, the proofreads, the jokes, and the back-up. And to my parents, for everything, every day of my life: you help me see the whole of the moon, to have faith in the magic of the night. This is for you.

When I pitched this book, I believed that it would have something to say about the world today – empires have long legacies and many were highlighted in the proposal. I expected the challenge of doing justice to those empires and their legacies would be difficult. I did not expect their relevance to be so overwhelmingly clear; I did not expect to write while watching the horrors inflicted on Gaza, while watching the US election of 2024, while watching so many people in so many places show again and again that they believe some lives are worth more than others. And yet, I also watched millions of people show extraordinary courage and perseverance every day: to keep going, to find joy and hope, to fight for each other and make a world where we are all free. 'We have on this earth that which makes life worth living' (roughly translated) is a line from one of my favourite poems, by Mahmoud Darwish. We live in the world our predecessors built, some of which is discussed in this book. I believe we can build a better one – one where everyone, everywhere is free to enjoy April's hesitation, the final days of September, and everything else on this earth that makes life worth living.

Rhiannon Garth Jones

Index

Page numbers followed by n indicate footnotes.

A

Abbasids 39, 56, 130, 173, 176, 179–84, 187–92, 225–6
Abd al-Malik, Caliph 174, 177, 190
Abd al-Rahman I, Caliph 179
Abd al-Rahman III, Caliph 174, 179–80
Achaemenids 222n
Actium, Battle of 14
Adams, John 197
Adrian I, Pope 50–1
Ahmed I, Ottoman Sultan 106, 108
Aksum 151n
    Aksumites 172
Al-Andalus 54, 56, 63, 75, 179, 184
Alamanni 48
Alexander the Great 23, 100n, 105, 107, 181, 222
Alexios 37
Algeria 8, 155, 157
Amman 130
Anatolia 15, 96, 99, 107, 113–14, 222
Anglo-Saxons 158n
Anna Komnene 29–30, 202
Anna Porphyrogenita 69–70, 72
Antioch 28, 171
antiquities 148–52
Apocalypse 74, 85
Appian 162
Aqueduct of Valens, Constantinople 29

Arabia 36, 98, 100n, 131, 169–73, 192–3
    'desert castles' 178–9
    early Islamic empires 173–6
    scholarship 187–90
archaeology 90–1, 148, 150–1, 154–5, 225–6
Aristotle 188, 207n, 221
Arminius, see Hermann
Arsakids 222
Artemis 3, 214
al-Asaad, Khaled 226
al-Assad, Bashar 226
Athanasius of Alexandria 157
Athens 110, 119, 199, 212
Attila the Hun 46
Augustine of Hippo 157
Augustus 21, 25, 48n, 57, 73, 147, 153–4, 164, 218–20
    importation of Egyptian obelisks 218–20
    Res Gestae Divi Augusti 93–4, 222–3
Aurelian 225
Australia 125
Austria 33, 55n, 81, 143
Austro-Hungarian Empire 143, 152
automata 108, 191

B

Baghdad 27, 56, 63, 130, 174, 180–9, 190–1, 214n, 227
Bangladesh 214
Baring, Evelyn, Lord Cromer, *Modern Egypt* 128–9
Basil II, HRE 69
Bayezid II, Ottoman Sultan 100

Bayt al-Hikma, Baghdad 190n
Bedouins 130–2, 178–9
Bellini, Gentile 98–9
Benu Huchaim 132
Berlin 150, 178, 199
Bessarion 68
Bilqis, Queen of Sheba 182–3
Black Death 59
Bodin, Jean 104
Bohemia 60n, 61
Bonaparte, Napoleon 142, 147
Botticelli, Sandro 13
Brandenburg Gate, Berlin 199
Britain 111, 117–18, 120n, 146n, 151–2,
    200, 206
  Britannia 118
British Empire 9, 117–19, 204n, 206, 227
  educated by empire 123–6
  educated for empire 119–23
  Mandate territories 129–32
  Roman response 132–8
  ruling like a Roman 126–9
  'unjust rule never lasts' 138–40
British Museum 150n
Brutus, Lucius Junius 161
Bukhara, Uzbekistan 192
Bulgaria 8, 152n
Burgundians 31, 32, 48
Byzantine architecture 170n
Byzantine Empire 17, 39
Byzantium 21–3, 30
  inventing Byzantium 108–12
  Russia 82–5, 87, 143n, 193

C
Caesar 65
Caesar, see Julius Caesar
Cairo, 137, 174, 187
calendars 18n, 174n
Cambridge University 121, 124n, 189–90
Canada 125, 214
Capitol Hill, Washington DC 195–6, 199
Caribbean 132, 136, 163, 214
Carrhae, battle of 222

Carthage 154n, 156–7, 162–3, 218n, 220–2
Cassius Dio 223
Catherine I of Russia 80–1
Catherine II (the Great) of Russia 66–7,
    76–80, 82, 85, 87, 99, 110, 191n, 199
  Greek Plan 81, 85, 110
Charlemagne 37n, 42, 57, 184n
  Charles, King of the Franks 48–54, 60,
    184n
Charles II 118
Charles V, HRE 100, 101–4
China 169, 187
Choniates, Niketas 38
Christianity 7–8, 12, 15, 72–3, 119, 171,
    225
  Anglican Christianity 121, 127
  Constantine I 20–4, 26–7
  Great Schism 1054 37n, 74n, 76n
  New Rome 28–30, 35
  Rome 27–8, 35
Churchill, Winston 124
Cicero 30, 62–3, 92, 121, 128–9, 134,
    137, 197, 208–9
Clarke, Austin 136
Clement VII, Pope 102, 103
Cleopatra 14, 218
Colston, Edward 216
Columbus, Christopher 216
Conring, Hermann 63–4
Constantine I (the Great) 20–7, 29, 38,
    46n, 55, 69, 104, 111
Constantine VI 49, 51
Constantine XI Palaiologos 97, 109
Constantinople 17, 169, 174, 183–4, 192,
    193, 227
  building the New Rome 20–4
  Catherine the Great 79, 81, 85
  denying Rome 38–9
  Fall of Constantinople 1204 18–20, 37–8
  life in New Rome 28–30
  New Rome 19–20
  New Rome inspired by Old Rome 24–8
  Ottomans 67–8, 81, 95–7
  Rome in the eyes of the Rus 69–71,
    74–6

Constantius 21
Córdoba 174, 179–80, 184–5, 187, 191
Corpus Juris Civilis 54
Crassus, Marcus Licinius 222
Croatia 8, 37, 143
#CrossTheRubicon 6, 195
Crusades 35–8, 157, 200n
Curzon, Lord 135
Cybele 15

D
Dallam, Thomas 108
Damascus 171, 174, 176–7, 179, 184
Declaration of Independence, USA 195, 200n
Defenestration of Prague (1419) 61n
despots 66n
dictators 153n
Diderot, Denis 201
Diocletian 11–12, 20, 21
Diviciacus 134
Dodecanese 151–2
Dome of the Rock, Jerusalem 170, 174, 177, 212
Donation of Constantine 55, 58
Dostoevsky, Fyodor 74n
Douglass, Frederick 196, 198, 209, 212
Dugin, Aleksandr 84–5, 85n, 86–7

E
Early Church Fathers 62
Egypt 23, 100, 157, 193
    British Empire 124, 126, 128–30, 132, 137–8
Egypt, ancient 3, 134, 148, 154
    Roman Empire 171, 218–20
Eirene, Empress 20, 48–52, 60
Elizabeth I 106–8, 118, 191n
Engels, Friedrich 162
England 36n, 55, 117, 118, 120n, 158n, 214n
English 33
Enlightenment 77, 79–80, 82, 113, 144, 199–201, 203, 206, 207n, 209–10, 213

environmental determinism 207
Ethiopia 151n, 155, 163–4
Etruscans 3, 134
Euclid, *Elements* 181
Euripides, *Oedipus Rex* 138

F
Fabius Maximus Cunctator, *see* Quintus Fabius Maximus Verrucosus
Fall of Rome 476 CE 15, 43–7, 74
fasces 141, 152–3
fascism 6, 141–5
    Carthage 162–4
    ideological resistance to 160–2
    inheriting Rome. collecting antiquities 148–52
    new sense of time 145–7
    return to Rome 155–60
    speeding up the future 152–5
Fatimids 39
Ferdinand II of Aragon 100
Ferdinand of Hungary 103–4
Fez, Morocco 192
First Crusade 35–8
First World War 114, 130, 152, 155, 161–2
Flaminio Obelisk, Rome 217–20
Floralia 13
foederati 45–7, 159
Forum of Constantine, Constantinople 29
Founding Fathers, USA 7, 196–9, 202, 210, 213
Fourth Crusade 25n, 37, 58, 75
France 8, 9, 23, 31, 35, 47, 55, 111, 146n, 152, 155, 158n, 175, 179n, 206, 224
Francis II, HRE 142–3, 147
Frankfurt 227
Franks 31–2, 36, 42, 48, 107, 158n
    Charles, King of the Franks 48–54, 60, 184n
    First Crusade 36n
Frederick I (Barbarossa), HRE 54, 56–8, 60, 79n
Frederick II (the Great) of Prussia 78, 191n

Freikorps 162n
French Martinique 214n
Frontinus Stratagemata 80
FSB 83–4

G

Gaius Julius Caesar, *see* Julius Caesar
Gaius Octavius 11–12
   see Augustus
Gaius Pompeius Magnus, *see* Pompey
Gaius Verres 128–9
Galen 188
Galla Placidia 45n
Garibaldi, Giuseppe 146
Gelasius I, Pope 15
Genghis Khan 136
George III 215n
George V 136
Gergiev, Valery 226
German Archaeological Institute 151n
Germany 2n, 8, 57, 63–4, 83, 141, 143,
   145, 148, 152, 200n
   German Empire 146–7, 150–1, 162, 227
   German Nazism 155–60
Gibbon, Edward, *The History of the Decline
   and Fall of the Roman Empire* 200
Gladiator 2
Gladstone, William 124
Godfrey of Viterbo 56–9, 60
Golden Palace, Baghdad 174
Gondophares 23n
Goths 4, 44, 48
Grand Tour 149n
Great Mosque of Damascus 177, 179
Great Schism 1054 37n, 74n, 76n
Greco-Turkish War 114n
Greece 34n, 110–12, 114–15, 149–50
Greece, ancient 33, 57, 79, 81, 114, 119,
   120n, 125, 158, 159n, 218n, 221
Greek 33–4, 39, 62, 72, 76, 121
Grimm, Jacob and Wilhelm 147n, 158

H

Habsburgs 64n, 101, 103–5

Hadrian 21
Hagia Sophia, Constantinople 29
Haiti 161n, 211
Hamilton, George 135
Hannibal Barca 160, 163–4
Harun al-Rashid 182–3, 184n, 191
Helena 26, 69
Heliopolis, Egypt 218
Herculaneum 3, 90–1, 153
Herero 157n
Hermann 61
Himyarites 171–2
Hippodrome, Constantinople 25, 104, 151
Hitler, Adolf 156, 158, 160, 204n
Holy Roman Empire 31n, 36n, 41–3, 72,
   76, 119, 142–3, 145, 147, 155, 159,
   169
   barbarian or Roman? 43–8
   Catherine the Great 66–7
   crowning of Charlemagne 43, 52–4
   Empress Eirene 48–51
   Ottoman Empire 98, 101–5
   reforming Roman religion 59–62
   Roman-ness re-thought 54–6
   studying the world through Roman
      textbooks 62–4
   Trojan Romans, Roman Germans 56–8
Homer 114, 121
   Iliad 99, 113
Horace 201
Horton, James Africanus Beale, *West
   African Countries and Peoples* 137
Hume, David 201
Hungary 101, 104, 143
Hürrem Sultan, Ottoman Sultana 100–1,
   106
Hussite Wars 61n, 67

I

Iberia 31, 35, 47, 49n, 59–60, 100, 169, 179
ibn al-Jahm, Ali 173
Ibn Sina 99
Imperial Civil Service 119–20, 123–4, 128
   classical education 120–22, 134–5

India 117, 119, 122, 187, 214
  British Empire 123–8, 132, 134–7
indigenous peoples 125, 151, 163, 198,
    209
  Americas 198n
International Eurasian Movement 86–7
Iran 130, 192n
Iraq 98, 130, 132, 169, 178, 180
Ireland 55, 117, 127n, 132–4
Isabella I of Castile 100
ISIS 5, 169, 193, 225–7
  Rumiyah 193n
Islam 6, 8, 9, 35, 169–73
  early Islamic empires 173–6
  rivalling Rome 180–3, 187–90
  Roman audience 183–7
  science, technology, engineering, and
    mathematics 190–3
  Umayyads 176–80
Istanbul, see Constantinople
Italian Empire 143, 146n, 151–2, 155,
    227
Italy 2n, 5, 6, 8, 18, 26, 28, 31, 39, 46–7,
    50–1, 55n, 57–8, 68, 71, 100–1,
    161n, 172, 185, 208, 224
  Fascist Italy 152–5, 156, 160, 162
  kingdom of Italy 145–7, 151–2
  modern Italy 141, 143
  Renaissance Italy 75, 119, 145
Ivan III of Russia 67, 70–1, 73, 74, 84
Ivan IV of Russia (the Terrible) 76

J
Jafnids 171
al-Jahiz 189
Japan 152
Jefferson, Thomas 195, 197, 200
  Notes on the State of Virginia 200n
Jerusalem 26n, 28, 36, 73, 130, 174,
    176–7, 184
Jesus Christ 15, 18n, 72n, 73
Jews 36, 49n, 60, 100, 172, 174n, 175–6,
    188, 225
John Paul II, Pope 177n

John the Baptist 177n
John the Grammarian 189
Johnson, Boris 139–40
Jowett, Benjamin 139
Julia Domna 48n, 171
Julius Caesar 6–7, 10–11, 12n, 14, 21, 25,
    30, 160, 100, 136, 137, 153n, 167,
    203, 209
  Commentarii de Bello Gallico 80, 121,
    203
Julius Nepos 45–6
Jupiter 14, 102, 177
Justinian I 29, 32, 48n, 79n, 83, 174
  Code of Justinian 54

K
Kaiser 65, 136n, 147
Kandahar, Afghanistan 23n
Kant, Immanuel 200, 201
Kaysar 65
Khalifa 98, 105, 176
Khan 98, 105

L
Latin 31–2, 39, 62–3, 72, 76, 121, 154
Leathes, Sir Stanley Mordaunt 121
Leo III, Pope 50–4, 55n, 60
Leo the Mathematician 189
Levitsky, Dmitry 66
Libya 8, 152
Livia 48n
Lombards 49n, 50, 224
Louis XV of France 199
Louverture, Toussaint 161n
Lucan 86
Lucas, Charles Prestwood 121n
  Greater Rome and Greater Britain 125–6
Lugard, Frederick 136–7
Lupercalia 13–14
Luther, Martin 60–1, 147
Luxemburg, Rosa 161, 162

M

Macaulay, Thomas Babington 121n, 127
   Lays of Ancient Rome 124
Madinat al-Zahra, Córdoba 174, 180
Madison, James 197, 199
Magna Mater 15
Maimonides 99
Mamluks 100, 130
al-Mamun, Caliph 189, 191
Mandate territories 129–32
al-Mansur 174, 181–2, 184, 188
Marcus Antonius 14, 218
Marcus Aurelius 77
Mars 107
Marx, Karl 162
al-Masudi 189
Medina 174n, 174, 184, 187
Mehmed II, Ottoman Sultan 95–100,
   106, 109
Mehmed III, Ottoman Sultan 106, 108,
   191n
Mehmed IV, Ottoman Sultan 105
Meroe 151n
Merovingians 47
Mesopotamia 130, 171, 175
   see Iraq
Michelet, Jules 122
Mikael, Käbbädä, *Annibal* 163–4
Miletus Gate, Berlin 150
Montesquieu, Charles 199, 200–1, 207n
Moore, Thomas 195
Morocco 175, 192n
Moscow 5, 7, 71, 73, 75–6, 83, 85, 227
Muawiyah, Caliph 176
Mughals 98, 136n
Muhammad, the Prophet 169, 170,
   172–4, 176n, 187, 193
al-Muqaddasi 177, 185
Murad III, Ottoman Sultan 106
Mussolini, Benito 27, 145, 152–5, 163n,
   204n
Mustafa I, Ottoman Sultan 106
al-Mutawakkil, Caliph 173–4, 183

N

Nama 157n
Namibia 157n
Napier, General Sir Charles James 139
Nasrids 171
Nazis 83, 155–60, 207n
Nehru, Jawaharlal, *Glimpses of World
   History* 135–6
neoclassical style 7, 77, 126n, 146, 199,
   202, 214, 217, 225
New Rome 19, 40, 43, 46–7, 202
   building the New Rome 20–4
   Crusades 35–8
   destruction of Constantinople 38–9
   Fall of New Rome 1204 18–20, 37–8
   gods and goddesses 24–5
   living in New Rome 28–30
   population increase 25
   religion 23–4
   strategic replacement for Old Rome
      24–8
   what's in a name? 30–5
New Zealand 125, 214
Nishapur, Iran 192
Normans 35–6

O

obelisks 148, 154, 217–20
   Flaminio Obelisk 219n
Odoacer 18, 43–4, 46, 47
Olga 69
Olympic Games 154, 224
One Thousand and One Nights 182n
Oratorio de Santa Maria 224
Orestes 44, 46
Orthodox Christianity 7–8, 17, 72–3
   Great Schism 1054 37n, 74n, 76n
   Russia 65, 67–71, 84n, 85, 109–10
Osman I of Anatolia 99
Osman II, Ottoman Sultan 106
Ostrogoths 31, 47
Otto I of Greece 111
Otto I, (the Great) HRE 54, 157

Ottoman Empire 9, 39, 59, 81, 130,
    150–2, 192–3, 225
  conquest of Constantinople 95–7
  expanding the empire 100–1
  inventing Byzantium 108–12
  remnants of Rome 112–16
  Renaissance rival 97–100
  Roman-style triumph 101–4
  Treaty of Lausanne 1923 114–15
  what's in a name? 104–8
Oxford University 120–1, 124n,
    125, 139

P

Palestine 130–1, 177–8
Palmerston, Henry John Temple, Lord
    126–7
Palmyra 5–6, 8, 155, 171, 225–7
pan-Africanism 160, 163
Pantheon, Rome 156
Paris 1, 199, 224
Parthians 23n, 222–3
Pasha, Ibrahim 101–4
Pasha, Ismail 128–9
Pasha, Mehib 109
Patrushev, Nikolai 84
Paul II, Pope 67, 70
Pavlovsk Palace, Saint Petersburg 199
Pergamon Altar, Berlin 150
Persia 81, 98, 100–1, 104, 105, 113, 122,
    134, 169, 171–6, 178–9, 183, 186–8,
    190–2, 218n, 220, 222–4
Peter III of Russia 67, 77–9
Peter the Great of Russia 77, 78, 80–1
Petra 171, 187
Petrarch, Francesco Africa 162–3
Philip I 171
Phoenicians 134, 156n
Photios 189
Phrygian Cap 224
Piazza del Popolo, Rome 217–19
Pius IV, Pope 217
Platonic philosophy 62n
Pliny the Elder 219n

Plutarch 14, 159n
Pompeii 3, 90–1
Pompey 167
population movements 114–16
Prophet's Mosque, Medina 177
Protestantism 41, 60–1, 63, 105–4, 133,
    145, 213
Ptolemy 171n
Publius Vergilius Maro, *see* Virgil
Punch 139
Punic Wars 156, 162n, 220–1
Putin, Vladimir 5, 7–8, 83–5, 226

Q

Quintus Fabius Maximus Verrucosus 221

R

racism 137, 157, 207n, 209, 211
Raqqa 174, 182–3, 191
Rashtrapati Bhavan, Delhi 126n
Ravenna 32, 44–6, 50, 174
Reconquista 59n, 100
Rembrandt 13
Renaissance 2n, 62–3, 75, 119, 192
  Ottoman Empire 97–100
Rhodes, Cecil 126
Risorgimento 145
Roma 145
Roman art 2–4, 24–5
Roman Catholic Church 8, 27, 49–50,
    72–3, 119, 143, 145, 213
  Great Schism 1054 37n, 74n, 76n
  Holy Roman Empire 41–3, 60–1
Roman literature 62–4
Roman-ness 28, 30–1, 152–3, 164, 212
  Britain 133n, 136
  Germany 145–8, 151
  Holy Roman Empire 48, 54–6, 58–9,
    61, 64
  Nazi Germany 155, 158
  Ottomon empire 105, 108–10
  Russia 65, 83
  Troy 114

USA 197, 209–10
Venetian Republic 25n
Romanitá 151n, 152–3
romanitas 43, 55, 57
Romanland 17, 19–20, 29, 30, 48, 59, 63,
  66n, 119, 143, 149, 153n, 192, 225
  Crusades 37–8
  destruction of Constantinople (1204)
    38–9
  Empress Eirene 48–51
  Ottoman Empire 96–7, 107, 109–12
  Roman-ness re-thought 54–6
  Third Russia 67–76, 79, 81–2, 84–5, 87
  what's in a name? 30–5
Rome 1–4, 10–12, 24–8, 120n, 198–9,
  201–5, 207–10
  cultural life 165–8
  destruction of Constantinople 38–9
  foederati 45–7, 159
  forms of government 10–12, 20–1
  from city-state to empire and back again
    39–40
  gods and goddesses 12, 13–15
  invading New Rome 35–8
  mos maiorum 4–5, 29
  population decline 25, 27, 31
  Roman Empire 89–94, 119, 130
  Roman tradition of statues 214–16
  Rome as concept 4–10, 227–8
  what's in a name? 30–5
Romeyka 115–16
Romulus 208
  Romulus and Remus 14
Romulus Augustulus 18, 25, 43–4, 46
Rousseau, Jean-Jacques 201
Roxelana, *see* Hürrem Sultan
Rus 67n
  Rome in the eyes of the Rus 69–71
  successive Romes 73–6
Russia 5–6, 7, 65–7
  Roman expressions for Russian rule
    76–80
  Roman rulers of Russia 80–3
  Sophia Palaiologina 67–71, 75–7, 84
  Third Rome revived 83–7

Russian Empire 9
  Ottoman Empire 98
Rutilius Claudius Namatianus 128n

S
al-Sabi, Hilal 186
Safavids 81, 98, 100–1, 104
Safiye Sultan, Ottoman Sultana 106–8
St Mark's Basilica, Venice 38
St Maurice 84n, 157–8
St Peter 31
Salafis 193
Sallust 63
Samarkand 174, 192
Samarra 173–4, 183, 189, 191
Sasanians 31, 81, 174, 190n, 222–4
  Veh Ardashie 181n
  Yazdegerd III 183
Saxons 48
scholarship 187–90
  science, technology, engineering, and
    mathematics 190–3
Scipio Africanus, Publius Cornelius 163n,
  221
Second Crusade 36n
Seleukids 222
Selim I, Ottoman Sultan 100
Selim II, Ottoman Sultan 100, 106
Seljuks 39
Seneca 63, 86, 92–3, 121, 140, 164, 199
Septimius Severus 48n, 226
Seti I of Egypt 218
Shakespeare, William 127
  Antony and Cleopatra 138
Shawqi, Ahmed, *The Death of Cleopatra*
  138
Sicily 32, 35, 92, 129n, 221
Sigerson, George 133–4
Sixtus V, Pope 217–19
skin colour 158, 205, 207, 209
slavery 161n, 163, 167n, 196, 198–9,
  204, 216
Smyrna, *see* İzmir 114
socialism 160, 162

Sol Invictus 26
Solomon 73, 100n, 174, 182–3, 191
Sophia Palaiologina 67–71, 75–7, 84
South Africa 125, 214
Soviet Union 83, 214n
Sparta 119, 158
Spartacus 160–2, 211
Spartakusbund 162
Speer, Albert 156
Star Wars 4
statues 1–4, 6, 14, 24–5, 29, 48, 77, 104,
    118, 120n, 126, 144, 154, 202, 211,
    213
  Roman tradition 214–16
  whiteness 3–4, 211, 213–14
Stoics 4, 62n, 93
Stuarts 119
Suleyman I, Ottoman Sultan (the
    Magnificent) 100–7, 170n
Sulla, Lucius Cornelius 153n
Syria 8, 155, 169, 170–1, 176, 178, 224,
    226

T
al-Tabari 176n
Tacitus 61, 63, 86, 92–4, 124, 127, 129,
    140, 155, 164, 199
Tadmor, Syria 224–5, 226
  see Palmyra
Tertullian of Carthage 157
Teutoburg Forest, Battle of the 61
Teutons 57–9, 61
Theodora 29, 48n, 174
Third Crusade 36n
Third Rome 5, 65–7, 71
  Roman expressions for Russian rule
    76–80
  Roman rulers of Russia 80–3
  successive Romes 72–6
  Third Rome revived 83–7
Thirty Year's War 61n, 64
Thornton, William 199
Tipu Sultan of Mysore 191n
Titian 13

Transjordan 130, 132
translatio imperii 56, 74
Treaty of Lausanne 1923 114–15
Treaty of Versailles 1930 130
Trevelyan, Charles 127
triumphs 80n, 148
  Roman-style triumphs 101–4, 156
Troy 56–9, 99, 107–8, 113–14, 154n, 220
Trump, Donald 6–7, 195
Tsar 65, 147
Tsargrad (Constantinople) 69, 71, 73–4,
    81, 85
Tudors 107–8, 119
Turkey 8, 57, 114–15

U
UK 6, 214
Umayyads 39, 130, 170, 176–80, 184,
    187, 192, 225
UNESCO 226
USA 1, 6, 152, 158n, 163, 169, 193,
    195–7
  Great Seal 225
  inheriting Rome 205–10
  inventing Western civilization 210–14
  Roman solution 197–201
  view from the Roman Republic 201–5
Uzbekistan 192n

V
Valentinian III 45
Vandals 31, 44, 47
Vatican City State 27n, 145n
Venetian Republic 25n, 37–8, 60, 98, 103
Venus 57
Victor Emmanuel II of Italy 146
Victor Emmanuel III of Italy 153
Viganò, Carlo Maria 8n
Virgil 57, 62
  The Aeneid 154n, 162–3, 220, 221
Visigoths 31, 32, 35, 47
Vittoriano, Rome 145
Vladimir I, King of the Rus 69–70, 72
Voltaire, François 41, 77, 200–1

W

Wahhabis 193
Wales 133n
al-Walid 177, 179
Warren, Joseph 200, 206, 210
Washington, George 197, 211–12
Weil, Simone 160
West Africa 132, 136–7
Wheatley, Phillis 211–12
White House, Washington DC 195–6
Wilhelm II of Germany 225
Williams, Eric 136
Winckelmann, Johann 2–3, 158, 210–11, 213–14

Y

Yazdegerd III 183

Z

Zeno 46
Zenobia of Palmyra 225
Zissu, Theodore 131
Zoe Palaiologina, *see* Sophia Palaiologina
Zoroastrians 174n, 175–6, 188